The Rou  D0096628

The Grand Canyon

written and researched by

Greg Ward

ROUGH GUIDES

NEW YORK · LONDON · DELHI

www.roughguides.com

Contents

Grand Canyon trails
insert following p.128

◀◀ Rainbow beyond Grand Canyon Village ◀ View from Point Imperial across the Marble Platform

Introduction to the

Grand Canyon

Although almost five million people come to see the Grand Canyon of the Colorado every year, it seems to remain beyond the grasp of the human imagination. No photograph, no set of statistics, can prepare you for such overwhelming vastness. At more than one mile deep, it's an inconceivable abyss; varying in its central stretch from four to eighteen miles wide, it's an endless expanse of bewildering shapes and colors, glaring desert brightness and impenetrable shadow, stark promontories and soaring never-to-be-climbed sandstone pinnacles.

 While no one is disappointed at that first stunning sight of the chasm, visitors often find themselves struggling to understand what can appear as a remote and impassive spectacle. They race frantically from viewpoint to viewpoint, imagining the next one will be the "best," the place from which the whole thing finally makes sense. This book is an attempt to guide you beyond that initial anxiety. More than anything, it's aimed at encouraging you to slow down, to appreciate whatever small portion of the canyon you may encounter at any one moment, and to allow enough time for the bigger picture to develop. You don't have to learn the names of all those buttes and mesas – dubbed Shiva Temple, Wotans Throne, and so on in a spate of late-Victorian fervor – and you may not ever be able to identify all the different rock strata or desert plants. The longer you linger at the canyon, however, the greater the chance you'll start to hear it speak.

Back in the 1920s, the average visitor would stay at the canyon for two to three weeks. These days, two or three hours is more typical, of which perhaps forty minutes are spent actually looking at the canyon. That's partly because most people now arrive by **car**. As the only part of the canyon you can reach in a car is the **rim**, seeing the canyon has thus come to mean seeing it from above, from a distance. If you really want to engage with the canyon, however, you need literally to get into it – to **hike** or ride a **mule** down the many inner canyon trails, to sleep in the backcountry campgrounds or in the cabins at **Phantom Ranch** on the canyon floor, to **raft** through the white-water rapids of the river itself.

Mapping and defining precisely what constitutes the "Grand Canyon" has always been controversial; **Grand Canyon National Park** covers a relatively small proportion of the greater canyon area. Only since 1975 has the park included the full 277-mile length

▲ Marble Canyon Lodge, near Lees Ferry

The Grand Canyon in figures

• The total length of the Colorado River is 1450 miles; within the Grand Canyon it measures 277 miles, from Lees Ferry to the Grand Wash Cliffs.

• The river is on average 300ft wide and 40ft deep, and its temperature remains at 48°F year-round.

• Grand Canyon National Park measures 1904 square miles or 1.2 million acres; that's roughly half the size of Yellowstone National Park, a third the size of Death Valley National Park, and a tenth the size of the largest US park, Wrangell–St Elias in Alaska.

• The canyon averages ten miles across and one mile deep. Its narrowest point is in Marble Canyon, at 600ft wide, while the maximum width from rim to rim is eighteen miles.

• The highest point on the North Rim, Point Imperial, is 8803ft high; on the South Rim it's Navajo Point, at 7498ft. The elevation at Phantom Ranch, on the central canyon floor, is 2400ft, while the west end of the canyon at Lake Mead lies at 1200ft.

Feet
9000
6000
4500
3000
1200
0

N

NEVADA

Salt Lake City

St George

Mesquite

LAKE MEAD
NATIONAL
RECREATION
AREA

Las Vegas

Henderson   Hoover
Dam

Boulder City

Lake
Mead

Pearce Ferry

Temple Bar

Colorado River

Searchlight

Chloride

Laughlin

Bullhead City

CALIFORNIA

Oatman

0   20 miles

Mount
Trumbull

GRAND CANYON–PARASHANT
NATIONAL MONUMENT

Guano
Point

DIAMOND BAR ROAD

GRAND CANYON
WEST

BUCK AND DOE ROAD

Diamond
Creek

PEARCE FERRY ROAD

ANTARES ROAD

STOCKTON HILL ROAD

Peach Springs

Antares
Point

Truxton
Valentine

Hackberry

Kingman

Los Angeles   Phoenix

of the Colorado River, from Lees Ferry in the east to the Grand Wash
Cliffs near Lake Mead in the west, and for most of that distance it remains
restricted to the narrow strip of the inner gorge. Ranchers whose animals
graze in the federal forests to either side, mining companies eager to exploit

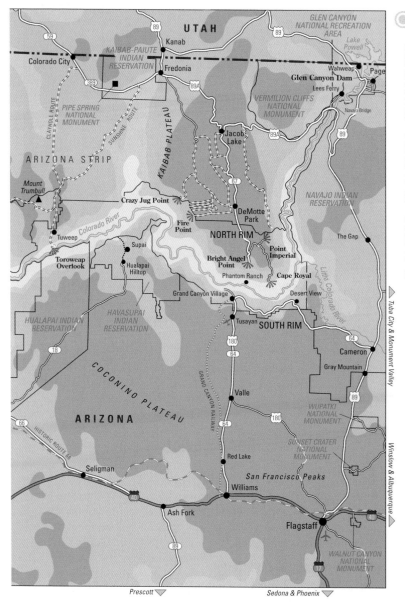

the mineral wealth hidden in the ancient rocks, engineers seeking to divert the river to feed the deserts of southern Arizona, and Native Americans who have lived in the canyon since long before the first Europeans reached North America have combined to limit the size of the park.

▲ Tranquil stretch of the Coloraco River

Where to go

The vast majority of visitors arrive at the **South Rim** – it's much easier to get to, offers far more facilities (mainly at **Grand Canyon Village**, inside the park), and is open year-round. Another lodge and campground sit atop the **North Rim**, where isolation enhances the aesthetic appeal, but at a thousand feet higher this entire area is usually closed by snow from mid-October through mid-May. On both rims, visitors spend most of their time gazing over the gorge from **overlooks** placed at strategic intervals along the canyon-hugging roads. Both also serve as starting points for countless **hiking trails** down into the canyon, and it's even possible to hike from one rim to the other, along the so-called corridor trails, a trek that takes a minimum of two days from rim to rim.

The drive from one rim to the other is 215 miles alone, while to complete a loop around the entire national park would require a drive of almost eight hundred miles and take you as far west as Las Vegas, Nevada. Even that long haul would bypass several of the region's most interesting sites, amid the baffling checkerboard of federal, state, Indian, and private lands that lies beyond the park boundaries. These encompass several **national monuments**, including two huge ones, **Vermilion Cliffs** and **Grand Canyon–Parashant**, created in 2000; two

> If you really want to engage with the canyon, you need literally to get into it

national recreation areas, **Glen Canyon** and **Lake Mead**, which bookend the canyon; two sections of the **Kaibab National Forest**, north and south of the river; and four neighboring **Indian reservations**, belonging to the **Havasupai**, the **Hualapai**, the **Kaibab Paiute**, and the **Navajo**. While most (though not quite all) provide recreational possibilities for visitors – detailed throughout this book – few offer any kind of accommodation or other facilities. For that, you need to call in instead at the many gateway towns that surround the canyon, from **Flagstaff** and **Williams** in the south to **Kanab** in the north.

When to go

There's no definitive answer as to which is the **best season to visit**. Summer on the South Rim can be murderously crowded and, for hikers especially, uncomfortably hot, so if you have the choice, and you plan to spend a lot of time out on the trails, spring and fall are preferable. That's less of an issue on the North Rim, which receives far fewer visitors and stays significantly cooler. In winter, the scope for outdoor activities is greatly reduced, and the North Rim is closed altogether, but the South Rim is transformed into a haven of peace and tranquility. In terms of **aesthetics**, the canyon can look radiant, flecked with snow, on a crisp winter's day; alive with color when the cacti and wildflowers blossom in spring; and suffused with a golden glow in fall, as the trees close to rim level start to turn.

The **climate** varies with both the **season** and the **altitude**. Although most people picture the canyon as being in barren desert, in fact both the North and South rims are set in cool, high forests. The **North Rim**, the higher of the two at 8000ft, receives so much snow that it's completely cut off between, roughly, late October and early May. Nights there remain distinctly chilly at the start and end of each season, and

▶ Dawn on the South Kaibab Trail

What to bring

Whatever time of year you visit, expect to need warm clothing, especially in the evenings, and something waterproof to keep off sudden rains. Temperatures vary so much, and so rapidly, that it makes sense to dress in layers. Detailed advice on what to bring if you're hiking appears on p.93, and if you're rafting on p.202. Otherwise, if you're touring by car, and just sightseeing without strenuous physical activity, no special gear is necessary. Be sure, however, that you have adequate protection from the sun, including a broad-brimmed hat, sunblock, and sunglasses.

only between June and August do normal daytime temperatures rise above 70°F (21°C).

The **South Rim** is a thousand feet lower, enough of a difference to allow visitor facilities to remain open year-round. However, temperatures still drop well below freezing at night between late October and April, so driving conditions can be treacherous, with occasional road closures, and the upper portions of hiking trails may be dangerously icy. Only between May and September can you expect daytime highs above 70°F (21°C).

The **inner canyon** is a very different proposition. At river level, almost 5000ft below the South Rim, thermometer readings in excess of 100°F (38°C) are recorded on most days between late May and early September, and it's unlikely to drop below 70°F (21°C) even at night. Winter temperatures are a little cooler than you might expect, because so little direct sunlight manages to reach the canyon floor, but it seldom freezes down there, and December highs remain well over 50°F (10°C).

▼ Sunset from Hopi Point

Precipitation is seldom severe enough to spoil a visit; the greatest risk of heavy rain comes in August, when afternoon thunderstorms sweep in (sometimes creating localized flash floods), but they're spectacular to watch and normally blow over fast. However, it must be said that any time of year you may turn up and find the canyon obscured beneath a layer of **cloud** or **fog**; on average around four times a year it remains invisible all day.

> In winter, the South Rim is transformed into a haven of peace and tranquility

Average temperatures and rainfall

	Jan	Feb	Mar	Apr	May	Jun	Jul	Aug	Sep	Oct	Nov	Dec
South Rim												
High (°F)	41	45	51	60	70	81	84	82	76	65	52	43
Low (°F)	18	21	25	32	39	47	54	53	47	36	27	20
Precipitation (inches)	1.32	1.55	1.38	0.93	0.66	1.81	1.81	2.25	1.56	1.10	0.94	1.64
Inner canyon												
High (°F)	56	62	71	82	92	101	106	103	97	84	68	57
Low (°F)	36	42	48	56	63	72	78	75	69	58	46	37
Precipitation (inches)	0.68	0.75	0.79	0.47	0.36	0.84	0.84	1.40	0.97	0.65	0.43	0.87
North Rim												
High (°F)	37	39	44	53	62	73	77	75	69	59	46	40
Low (°F)	16	18	21	29	34	40	46	45	39	31	24	20
Precipitation (inches)	3.17	3.22	2.65	1.73	1.17	1.93	1.93	2.85	1.99	1.38	1.48	2.83

To convert Fahrenheit to Celsius, subtract 32, multiply by 5, and divide by 9. To convert inches to millimeters, multiply by 25.4.

things not to miss

With so many things to see and do in the Grand Canyon area, it's sometimes difficult to plan your day. What follows is a selection of some of the most popular and worthwhile sights and activities in and around the canyon. They're arranged in four color-coded categories to help you find the best to do, see, and experience. All highlights have a page reference to take you straight into the guide, where you can find out more.

01 **Bright Angel Point** Page **74** • This superb North Rim overlook is located at the tip of a slender rocky outcrop just a short walk from the Grand Canyon Lodge.

02 Flagstaff Page **153** • The liveliest and most appealing of the gateway towns, this high-desert crossroads remains redolent of the Wild West.

03 Toroweap Point Page **145** • The remotest major overlook within the national park, at the far west end of the North Rim, Toroweap is perched above sheer 3000ft cliffs and offers unique and extraordinary views into the inner gorge.

05 Dining Room at Grand Canyon Lodge Page **72** • Thanks to both its good food and superb sunset views of the canyon, the North Rim's only restaurant is often booked up months in advance.

04 Bright Angel Trail Page **96** • It's the most popular hiking trail within the park precisely because it provides such a superb introduction to life below the rim.

06 The Colorado near Phantom Ranch Page **45** • Unless you're on a long-distance backpacking expedition, by far the best way to see the river close up is by spending a night in the vicinity of Phantom Ranch.

07 **Helicopter flight at Hualapai** Page **190** • The so-called "Grand Canyon West" on the Hualapai Indian Reservation is the only place where it's possible to fly right down into the canyon and land beside the river.

09 **Antelope Canyon** Page **124** • Irresistible if often all too crowded slot canyon, just outside Page near the Glen Canyon Dam, that's a magnet for photographers.

08 **South Kaibab Trail** Page **99** • Even if you don't make the entire hair-raising descent to the Colorado, this trail offers perhaps the finest day hikes into the canyon.

10 **Desert View Watchtower** Page **65** • Circular mock-Puebloan tower, blending into the rocks at the east end of the South Rim, that harks back to the golden years of Western tourism while still providing stunning views.

12 Rafting Page **197** • A rafting expedition through the Grand Canyon, which can take from three days to three weeks, ranks among the world's greatest outdoor experiences.

11 Condors at the South Rim Page **53** • The majestic silhouette of a California condor, soaring on its nine-foot wings above the canyon, makes an unforgettable spectacle.

14 Shoshone Point Page **62** • This little-known South Rim viewpoint, accessible only on foot, provides a rare opportunity to experience a one-on-one encounter with the Grand Canyon.

13 North Rim Campground Page **73** • The most spacious, least-crowded, and all-around nicest of the national park campgrounds, in a lovely wooded setting above a dramatic side canyon.

15 Wupatki National Monument Page **162** • The finest archeological remains in the Grand Canyon region stand at Wupatki, not far from Flagstaff.

16 **Cape Royal** Page **81** • Thrusting south from the tip of the North Rim's Walhalla Plateau, Cape Royal is the perfect vantage point from which to appreciate the canyon's overall shape.

17 **Mule ride to Phantom Ranch** Page **57** • If you fancy yourself as the star of a real-life Western movie, what better place could there be to saddle up?

19 **El Tovar** Page **45** • The jewel of Grand Canyon Village, this historic hotel provides the South Rim's best food and lodging.

18 **Lees Ferry** Page **130** • This scenic little outpost, the launching point for all Grand Canyon rafting trips, boasts its own fascinating and romantic history.

20 **Havasu Falls** Page **180** • Hikers who make the trek down into the Havasupai Indian Reservation are rewarded with the astonishing sight of lush turquoise waterfalls buried deep within the canyon.

Basics

Basics

Getting there

Almost all independent travelers who visit the Grand Canyon, including those who have flown to the US from overseas, arrive by car. You can travel directly to the canyon by plane or train (from Las Vegas or Williams, respectively), but be prepared to pay an expensive excursion fare. While there is limited bus service to the South Rim from both Flagstaff and Williams, it's not easy to tour the park as a whole unless you have your own vehicle. Public transportation to the North Rim is virtually nonexistent.

By air

For international travelers, as well as US and Canadian citizens who live beyond reasonable driving distance from the canyon, the most cost-effective way to visit is to fly to **Las Vegas** or **Phoenix**, rent a car, make a loop tour, and fly home from the same airport. Not that the Grand Canyon is particularly close to either city – Phoenix is 220 miles from the South Rim, by way of Flagstaff, and 345 miles from the North Rim, via Flagstaff and Navajo Bridge; Las Vegas is 285 miles from the North Rim, via St George, and 290 miles from the South Rim, via Kingman and Williams. Las Vegas is the better bet, as it offers low airfares and car rental rates and welcomes more direct flights from overseas, although Phoenix's Sky Harbor International Airport is equally well served by major domestic carriers.

Note that while there is a small airport at **Tusayan**, near the South Rim, it almost exclusively hosts sightseeing flights from Las Vegas (see p.25); none of the national airlines serves the airport.

Flying from elsewhere in the US

Flights to the Southwest are most expensive in summer, which despite soaring temperatures is peak season. Prices drop during the "shoulder" seasons (September to late December and March to May) and are cheapest in low season (January and February).

Start by checking fares on Southwest Airlines and JetBlue. You'll often find the best bargains on flights to Las Vegas. It should be possible to find fares for around $100 from Los Angeles, $200 from Seattle, and $300 from New York; even a two-week fly-drive trip from New York to Las Vegas should cost well under $500 per person. Note that these prices assume midweek travel; flying to Las Vegas on a weekend can add a hefty premium.

A round-trip from New York to Phoenix should cost about $300–350; equivalent figures from Chicago might be $250–300 and from Los Angeles just under $100. Sample fares from Montréal to Phoenix start from CAN$600, and from Vancouver CAN$350.

Flying from the UK or Ireland

Just two nonstop flights serve Phoenix and Las Vegas from the UK. British Airways flies from London Heathrow to Phoenix daily except Wednesdays, while Virgin Atlantic flies from London Gatwick to Las Vegas daily except Saturdays. Typical round-trip fares range from around £335 in winter up to £550 in summer; flying time on each is a little under eleven hours there and ten hours back.

Most other transatlantic carriers also fly to Phoenix or Las Vegas for similar or slightly lower fares, but all require at least one stop en route. From Britain, you can either fly nonstop to the West Coast, then double back toward the Southwest, or touch down on the East Coast and then fly west; timewise, it makes little difference. If you'd rather keep your flying time to a minimum, consider flying nonstop to California and driving to the Southwest from there, taking advantage of that state's low car rental rates. Both British Airways and Virgin fly twice daily from

London to Los Angeles, while American, United, and Air New Zealand fly once daily.

From Ireland's Dublin and Shannon airports, Aer Lingus flies to Boston, Chicago, Los Angeles, New York, and Washington, and Delta services Atlanta. Alternatively, you can fly to London and take your pick of transatlantic routes.

Flying from Australia or New Zealand

There are no direct flights to the Southwest from Australia or New Zealand, so you'll have

Airlines

	Website	US	UK	Australia
Aer Lingus	ⓦ www.aerlingus.ie		☎ 0870/876 5000	
Air Canada	ⓦ www.aircanada.ca	☎ 1-888/247-2262		
Air New Zealand	ⓦ www.airnewzealand.com	☎ 0800/028 4149		☎ 13 2476
Alaska Airlines	ⓦ www.alaska-air.com	☎ 1-800/252-7522		
America West	ⓦ www.americawest.com	☎ 1-800/235-9292	☎ 02/9267 2138	
American Airlines	ⓦ www.aa.com	☎ 1-800/433-7300	☎ 0845/778 9789	☎ 1300/130 757
American Trans Air	ⓦ www.ata.com	☎ 1-800/435-9282		
British Airways	ⓦ www.ba.com		☎ 0870/850 9850	☎ 1300/767 177
Continental Airlines	ⓦ www.continental.com	☎ 1-800/523-3273	☎ 0800/776464	
Delta Airlines	ⓦ www.delta.com	☎ 1-800/221-1212	☎ 0800/414767	☎ 02/9251 3211
Frontier Airlines	ⓦ www.flyfrontier.com	☎ 1-800/432-1359		
Hawaiian Airlines	ⓦ www.hawaiianair.com	☎ 1-800/367-5320		
Japan Airlines	ⓦ www.jal.com			☎ 02/9272 1111
JetBlue	ⓦ www.jetblue.com	☎ 1-800/538-2583		
Mesa Airlines	ⓦ www.mesa-air.com	☎ 1-800/637-2247		
Northwest/KLM	ⓦ www.nwa.com	☎ 1-800/225-2525	☎ 0870/507 4074	
Qantas	ⓦ www.qantas.com.au		☎ 0800/0014 0014	☎ 13 1313
Scenic Airlines	ⓦ www.scenic.com	☎ 1-800/634-6801		
Skywest	ⓦ www.skywest.com	☎ 1-800/453-9417		
Southwest	ⓦ www.southwest.com	☎ 1-800/435-9792		
United Airlines	ⓦ www.ual.com	☎ 1-800/241-6522	☎ 0845/844 4777	☎ 13 1777
US Airways	ⓦ www.usair.com	☎ 1-800/428-4322		
Virgin Atlantic	ⓦ www.virgin-atlantic.com		☎ 0870/380 2007	

Visa requirements for foreign travelers

to fly to one of the main US gateways and pick up a connecting flight or a rental car.

The cheapest route to the US, and the one offering the most flights from Australia and New Zealand, services Los Angeles, which provides plenty of onward flights to Las Vegas and Phoenix. Qantas, American Airlines, and Air New Zealand fly to LA at least twice daily, while United flies once a day; other airlines that serve LA include Japan Airlines and Singapore Airlines.

By car

Most drivers approach the Grand Canyon along **I-40**, which on its east-west route across Arizona passes south of the canyon through both **Flagstaff** and **Williams**. From Flagstaff, **US-180** winds northwest past the San Francisco Peaks about eighty miles to the **South Rim**; from Williams, **AZ-64** leads due north sixty miles to the South Rim, merging with US-180 in Valle about midway. Drivers from southern Arizona can reach Flagstaff by taking I-17 north from Phoenix.

To reach the South Rim from the east, drivers take AZ-64 west from **US-89** at **Cameron**; you'll reach Desert View after 34 miles and Grand Canyon Village 25 miles later. This is the obvious route if you've been exploring southern Utah or the Four Corners region, and it's also the most direct route from the North Rim.

The isolated North Rim is accessible via **US-89A** through **Jacob Lake**, which sits roughly eighty miles southwest of **Page**, Arizona, and 92 miles southeast of the I-15 corridor between Las Vegas and Salt Lake City (**St George**, Utah, is the nearest

town along the interstate). The final 44 miles south from Jacob Lake to the North Rim are on **AZ-67**, which is closed by snow for a protracted, unbroken period between late fall and early May, during which time all facilities at the North Rim shut down.

By rail

The closest that Amtrak **trains** (☎1-800/872-7245, ⓦwww.amtrak.com) come to the South Rim are the stations at **Flagstaff** and **Williams** (see p.155 and p.165 for more). Bus connections are detailed below.

From a separate station in the heart of Williams, the historic **Grand Canyon Railway** (☎928/773-1976 or 1-800/843-8724, ⓦwww.thetrain.com) offers daily service to the South Rim. Operated by a **steam locomotive** in summer, it's more of a themed Western attraction than an efficient means of transportation. Passengers are not required to return to Williams the same day, so many take the railway to enable a multi-night stay at the canyon. Round-trip fares range between $60 and $155. (For full details, see p.40.)

By bus

Regularly scheduled Greyhound **buses** ply the I-40 corridor south of the canyon, heading east from Las Vegas, Los Angeles, and San Francisco and west from Albuquerque and beyond (☎1-800/231-2222, ⓦwww.greyhound.com). The closest stops to the canyon are at **Williams** and **Flagstaff**.

Operated by **Open Road Tours & Transportation** (☎928/226-8060 or 1-877/226-8060, ⓦwww.openroadtours.com), two daily

Package tours

Although many national and international **tour companies** include the Grand Canyon on their Western US itineraries, most only stop for an hour or two, usually along the South Rim. Such tours do not merit inclusion in this book.

However, local tour companies that operate more extensive tours to and around the canyon are listed on p.25.

buses in each direction connect Flagstaff and Williams with the **South Rim** (fares and timetables are detailed on p.41). Departing from Flagstaff's Amtrak station, the route stops at the Grand Canyon Railway's Williams Depot and the Grand Canyon IMAX Theater in Tusayan and winds up at the Maswik Lodge in Grand Canyon Village. Open Road also

runs five daily buses between Flagstaff and **Phoenix**.

The only scheduled bus service – or, indeed, public transportation of any kind – to the **North Rim** is the Transcanyon Shuttle, a daily van service along the 215-mile route between the North and South rims. For more details, see p.71.

Information, websites, and maps

There's no single perfect source for information on the entire Grand Canyon region; that's the point of this book, after all. In addition to the national park itself, the area includes assorted other federally managed national monuments, national forests and the like; several Indian reservations; and four separate counties of Arizona.

Park information

The best place to find advance information about Grand Canyon National Park is the Park Service website (Ⓦ www.nps.gov/grca), which provides information about park fees, facilities, activities, and programs. However, Xanterra Parks & Resorts (PO Box 699, Grand Canyon, AZ 86023; ☎303/297-2757 or 1-888/297-2757, Ⓦ www.grandcanyon lodges.com) operates all in-park accommodations (see p.28).

Once you arrive, the top information source is the free park newspaper, *The Guide*, which rangers distribute at all entrance stations. Published in separate editions for the North and South rims, it provides current operating hours for all park facilities, detailed hiking advice, a schedule of upcoming ranger talks, and plenty of background on park geology,

natural history, and other issues. Rangers also hand out a glossy **park brochure**, which includes useful maps, the **Accessibility Guide** (see p.31), and the **Backcountry Trip Planner** (upon request), which features full details on backpacking and camping opportunities. To obtain these materials in advance **by mail**, write to PO Box 129, Grand Canyon, AZ 86023.

Although *The Guide* probably lists most of what you need to know, consider stopping at one of the park **visitor centers**, detailed throughout this book. The main ones are the **Canyon View Information Plaza** on the South Rim (daily: May–mid-Oct 8am–6pm, mid-Oct–April 8am–5pm; ☎928/638-7888; see p.41) and the **North Rim Visitor Center** (May–mid-Oct daily 8am–6pm; ☎928/638-7864; see p.71). To prevent waste, rangers don't display all available leaflets, but they can supply additional printed information on a range of topics, such as rafting or flight-seeing, the Havasupai Indian Reservation, or backcountry hiking and driving routes. They also track current trail and road conditions, so be sure to ask if you're planning a specific adventure.

Complementing the official Park Service publications are the varied books, brochures, and maps at the Grand Canyon Association **bookstores**, which operate across the plaza at Canyon View, at Desert View, and at several other locations along the South Rim, as well as at *Grand Canyon Lodge* on the North Rim. A wide selection is available both by mail (PO Box 399, Grand Canyon, AZ 86023; ☎928/638-0199) and online at ⓦwww.grandcanyon.org.

Useful contacts and websites

Arizona Daily Sun 1751 S Thompson Ave, Flagstaff, AZ 86001 ☎928/774-4545, ⓦwww .azdailysun.com. Flagstaff's daily newspaper is the best source for up-to-the-minute news about issues that affect the entire Grand Canyon region; its website includes a searchable archive of past issues.
Arizona Office of Tourism PO Box 24548, Phoenix, AZ 85002 ☎602/230-7733, ⓦwww .arizonaguide.com. Comprehensive statewide travel information, available by mail and online.
Grand Canyon Association PO Box 399, Grand Canyon, AZ 86023 ☎928/638-2481, ⓦwww .grandcanyon.org. This nonprofit organization runs the in-park bookstores; its website is the best online source for Grand Canyon books and souvenirs.
Grand Canyon National Park PO Box 129, Grand Canyon, AZ 86023, South Rim ☎928/638-7888, North Rim ☎928/638-7864, ⓦwww.nps .gov/grca. The Park Service not only mails out copies of its newspaper, *The Guide*, and other information, it also maintains a regularly updated online database of everything you might need to know, with links to rafting operators, tour companies and the like.
Grand Canyon Pioneers Society PO Box 2372, Flagstaff, AZ 86003-2372 ⓦwww.kaibab.org/gcps. This group of Grand Canyon enthusiasts organizes outings and activities in the region and publishes a

monthly newsletter, *The Ol' Pioneer*, which details members' latest historical research.
High Country News 119 Grand Ave, PO Box 1090, Paonia, CO 81428 ☎970/527-4898, ⓦwww.hcn .org. Biweekly newspaper devoted to Western US environmental issues, with special reference to national parks and public lands. Its searchable online archive covers all the latest Grand Canyon news.
Xanterra Parks & Resorts PO Box 699, Grand Canyon, AZ 86023 ☎303/297-2757 or 1-888/297-2757, ⓦwww.grandcanyonlodges .com or ⓦwww.grandcanyonnorthrim.com. The concessionaire that operates the in-park lodges on both the South and North rims offers advance reservations by mail, phone, or online.

Maps

The best general-purpose **road map** for the region covered in this book is the *Guide to Indian Country*, available free to members of the American Automobile Association and sold throughout the Southwest for $4.95. However, it is not reliable for dirt roads and backcountry routes. If you plan to explore the isolated plateaus north of the Colorado, either on the North Rim or the Arizona Strip, be sure to pick up either the *North Kaibab Ranger District* map, published by the Kaibab National Forest, or the BLM Arizona Strip Field Office *Visitor Map*, available from visitor centers in Jacob Lake (see p.136) and on the North Rim.

For **hiking**, it's important to have an accurate **topographical** map. The best one for the canyon as a whole is the waterproof and tearproof 1:73530 *Grand Canyon National Park*, published by National Geographic–Trails Illustrated (ⓦmaps.nationalgeographic .com/trails; $9.95). Earthwalk Press produces a more detailed 1:24000 *Bright Angel Trail* map of the corridor trails ($3.95). For even greater resolution, get hold of the appropriate **US Geological Survey** quadrant maps, each of which covers a square parcel measuring seven by seven miles (☎1-888/275-8747, ⓦwww.usgs.gov). Orders cost $4 per map plus $5 postage.

Transportation and tours

The South Rim is the only part of the Grand Canyon accessible via public transportation. In fact, the Park Service would prefer that you not bring a car, and hikers in particular can happily stay several days on the South Rim without need of one.

As detailed on p.43, free shuttle buses link the various lodges and other facilities in Grand Canyon Village; run west to several viewpoints along Hermit Road; and also head east to Yaki Point, the trailhead for the South Kaibab Trail. Commercial tour buses also make the 52-mile round-trip out to Desert View.

Driving

Public transportation may run to those popular spots, but if you hope to explore the other places covered in this book, there's little choice but to **drive**. That's the only way to take in various sights on the "road between the rims," detailed in Chapter Four; to admire the views from the North Rim overlooks, in Chapter Two; to visit the stunning overlook at Toroweap, in Chapter Five; or to reach the remote Havasupai Indian Reservation, in Chapter Seven.

While the main roads up to the South Rim from I-40 are busy and well maintained, at times you'll find yourself crossing very empty **desert**. Be sure to have two gallons of water per person in the car, and also carry flares, matches, a first-aid kit, compass, shovel, air pump, and extra gas. Take care driving at **night**; much of the land that borders the Grand Canyon is open range, and livestock can wander onto unlit roads. If your car engine **overheats**, don't turn it off; instead, try to cool it quickly by switching off the air conditioning and turning up the heat full blast. If you do have car problems, it's best to stay with your vehicle, as you'll be harder to find wandering around alone. Note that most of the region is too remote for **cell phones** to pick up a signal; satellite phones are somewhat more reliable.

Further details regarding specific roads are available in the relevant chapters.

Cycling

For all but the hardiest of adventurers, it's only realistic to see **cycling** in the Grand Canyon region as an enjoyable complement to driving. Consider the South Rim, where roads closed to private vehicles remain open to cyclists. Elsewhere, the logistical problems of touring solely by bike in desert conditions, where sixty miles might separate even the smallest settlements, are simply too overwhelming. Note that hiking trails in the national park are off-limits to cyclists.

Flight-seeing tours

Air tours of the Grand Canyon operate from two main bases – **Las Vegas** and **Tusayan**, close to the South Rim, whose tiny airport nevertheless ranks as Arizona's second busiest. Nearly 100,000 flights, carrying almost a million passengers, take off each year.

Despite its popularity, controversy has long surrounded the flight-seeing industry, as flying conditions in the canyon vicinity are unusually hazardous. Light aircraft especially can struggle with the takeoff altitude at Tusayan of 7000ft, followed by fierce and unpredictable air currents over the canyon itself. The **safety record** is, to say the least, alarming. In 1956, 128 people died in what was then the worst crash in US aviation history, when two commercial passenger planes collided above the confluence of the Colorado and Little Colorado rivers. Since

For a recorded message about road and weather conditions in the Grand Canyon region, call ☎928/638-7888; for conditions statewide, call ☎1-888/411-7623.

then, a further sixty crashes have claimed around 230 more lives.

Both for safety reasons and to diminish the barrage of **noise** within the park, strict **regulations** govern flights over the national park. Airplanes and helicopters must fly at different altitudes; no one is allowed to fly below rim level; and 75 percent of the park, including airspace over the South Rim overlooks and central rim-to-rim corridor, is completely off-limits. The number of overflights has also been restricted, though that only means it can't exceed its already high current level.

Only you can judge whether a flight is worth either the risk or the expense. Yes, in a sense you'll see more of the canyon, but from an even more remote, and potentially alienating, distance than from a rim overlook. For many visitors, the issue at the Grand Canyon is to find a way to engage with and understand this vast, incomprehensible landscape. Taking a scenic flight is unlikely to help. On the other hand, it is an undeniably exciting adventure, and, after all, you are on vacation.

Tours and operators

Helicopter companies based in Tusayan include **Papillon** (☎928/638-2419 or 1-800/528-2418, ⊛www.papillon.com) and **Maverick** (☎928/638-2622 or 1-800/962-3869, ⊛www.maverickhelicopter.com). Each typically flies three standard routes: a half-hour western tour, straight across the canyon and back a few miles west of the village, for around $100 per adult ($70 per child); a forty-minute eastern tour, along the rim as far as the confluence of the Colorado and Little Colorado rivers, for roughly $145 ($100/child); and a fifty-minute loop that combines the prior routes and crosses the North Rim forest, for $170 ($120/child). Papillon also runs amazing $455 day trips to the Havasupai Indian Reservation (see p.178).

The main **airplane,** or fixed-wing, tour operators at Tusayan are **Air Grand Canyon** (☎928/638-2686 or 1-800/247-4726, ⊛www.airgrandcanyon.com) and **Grand Canyon Airlines** (☎928/638-2359 or 1-866/235-9422, ⊛www.grandcanyonairlines.com). While planes can cover much greater distances than helicopters, they're obliged to keep at least a thousand feet above rim level, thus tend not to offer as good views. Fixed-wing tour prices are lower, however, ranging from $75 per adult ($45 per child) for a half-hour up to around $175 ($95) for ninety minutes.

Helicopter tours from **Las Vegas** to the South Rim typically cost $300 per person and up. Operators include **Air Vegas Airlines** (☎702/736-3599 or 1-800/255-7474, ⊛www.airvegas.com) or **Maverick Helicopter Tours** (☎702/261-0007 or 1-888/261-4414, ⊛www.maverickhelicopter.com). **Scenic Airlines** (☎702/638-3200 or 1-800/634-6801, ⊛www.scenic.com) offers airplane tours for about $250.

Several Las Vegas–based companies also fly to the **West Rim** at **Grand Canyon West** (see p.190), which lies on Hualapai land and is not governed by the same regulations as the rest of the canyon. That enables helicopters, run by both **Papillon** (☎702/736-7243 or 1-888/635-7272, ⊛www.papillon.com) and **Sundance** (☎702/736-0606 or 1-800/653-1881, ⊛www.helicoptour.com), to descend below the rim and land beside the Colorado River.

Ground tours

Bus tours along the South Rim, run by Xanterra under the old Fred Harvey banner, are detailed on p.43. However, outfitters in several nearby towns offer guided day trips and longer excursions to other parts of the canyon. Operators detailed in relevant chapters throughout the book include Canyon Country Out-Back Tours (☎435/644-3807 or 1-888/783-3807, ⊛www.ccobtours.com) and Canyon Rim Adventures (☎435/644-8512 or 1-800/897-9633, ⊛www.canyonrimadventures.com) in **Kanab** (see p.142); Marvelous Marv's Tours (☎928/635-4061 or 1-800/655-4948, ⊛www.marvelousmarv.com) in **Williams** (see p.165); and the *DuBeau International Hostel* (☎928/774-6731 or 1-800/398-7112; see p.157) and *Grand Canyon International Hostel* (☎928/779-9421 or 1-888/442-2696, ⊛www.grandcanyonhostel.com; see p.157) in **Flagstaff**, which run joint trips.

For true expert guidance and an introduction to the canyon backcountry, consider a guided hiking trip with the **Grand Canyon**

Field Institute (☎928/638-2485, ⓦwww .grandcanyon.org/fieldinstitute; see p.94) or one of the multitude of educational programs arranged by Flagstaff's **Museum of Northern Arizona** (☎928/774-5213, ⓦwww.musnaz.org).

Costs and money

This book lists detailed price information for lodging and dining throughout the region. Accommodation rates are coded according to the system explained on p.28, which excludes any applicable local taxes, while restaurant prices only account for food, not drinks or tip. For museums and similar attractions, the entrance fees quoted are for adults; unless otherwise specified, assume that children get in half-price.

Grand Canyon National Park: Admission charges and fees

The **entrance fee** to Grand Canyon National Park is payable when you cross the park boundary at one of the three main entrance stations. Two anchor the South Rim: one just north of **Tusayan** on US-180/AZ-64, en route from Williams and Flagstaff, the other just east of **Desert View**, on AZ-64 west of Cameron. The North Rim equivalent is 30 miles south of **Jacob Lake** on AZ-67.

Admission is valid for seven days and currently costs **$25** for one private, noncommercial vehicle and all its passengers, or **$12** per individual if you arrive on foot, bicycle, or motorcycle.

It's also possible to buy various **passes** at the entrance stations, which supersede the usual admission fee. The **Grand Canyon Pass** ($40) entitles the bearer and any passengers in the same vehicle, or any accompanying family members if you arrive by some other means, to unlimited admission over the following year. If you plan to visit any other national parks or monuments in coming months, it makes more sense to buy a **National Parks Pass** ($50), which grants the bearer and fellow passengers unrestricted access to all such parks and monuments for a year from the purchase date. This is a slightly cheaper alternative to the annual **Golden Eagle** pass ($65), which also covers sites managed by the US Fish & Wildlife Service, the Forest Service, and the Bureau of Land Management. For most Grand Canyon visitors who are unlikely to visit such sites, the extra $15 is not worth paying.

None of the passes or fees mentioned above covers or reduces charges for such activities as **camping** (from $4 per person or $10 per group per night at park campgrounds; see p.28), **backcountry hiking** ($10 per permit plus $5 per night; see p.92), or private **rafting** trips ($100 per group permit plus $100 per person; see p.204).

Two other passes grant **free access** for life to all national parks and monuments, again to the holder and any accompanying passengers, and also secure a fifty percent discount on camping fees. The **Golden Age Passport**, available at the entrance stations, is issued to any US citizen or permanent resident aged 62 or older for a onetime processing charge of $10, while the **Golden Access Passport**, available only at the visitor centers and the Tusayan Museum, is issued free to permanently disabled US citizens or permanent residents.

Costs

Prices in the Southwest are broadly similar to those found elsewhere in the US. Food and lodging are generally cheaper here than in major US cities and tourist regions, while gas and groceries, especially in remote places, are a bit more expensive. Most visitors from Europe and Australasia feel their money goes further in the US than it does at home. However, if you're used to traveling in the less expensive European countries, let alone the rest of the world, don't expect to scrape by on the same minuscule budget in the US.

Most visitors drive to the park. If you can't bring your own vehicle, car rental will cost you around $150 (£87/€125) per week. Lodging costs are more flexible. For most of the year in towns away from the canyon, you should have no problem finding a motel room for under $60 (£35/€50), though even the cheapest peak-season rates in or near the park are more like $80 (£46/€68). Although a few hostels in the region offer dorm beds for around $16 (£9/€14) per person per night, they're by no means common and really don't save that much money for two or more travel companions. Camping is not only cheap (federal and state park campgrounds range from free to perhaps $12 (£7/€10) per night), but also the only option in many wilderness areas.

As for food, $20 (£12/€17) per day is enough to support an adequate diet, comprising perhaps one full meal at a local diner supplemented by a stash of groceries, while for $30 (£17/€25) per day one can eat pretty well.

The most economical possible vacation, therefore, with two people sharing a rental car, camping in state and federal parks most nights, and eating one restaurant meal per day, will run a minimum of $300 (£175/€250) per person per week.

For advice on tipping and taxes, see p.32.

Cash, cards, and checks

Expect to pay most of your major expenses by credit or debit card; hotels and car rental agencies usually demand a credit card imprint as security, even if you intend to settle the bill in cash, and you'll be at a serious disadvantage if you don't have one. Visa, MasterCard, Diners Club, American Express, and Discover are widely accepted.

You'll also need to carry some cash. If you have a MasterCard or Visa, or a cash-dispensing card linked to an international network such as Cirrus or Plus (check with your home bank in advance), you can withdraw cash from appropriate automatic teller machines (ATMs). Also consider carrying US dollar travelers' checks, which offer the security of knowing that lost or stolen checks will be replaced. Checks issued by American Express, Visa, and Thomas Cook are universally accepted as cash in shops, restaurants, and gas stations, and any change from your transactions will be rendered in hard currency. Carry plenty of $10 and $20 denominations, and don't be put off by "no checks" signs, which only refer to personal checks. Foreign travelers should *not* bring travelers' checks issued in their own currency, as banks may not exchange them, and few businesses are likely to accept them.

Accommodation

Not surprisingly, most visitors to the Grand Canyon who stay longer than a few hours hope to find accommodation within the national park. Both the South and North rims host comfortable, attractive hotels, known in traditional park parlance as lodges.

Lodges and motels

The six **lodges** along the **South Rim** collectively offer about a thousand rooms, the best of them in the venerable *El Tovar* and *Bright* *Angel Lodge*. The similarly appealing *Grand Canyon Lodge*, the only North Rim option, provides another two hundred rooms. You'll find detailed reviews of each lodge in the relevant chapters of this book. Note that very few rooms – to be specific, around half a dozen rooms on the South Rim and four on the North – offer direct canyon views.

All the lodges are run by concessionaire **Xanterra**, which until recently was known as Amfac and which still uses the old **Fred Harvey** name in its marketing. For **reservations** at all lodges, as well as at Phantom Ranch on the canyon floor (see p.107) and the RV campground in Grand Canyon Village (see p.47), contact Xanterra Parks & Resorts, PO Box 699, Grand Canyon, AZ 86023 (same day ☎928/638-2631, advance ☎303/297-2757 or 1-888/297-2757, ⊛www.grandcanyonlodges.com). **Room rates** are set by the Park Service; a typical charge for a double, en suite room runs from $70 to $130 between mid-March and mid-November, and perhaps $10–20 less in winter. Demand, especially in summer, far exceeds supply on both rims, so make your reservations as far in advance as possible.

Just outside the park at the South Rim, the gateway community of **Tusayan** offers another thousand rooms split among several large chain motels, only worth considering if in-park options are booked. While rates are similar to those found in the park, the facilities are often much more modern. You'll find further congregations of motels along I-40 in **Flagstaff** and **Williams** – though at eighty and sixty miles, respectively, from the canyon, these are too far away to make convenient bases for multi-day stays.

At the **North Rim**, few options exist outside the *Grand Canyon Lodge*. **DeMotte Park**, seventeen miles north of the canyon, and **Jacob Lake**, 44 miles north, offer one small motel each, and you'll find several more in both **Fredonia**, Arizona and **Kanab**, Utah, neighboring towns another thirty miles north.

There are also a number of attractive roadside lodges and motels scattered along the 215-mile road that connects the North and South rims, particularly in **Cameron** and **Marble Canyon**.

Camping

The National Park Service maintains appealing, well-equipped **campgrounds** on both sides of the canyon. Fees run between $10 and $15 per night per vehicle and as little as $4 for individual backpackers. Spherix (same day ☎928/638-2611, advance ☎1-800/365-2267 or ☎301/722-1257 from outside the US, ⊛www.reservations.nps .gov) handles reservations for both **Mather Campground** (see p.47), in Grand Canyon Village on the South Rim, and **North Rim Campground** (see p.73), a mile north of the *Grand Canyon Lodge*. Xanterra (☎303/297-2757 or ⊛www.grandcanyonlodges.com) oversees **RV camping** at **Trailer Village** (see p.47), in Grand Canyon Village. The summer-only **Desert View Campground** (see p.47), on the South Rim, is first-come, first-served.

Backcountry camping within the park, particularly below the canyon rim, is by permit only under tight Park Service restrictions (for full details, see p.92).

Camping possibilities **outside the park** are detailed wherever relevant in this book; see p.47 for options close to the South Rim, p.136 for the North Rim, and p.181 for the Havasupai Indian Reservation.

Accommodation price codes

All accommodation rates in this book have been coded using the symbols below. These indicate the **least expensive double room** in each establishment, **excluding taxes**, which are 6.38 percent inside the park, and from five to fifteen percent outside. Significant seasonal variations are noted, as are establishments that hold rooms at widely differing prices. Note that hostels offer inexpensive individual dorm beds, as well as standard rooms.

❶ up to $30	❹ $60–80	❼ $130–175
❷ $30–45	❺ $80–100	❽ $175–250
❸ $45–60	❻ $100–130	❾ $250+

Post, phones, and email

So long as you bear in mind that the Grand Canyon is basically a remote, rural destination, communications to and from the region are much as you'd expect anywhere in the United States.

Telephones

It's usually easy to find a public phone in the Southwest. As a rule, local calls cost 35¢, but you may have to feed in nine or ten quarters just to call the next town down the highway, and long-distance calls can cost far more. Some budget motels offer guests free local calls, but in general calls from motel rooms are even more expensive.

To save money on calls when you're on the road, it's well worth buying a **prepaid phone card**, available in various denominations from gas stations, supermarkets, and other outlets. These offer sizable savings on conventional phone rates – not least because they're normally accessed via a toll-free number that incurs no additional charge when called from a motel room.

Mail

You'll find **post offices** in the national park at both the South Rim (in Market Plaza; see p.49) and North Rim (in the *Grand Canyon Lodge*; see p.74), as well as in towns throughout the region; blue mailboxes stand at many street corners. Typical hours at post offices outside the park are Mon–Fri 9am–5pm and Sat 9am–noon. Ordinary mail

within the US costs 37¢ for a letter weighing up to an ounce. Airmail between the US and Europe or Australia costs 70¢ for postcards or aerograms and 80¢ for letters weighing up to half an ounce (a single thin sheet), and delivery generally takes about a week.

Internet access

Public Internet access in the canyon region is not as widely available as one might expect, though many of the South Rim park lodges (see p.49) provide email stations, as do hostels that cater to international travelers. Most public libraries offer free access, and self-styled "alternative" cafés here and there will let customers go online. On the road, however, it's not as easy to stay in touch.

If you're carrying a Wi-Fi–equipped laptop computer, you could simply cruise the streets looking for access, while those dependent on modems can usually plug in at even the cheapest motel (though you may have to shift that supposedly immovable bed to reach the socket). A greater concern among international travelers is whether one's Internet service provider is reachable via a toll-free or at least local call in the US, rather than having to make an international

Useful numbers and phone codes

Emergencies ☎911; ask for the appropriate emergency service: fire, police, or ambulance.
Directory information ☎411
Long-distance directory information ☎1-(area code)/555-1212
Directory enquiries for toll-free numbers ☎1-800/555-1212

International telephone calls
To make calls **TO THE US** from the outside world (excluding Canada), first dial 1.
To make international calls **FROM THE US**, dial 011 followed by the country code:

Australia 61	**Ireland** 353
New Zealand 64	**UK** 44

call just to log on – rarely an issue with larger ISPs, such as AOL. The useful website ⓦwww.kropla.com explains how to plug in your laptop while traveling and provides phone country codes and information about electrical systems worldwide.

Health and safety

By far the most important health and safety issues facing visitors to the Grand Canyon relate to hiking and backcountry survival, particularly below the rim.

Chapter Three addresses such concerns in depth, including water and food, wildlife, what to carry, and security precautions.

If you're planning any form of backcountry adventure, whether driving, hiking, or rafting, be sure to supplement the advice in this book with tips and information on current road or trail conditions from rangers at any of the park visitor centers.

Insurance

In view of the high cost of medical care in the US, all visitors from overseas should purchase some form of travel insurance. American and Canadian citizens should check existing coverage limits – some homeowner's and renter's policies are valid on vacation, and credit cards such as American Express often include medical or other insurance, while most Canadians are covered under their provincial health plans for medical mishaps abroad. Supplemental trip cancellation/interruption insurance is generally available for about $6 per $100 of coverage.

Rough Guides travel insurance

Rough Guides has teamed up with Columbus Direct to offer travel insurance that can be tailored to suit your needs.

Readers can choose from many different travel insurance products, including a low-cost backpacker option for long stays; a typical holiday package option; and many others. There are also annual multi-trip policies for those who travel regularly, with variable levels of cover available. Different sports and activities (trekking, skiing, etc) can be covered if required on most policies.

Rough Guides travel insurance is available to the residents of 36 different countries with different language options to choose from via our website – ⓦwww.roughguides insurance.com – where you can also purchase the insurance. Alternatively, UK residents should call ☏0800 083 9507; US citizens should call ☏1-800/749-4922; Australians should call ☏1 300 669 999. All other nationalities should call ☏44 870 890 2843.

Travelers with disabilities

For travelers with disabilities, the South Rim of the Grand Canyon is a much more convenient destination than the North Rim, offering a wider range of accessible overlooks, accommodations, and other facilities.

The park *Accessibility Guide*, available at all visitor centers or by mail from PO Box 129, Grand Canyon, AZ 86023, includes maps and information about wheelchair-accessible buildings and rim trails; such details are also available online at Ⓦ www.nps .gov/grca/pphtml/accessibility.html. Broadly speaking, all in-park lodgings on both rims, except *Yavapai Lodge* on the South Rim, are accessible, while some of the older, historic structures along the South Rim, such as Hopi House and Kolb Studio, are not.

Electric cart service is available upon request for travel between the Canyon View Information Plaza and Mather Point; inquire at the parking lot or in the visitor center. Loaner wheelchairs are also available at the visitor center.

Although most of the South Rim's free **shuttle buses** (see p.43) are not wheelchair-accessible, visitors can call Ⓣ 928/638-0591 two days in advance to arrange transport in

an accessible vehicle. Alternatively, stop by the entrance station, Canyon View Information Plaza, Yavapai Observation Station, or Kolb Studio to obtain a temporary **accessibility permit**, which allows private vehicle access to shuttle-only areas, notably Hermit Road (see p.57). The *Accessibility Guide* includes a map of "windshield views," where you can see the canyon without leaving your vehicle.

On the **North Rim**, *Grand Canyon Lodge* is accessible and provides loaner wheelchairs. The viewpoints at Point Imperial and Cape Royal are accessible along level paved paths, but the undulating, uneven trail out to Bright Angel Point is not recommended.

Both the park **bus tours** (see p.43) and **mule rides** (see p.55 & p.71) can accommodate travelers with disabilities; call Ⓣ 928/638-2631 for full details. So, too, can several of the **rafting** operators listed on p.202 onward.

Directory

Electricity The US electricity supply is 110 volts AC, with standard two-pin plugs – foreign visitors will need an adapter and voltage converter to use their electrical appliances.

Emergencies Dial Ⓣ 911.

ID Carry ID at all times. Two pieces should suffice, one of which should bear a recent photo; a passport and credit card(s) are your best bets. Not having a license with you while driving is an arrestable offense.

Senior travelers Anyone over age 62 with suitable ID can take advantage of certain discounts. Amtrak and Greyhound, for instance, offer slightly reduced fares to older passengers. US residents aged 50 or over can join the American Association of Retired Persons, 601 E St NW, Washington DC 20049 (Ⓣ 202/434-2277 or 1-800/424-3410, Ⓦ www.aarp.org), which organizes group travel for senior citizens and can provide discounts on accommodations and car rental. Elderhostel, 75 Federal St, Boston, MA 02110 (☎1-877/426-8056, ⊛www.elderhostel.org), operates educational programs and activities in the Southwest for persons 60 and over and their companions. For information about Golden Age Passports, which grant US citizens or residents aged 62 or older free admission to national parks, see p.26.

Tax Though added to virtually everything you buy in a shop, sales tax isn't included in the marked price. While local sales taxes vary, Arizona's base rate is 5.6 percent – except on Indian reservations, which do not levy a sales tax. Most towns also charge lodging taxes of between five and fifteen percent.

Temperature Always given in Fahrenheit; to convert to Celsius, subtract 32, multiply by 5, and divide by 9.

Time zones Arizona is on Mountain Time, two hours behind Eastern Time and seven hours behind Greenwich Mean Time. When it is 2pm at the Grand Canyon, it is 4pm in New York and 9pm in London. In winter, the time at the canyon is the same as in New Mexico, Utah, and Colorado, while Nevada and California are on Pacific Time, another hour behind. Between the first Sunday in April and the last Sunday in October, New Mexico, Utah, Colorado, and Nevada switch to daylight saving time and advance their clocks by one hour. Arizona, however, does not, so in summer the time is an hour behind New Mexico and Utah and the same as in Nevada. Confusingly, the Navajo Nation in northeast Arizona does shift to daylight saving time, putting it an hour ahead of the rest of Arizona in summer.

Tipping Restaurant waitstaff depend on tips for the bulk (and sometimes all) of their earnings; fifteen to twenty percent is the standard rate. Ten percent is acceptable for bar staff.

Traveling with children The canyon is a demanding place, so if you're traveling with young children, pay constant attention to their safety. For kids old enough to be trusted near the drop-offs, however, the national park makes a wonderful destination. Rangers at the South Rim in particular offer a wide range of activities for kids, from daily talks and walks (see p.42) to the Junior Ranger program, in which children aged 4 to 14 can complete activity books to attain the coveted title and badge. Be especially cautious when hiking with children; it's difficult and dangerous enough for adults without having to carry exhausted little ones. When in doubt, stick to the above-rim trails recommended on p.87. Finally, don't underestimate the sheer amount of driving involved if you plan to visit to both rims; consider interrupting your journey with an overnight stay in either Marble Canyon or Page.

Guide

Guide

1

South Rim

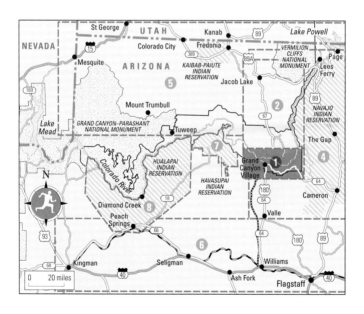

CHAPTER 1 # Highlights

✳ **Grand Canyon Railway** For families in particular, a ride on the steam train up from Williams makes a memorable introduction to the national park. See p.40

✳ **Cabins at Bright Angel Lodge** The attractive, bargain-priced cabins at this rim-edge option are often reserved well in advance, but a cancellation could grant you a real treat. See p.45

✳ **El Tovar** This rustic, century-old lodge oozes charm and offers the choicest eating and accommodation on the rim. See p.45

✳ **Mather Point** The overlook closest to the park visitor center is an ideal spot to get your first view of the abyss. See p.50

✳ **Condors** To witness North America's largest bird swooping over the canyon rim is an unforgettable experience. See p.53

✳ **Hopi Point** Though often crowded at sunset, Hopi Point offers some of the finest canyon views. See p.59

✳ **Hermits Rest** Architect Mary Jane Colter was responsible for this inviting little rest stop along the rim. See p.61

✳ **Shoshone Point** Only accessible on foot, this beautiful viewpoint offers a rare opportunity to be alone with the canyon. See p.62

✳ **The Watchtower** Another Colter tour de force, this mock-Pueblo tower with stunning canyon views blends into the rocks at the east end of Desert View Drive. See p.65

△ Sunset at Mather Point

1

South Rim

When people casually mention visiting "the Grand Canyon," it's almost certainly the **South Rim** to which they're referring. To be more precise, it's the thirty-mile stretch of the South Rim served by a paved road, and most specifically of all it's **Grand Canyon Village**, the small community sandwiched between the pine forest and the rim that holds a **visitor center** and most of the park's **lodges** and **restaurants**. In fact, of the almost five million people who visit the national park each year, nine out of ten head for this same tiny spot along the rim. Even an area as vast as the Grand Canyon can find it hard to handle the human influx.

The reason so many people come here is not, however, because this is a uniquely wonderful spot from which to see the canyon. In terms of views, it's as good a place as any to start, and every visit begins with an eager rush to catch that first breathtaking glimpse of the abyss. But really Grand Canyon Village just happens to be where the tourist facilities have come to be concentrated.

Tourism to the South Rim sparked toward the end of the nineteenth century, when miners prospecting along the rim put up paying guests in simple cabins and inns. Then, in 1901, a railroad was laid down north from Williams to the site that was to become Grand Canyon Village, and lodges, campgrounds, and other amenities sprang up around the station. Even after car visits supplanted train travel, the convenience of having everything in one place continued to outweigh overcrowding issues. The situation persisted for a hundred years, until, as the millennium approached, it looked as though the village could no longer take the strain, despite the emergence of nearby **Tusayan** as a rival lodging hub.

Despite universal consensus that something had to be done, the situation remains far from resolved; it has barely even improved. Planners did craft an ambitious transportation scheme, under which private vehicles were to be banned from both the village and canyon overlooks, obliging visitors to instead explore the South Rim on a proposed **light rail** network. The plan has barely been implemented – and as visitor numbers have failed to increase in line with the dire predictions of the 1990s, it seems unlikely it ever will. All that's really happened is construction of the large, open-air **Canyon View Information Plaza**, though it sits well away from the village center and back from the rim. It may look great, but it's done nothing to relieve traffic congestion and fails to meet even the basic requisite of being an easy first stop.

The first half of this chapter covers South Rim practicalities; jump to "Exploring the South Rim" (p.49) for descriptions of the sights, overlooks, and scenic drives.

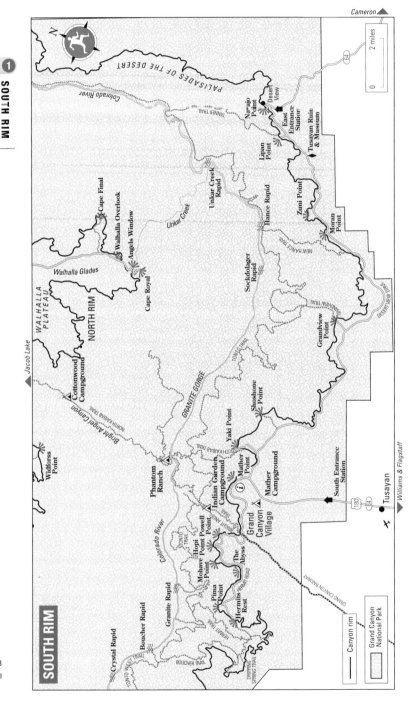

SOUTH RIM

On a positive note, the canyon is as majestic as ever, to be admired from countless differing vantage points not only within the village, but also along the eight-mile **Hermit Road** to the west and 23-mile **Desert View Drive** to the east. The village facilities maintain a pretty high standard – especially such historic properties like *El Tovar* and *Bright Angel Lodge* – and are generally well priced. The village itself is also a lot more attractive than one might imagine, and once the day-trippers have gone, it rarely feels as crowded as the horror stories might suggest.

Arrival

The vast majority of visitors make their way to the South Rim via either **Williams** (58 miles south; see p.164) or **Flagstaff** (81 miles southeast; see p.156). Both towns straddle I-40 and are served by cross-country Amtrak **trains**. In the absence of direct Amtrak service to the canyon, a separate **excursion train** runs from Williams up to the rim, while **buses** also run between Flagstaff and the canyon, calling at Williams en route. Direct **flights** to Tusayan's small airport are available from Las Vegas and other points in the Southwest.

By car

The two main roads up to the South Rim – **AZ-64** from Williams, also known as the Bushmaster Memorial Highway, and **US-180** from Flagstaff – merge at **Valle**, a tiny community 25 miles south of **Tusayan**, which lies just outside the park. Just north of Flagstaff, US-180 threads through the dramatic San Francisco Peaks, making it the more scenic drive of the two. Both roads, however, tick off most of their length across the **Coconino Plateau**, which is covered by the world's largest **ponderosa pine forest**. Crossing this flat expanse, you get no sense of the impending abyss until you reach the very edge of the canyon, close to Mather Point.

You can also drive to the park from the **east** along the 34-mile section of AZ-64 that branches off from US-89 at **Cameron** (see p.121). Coming this way, you'll reach the canyon at Desert View and pass the East Rim overlooks en route to the village, 25 miles farther on. The obvious route to follow if you're coming in from the north, it also serves as an alternative approach from Flagstaff if you'd like to add Sunset Crater and Wupatki national monuments to your itinerary (see p.162).

Parking

Parking in and around Grand Canyon Village is seldom easy. Guests staying at the various lodges – especially *Bright Angel*, *Maswik* and *Yavapai* – should have no trouble parking near their rooms overnight, but finding a space in the middle of the day can be murder. Ludicrously, there's no parking at all at the visitor center and very little at nearby Mather Point. Of the five free public lots in and around the village, your best bets are unpaved Lot D, across the tracks from the railway station (take the first left after crossing the tracks near the Hermit Road shuttle stop), and Lot A, across the main road from Market Plaza.

Current **admission fees** to Grand Canyon National Park, payable at the entrance stations just north of Tusayan and just east of Desert View, are detailed on p.26.

By train

Amtrak **trains** (℡1-800/872-7245, ⓦwww.amtrak.com) stop at the stations in **Flagstaff** and **Williams**. Schedules vary slightly year to year, but according to the latest summer timetable, westbound trains from Chicago via Albuquerque stop at Flagstaff at 8.51pm and Williams Junction at 9.33pm daily, while east-bound trains from Los Angeles are due at Williams Junction at 4.20am and Flagstaff at 4.56am daily. Winter service runs one hour later. Bus connections are detailed below.

Grand Canyon Railway

The **Grand Canyon Railway** (℡928/773-1976 or 1-800/843-8724, ⓦwww .thetrain.com), which celebrated its centennial in 2001, runs for 65 miles from **Williams** to a picturesque wooden station in the heart of Grand Canyon Village. When the line first opened, it heralded the start of mass tourism to the canyon, but by 1968 it had been driven out of business by the growth of private automobile travel. Restored in 1989, the railway is now a tourist attraction in its own right. Riding in historic cars of varying degrees of comfort, passengers are entertained throughout the day by Wild West shootouts, holdups, pistol-packing marshals, singing conductors, and the like. The scenery en route – part desert scrubland, part pine forest – is far from spectacular, and you'll never actually see the canyon from the train, but it's still a fun and memorable way to visit the park without having to drive.

Operating daily year-round (except Christmas Eve and Christmas Day), the train leaves central Williams (not the Amtrak station) at 10am and arrives at the village at 12.15pm, while the return trip leaves at 3.30pm and reaches Williams at 5.45pm. Sadly, it's only pulled by a **steam locomotive** between late May and the end of September; a diesel locomotive does the job the rest of year. Five types of passenger cars are in service, offering such amenities as larger, more comfortable seats and complimentary food and beverages. Round-trip fares range from $60 in coach ($35 for ages 11–16, $25 ages 2–10) up to $155 (under

△ Grand Canyon Railway locomotive leaves Grand Canyon Village

Horseback riding

Just outside the South Entrance at Moqui Lodge (itself permanently closed), **Apache Stables** (☎928/638-2891, ⓦwww.apachestables.com) charges $30.50 for a one-hour trail ride through the Kaibab National Forest or $55.50 for two hours. Evening offerings include campfire rides on horseback for $40.50 or by wagon for $12.50. To see the canyon itself, take the four-hour East Rim ride ($95.50).

17, $130) in the Luxury Parlor Car. The railway does not accept Amtrak passes of any kind, and unless you have a National Parks Pass, you'll face an additional $8 park admission fee.

Most passengers ride the railway on day-trips up from Williams, but you can break up the round-trip by staying at the village for one or more nights. You can also make the journey in reverse and visit Williams. Available package deals include lodging and dining discounts in Williams and/or the village, while Christmastime heralds special hour-long evening trips to meet Santa Claus at the North Pole (which, incidentally, is not at the Grand Canyon).

By bus

Open Road Tours & Transportation (☎928/226-8060 or 1-877/226-8060, ⓦwww.openroadtours.com) runs two **bus services** each day from the Amtrak station in **Flagstaff**, via the Grand Canyon Railway depot in **Williams** and the Grand Canyon IMAX Theater in **Tusayan**, to the **Maswik Lodge** in Grand Canyon Village. The first bus leaves Flagstaff at 8.30am daily, calling at Williams at 9am and reaching Maswik at 10.15am; the second leaves Flagstaff at 3pm and Williams at 3.30pm, reaching Maswik at 4.45pm. Return services leave Maswik at 10.45am and 5.45pm, arriving at Williams at noon and 7pm and Flagstaff at 12.30pm and 7.30pm, respectively. Tickets cost $27 each way from Flagstaff for adults, or $22 from Williams, and $19/$17 for accompanied children under 12.

Guided **bus tours** to the park from Flagstaff and Williams are detailed on p.155 and p.165, respectively.

By air

Tiny **Grand Canyon National Park Airport** sits just outside the park boundary in Tusayan, six miles south of the canyon rim. Used primarily by flight-seeing tour companies (see pp.24–25), it also welcomes scheduled flights and excursions, primarily from **Las Vegas**. While such flights don't pass directly over the park, they still offer good views. Standard fares run about $150 one way and $250 round-trip, but special offers can reduce that to as little as $60 and $100, respectively. The major Vegas operators are Scenic Airlines (☎702/638-3300 or 1-800/634-6801, ⓦwww.scenic.com), and Air Vegas (☎928/638-9351, 702/736-3599 or 1-800/255-7474, ⓦwww.airvegas.com).

Most Tusayan hotels offer guests courtesy pickup service. You won't find a **car rental** outlet at the airport, but the Enterprise branch in Flagstaff (☎928/774-9407, ⓦwww.enterprise.com) will deliver a car there for around $150.

Information

While the **Canyon View Information Plaza** may seem an obvious first stop at the South Rim, finding a parking spot anywhere near it in midsummer can be all but impossible. Save yourself the trouble by instead picking up a copy of the park's **free newspaper**, *The Guide*, available at the two **entrance stations** and in all park **lodges**.

As well as listing current operating hours and shuttle schedules, *The Guide* outlines a full program of **park activities**, such as ranger talks and guided hikes. On a typical day in high season, more than a dozen such talks or hikes are on offer, at venues ranging from shuttle bus stops and overlooks to the visitor center or canyon rim in the village. All are free of charge, and it's well worth scheduling your day to coincide with whatever's going on.

Apart from the plaza, you'll find **information desks** at Kolb Studio, Yavapai Observation Station, Tusayan Museum, and Desert View. For details about the **Backcountry Office**, which issues permits for backpacking and camping in the canyon, see p.93.

Canyon View Information Plaza

Opened in 2000, **Canyon View Information Plaza** (daily: May to mid-Oct 8am–6pm, mid-Oct to April 8am–5pm; ☎928/638-7888, ⓦwww.nps.gov /grca) is across the main road from Mather Point, just west of the junction of AZ-64 and the spur road to the village. Despite its name, the plaza sits well back from the rim and offers no canyon views. What it does provide are extensive, well-illustrated open-air interpretive displays and trail guides, helpful rangers, and an excellent separate bookstore run by the Grand Canyon Association.

For all its impressive scope, the plaza was not in fact built to serve as the main park visitor center, but rather as the terminus of a proposed **light rail** system. It was envisaged that people would leave their cars in huge parking lots at Tusayan, be ferried here on trains, then transfer to the park shuttle buses. The outdoor information panels were erected to give passengers something to read while waiting at the plaza. Officially, the Park Service still plans to build a dedicated visitor center in the heart of the village.

Construction of the light rail network, on the other hand, has been indefinitely postponed. At some point, a new bus system may serve the same purpose, but for now the plaza remains bizarrely inaccessible, in that it has no parking lot of its own. Instead, those able to find a space at Mather Point must walk the few hundred yards back to the plaza; electric cart service is available for disabled visitors.

Parking at Mather Point is officially restricted to one hour, though that policy doesn't appear to be enforced. Anyway, as space is limited, many summertime visitors simply end up parking on either side of the road itself. *The Guide* suggests you park in the village and catch a shuttle bus back to the plaza, though that takes far more time than it's worth. Be forewarned that while the plaza is accessible on foot from *Yavapai Lodge*, it's a solid mile, whatever impression you may gather from official maps.

Getting around

The ongoing failure to implement an efficient, user-friendly **public transportation** system on the South Rim – and thus persuade visitors *not* to use their private vehicles – means that getting around Grand Canyon Village can still be a frustrating experience. Almost all new arrivals drive straight to the village center. Many soon discover that the **shuttle bus** is a slow and awkward alternative and remain dependent on their cars. If visitors stayed long enough to acclimate to the shuttles, it might help, but for now only the **Hermits Rest Route** service, which ferries sightseers to overlooks west of the village, is an unqualified success.

Driving

Despite the parking shortage in high season, **Grand Canyon Village** is always accessible to private vehicles. So, too, is **Desert View Drive** east to the Watchtower. However, both **Hermit Road**, west of the village, and the short access road to **Yaki Point**, the first overlook east of Mather Point and jumping-off point for the popular **South Kaibab Trail**, are only open to private vehicles in winter (Dec–Feb).

Park shuttle buses

The Guide lists current schedules for the three Park Service shuttle routes. The busiest, the **Village Route**, loops between Grand Canyon Village and Canyon View Information Plaza, stopping at *Maswik* and *Yavapai* lodges and Mather Campground, as well as Yavapai Observation Station. Starting an hour before sunrise, buses run at half-hour intervals until 6.30am, and then at ten- to fifteen-minute intervals until 11pm in summer (May–Sept) or 10pm otherwise.

The whole circuit takes up to an hour to complete, a ridiculous span considering the short distances – perhaps to deter visitors from traveling around the village in the first place. The shuttle is most useful for travel between the campground or *Yavapai Lodge* and the *Bright Angel Lodge* area, though even the simplest trip from point A to B seems to involve a detour to C and D. Unless parking is impossible, it's far quicker to drive. Wherever you're staying, consider visiting the information plaza when you first arrive rather than returning to it by bus.

The **Kaibab Trail Route** offers service between the information plaza and **Yaki Point**, a couple of miles east of the village off Desert View Drive. Buses run at half-hour intervals from an hour before sunrise until an hour after sunset. To use this route, you must first take a Village Route shuttle to the plaza.

If you're planning to hike the **South Kaibab trail** (see p.99) from Yaki Point, it's a lot quicker to catch the early-morning **Hikers' Express**, which runs to the trailhead from *Bright Angel Lodge* and the Backcountry Information Center. The shuttle departs at 4am, 5am, and 6am daily from June to August; 5am, 6am, and 7am in May and September; 6am, 7am, and 8am in April and October; 7am, 8am, and 9am in November and March; and 8am and 9am from December to February. Note that you can also use a **taxi** on this route (see p.44).

Finally, from March through November, buses on the **Hermits Rest Route** follow Hermit Road, an eight-mile drive west of the village that comprises eight canyon overlooks. Allow at least two hours to linger and enjoy the views. (See p.57 onward for a description of the overlooks and advice on how best to use the shuttle.) Buses run from an hour before sunrise until an hour after sunset, at ten- to fifteen-minute intervals between 7.30am and sunset and half-hour intervals otherwise. Note that demand is always high as sunset approaches; get to your stop at least an hour in advance for the trip out.

Park bus tours

As well as managing the park lodges, Xanterra also operates guided **bus tours** along the South Rim. To make a reservation or check the current schedule (cued to sunrise and sunset), contact the transportation desk at any lodge or call

☎928/638-2631. Adults can take any two tours (not necessarily on the same day) for $35, while accompanied children under the age of 17 ride for free on all in-park tours.

The **Desert View Tour** skirts the East Rim along Desert View Drive – a route open to private vehicles but not served by park shuttle buses. Stops include Yavapai Observation Station, Lipan Point, and Desert View at road's end. The 52-mile round trip takes just under four hours and costs $29. The evening run coincides with sunset at Desert View.

West of the village, the **Hermits Rest Tour** is a two-hour jaunt along Hermit Road that costs $16.75. As it follows virtually the same route as the free Hermits Rest Route shuttle (see p.43), including some but not all the same stops, you're basically paying for the rather banal commentary.

Shorter **Sunrise** and **Sunset** tours head east and west of the village, respectively, with an adult fare of $12.75.

It's also possible to take a tour down to Williams, traveling there by bus and back on the **Grand Canyon Railway** (see p.40). The fare is $49 for adults and $29 for children under the age of 17.

Taxis

If you're pressed for time, consider taking advantage of the local 24-hour **taxi** service (☎928/638-2822). In particular, a taxi can spare you the lengthy wait for a shuttle bus to the South Kaibab trailhead at Yaki Point; expect to pay around $8.

Cycling

The park's transportation master plan calls for a bicycle rental facility at the information plaza and construction of a 73-mile **Grand Canyon Greenway**, which would enable cyclists to follow the rim in both directions and zip around Grand Canyon Village. At present, bike rental remains unavailable, and only a few segments of the Greenway are ready, including a stretch of the Rim Trail on either side of Mather Point and a trail that links the information plaza with the village. However, cyclists are permitted on all public highways and on Hermit Road.

Accommodation

Roughly two thousand **rooms** are available in the immediate vicinity of the South Rim – half of them in and around **Grand Canyon Village**, the other half in the dull gateway town of **Tusayan**, seven miles south of the rim. Demand far outstrips supply in the high season. Given the choice, the best place to stay has to be on the very lip of the canyon, though fewer than three hundred rooms stand at all close to the rim, and only a handful offer canyon views.

While motels in Tusayan are often more modern and better equipped, even basic in-park rooms away from the rim make more convenient bases, and as the Park Service sets all rates, some of the rates available within the park are an extraordinarily good value.

Grand Canyon Village

Xanterra Parks & Resorts, PO Box 699, Grand Canyon, AZ 86023 (same day ☎928/638-2631, advance 303/297-2757 or 1-888/297-2757, ⓦwww .grandcanyonlodges.com) handles **reservations** for all accommodations within

Grand Canyon Village and down at Phantom Ranch (see p.107), as well as on the North Rim. The nicest lodgings are two venerable Fred Harvey properties just north of Grand Canyon Village – the magnificent **El Tovar** and the almost as attractive **Bright Angel Lodge**.

As the rates set by the National Park Service depend almost entirely on in-room amenities rather than the view, it may be no more expensive to stay in a quaint rim-side cabin than in a charmless motel room a mile from the edge. There are, however, far more of the latter than the former; in fact, the number of rooms with unobstructed canyon views barely reaches double figures. During busy periods – roughly early May through late September – the best rooms are often booked up to thirteen months in advance, and by June it would be very unusual to find any available same-day bookings.

Rates listed here apply during high season; in the depths of winter, prices for rooms near the rim drop by about $20 per night, while rates at *Maswik* and *Yavapai* lodges can slide as much as $40. Bear in mind that once you've made your booking, it's well worth making repeated follow-up calls to see if any cancellations have become available; you could easily end up getting a nicer room at *Bright Angel Lodge*, for example, for half the asking price of *Yavapai Lodge*.

Lodges

Bright Angel Lodge Designed by Mary Jane Colter and built in 1935, the *Bright Angel* complex consists of an imposing central lodge and a westward sprawl of rustic but comfortable detached log cabins. Staying in a cabin makes for a delightful experience, whether you're in a Rim Cabin with a tremendous view or one of the cheaper Historic Cabins, set back closer to the mule corral. Though reasonably sized, appealingly furnished, well priced, and equipped with phones, many of the lodge rooms share bathrooms and/or toilets; a few do offer private showers. Best of all is the Buckey O'Neill Suite, which boasts a large living room with working fireplace and two front doors that open on the rim. Lodge rooms and Historic Cabins ❸, Rim Cabins ❻, Buckey O'Neill Suite ❾

El Tovar Named for an early Spanish explorer, this log-construction rim-side hotel remains the centerpiece of Grand Canyon Village. Extensively refurbished to celebrate its centennial in 2005, it continues to exude the same combination of rough-hewn charm and elegant sophistication that made it the very peak of fashion when it first opened. Only three suites offer extensive canyon views; the rest of the 78 tastefully furnished guest rooms come in two different sizes, but are otherwise very similar, with no extra charge for those offering partial glimpses of the abyss. Almost all provide just one bed. Standard ❼, larger ❽, suites ❾

Kachina Lodge Anonymous but perfectly adequate motel-style rooms, each with two queen-size beds and recently renovated, set in a low and utterly undistinguished two-story block separated by twenty yards of grass from the rim. Although the lodge makes no formal claim of canyon views, in fact the upper-floor rooms on the canyon side – which cost $10 extra – provide great panoramas. Registration is handled in the lobby of the adjoining *El Tovar*. ❼

Maswik Lodge Set a few hundred yards back from the rim at the southwest end of the village, the large *Maswik* complex includes two distinct blocks of motel-style rooms, which are often booked by tour groups, as well as a cluster of basic summer-only cabins, each of which holds two double beds. When split among four travelers, the cabins are the closest the village comes to budget lodgings. Rooms in the *Maswik North* building are considerably nicer than those in the smaller, cramped *Maswik South*. Cabins and Maswik South ❺, Maswik North ❻

Thunderbird Lodge Both the *Thunderbird* and the identical *Kachina Lodge* next door were built of gray brick in the 1960s and intended to last only ten years. Both are still going strong without being in any way distinctive. Run from the front desk of *Bright Angel Lodge*, the *Thunderbird* offers 55 rooms with twin beds, 37 of which are on the canyon side of the building and cost $10 extra. ❼

Yavapai Lodge With 358 rooms, *Yavapai* is the largest of the in-park lodges and the last to fill up, so it's the most likely to be available if you try to book on short notice. The main drawback is that it's half a mile from the rim, and twice that – farther than you'd want to walk, especially at night – from Grand Canyon Village, which leaves guests without vehicles all too dependent on the slow park shuttles. In late fall and early spring, either of the lodge's two similar sections, *Yavapai East* or *Yavapai West*, may be closed, while the whole lodge shuts down in winter. Despite the lackluster complex, the rooms themselves are perfectly decent motel-style accommodations, most with twin beds. As they're set back in the woods in smallish blocks, they're also fairly quiet. Yavapai West **5**, Yavapai East **6**

Outside the park: Tusayan

Straddling the highway a mile outside the park entrance and seven miles south of Grand Canyon Village, **TUSAYAN** is an unattractive commercial strip that holds little beyond the Grand Canyon IMAX Theater, a few stores and restaurants, and half a dozen large **hotel/motels**. Although it has traditionally functioned as an overspill when in-park accommodations are booked, large tour operators have come to prefer Tusayan for a higher standard of amenities and a greater ease in feeding, entertaining, and generally managing groups. No independent visitor, however, would or should choose to stay in Tusayan rather than the village. Listed below are high-season rates, which often drop significantly in low season.

Hotels and motels

Best Western Grand Canyon Squire Inn PO Box 130, Grand Canyon, AZ 86023 ☎928/638-2681 or 1-800/622-6966, ⌨www.grandcanyonsquire.com. While Tusayan's most lavish option bills itself as the canyon's "only resort hotel," with an outdoor pool, indoor spa, and even its own four-lane bowling alley, its rates compare favorably with those of its neighbors. Most rooms are spacious and very comfortable, if unremarkable; paying a little extra gets you an enormous deluxe room with oval bath. **6**

The Grand Hotel PO Box 3319, Grand Canyon, AZ 86023 ☎928/638-3333 or 1-888/634-7263, ⌨www.grandcanyongrandhotel.com. The overall look of this modern hotel is a nod toward traditional park lodges. Once you get past the very smart public spaces, however, the rooms themselves are no better than those at its cheaper neighbors or lesser in-park options, although there is a nice figure-eight indoor pool, and it's also home to the *Canyon Star* restaurant (see p.48). **7**

Holiday Inn Express PO Box 3245, Grand Canyon, AZ 86023 ☎928/638-3000 or 1-888/473-2269, ⌨www.ichotelsgroup.com/h/d/6c/1/en/hd/gcnaz. Unexciting but perfectly acceptable chain motel on the highway, with no pool or restaurant. **6**

Quality Inn & Suites Canyon Plaza PO Box 520, Grand Canyon, AZ 86023 ☎928/638-2673 or 1-800/995-2521, ⌨www.grandcanyonqualityinn.com. Though it's not very conspicuous from the highway, tucked behind the IMAX theater and the *Red Feather Lodge*, the *Quality Inn* is actually huge, with 176 rooms and 56 suites, plus an outdoor pool, an indoor spa, and a large but uninspiring restaurant in its central atrium. **7**

Red Feather Lodge PO Box 1460, Grand Canyon, AZ 86023 ☎928/638-2414 or 1-800/538-2345, ⌨www.redfeatherlodge.com. This long-established motel was joined a few years ago by a large new hotel block; they share a pool, the rates aren't bad, and the newer rooms offer a reasonably high standard. Motel **5**, hotel **6**

Seven Mile Lodge PO Box 56, Grand Canyon, AZ 86023 ☎928/638-2291. The last remaining little roadside motel in Tusayan, this twenty-room place is very plain beyond its kachina doorway and hanging flowers, but it's the least expensive option around. Reservations are not accepted; rooms are simply doled out from 9am daily. Despite the slight premium charged for housing three or four guests in the same room, it's still great value for groups of (close) friends. **4**

Farther afield

If even Tusayan is booked up, it's worth considering the large *Grand Canyon Inn* (☎928/635-9203 or 1-800/635-9203, ⌨www.grandcanyoninn.com; **5**), beside the Chevron station at the intersection of AZ-64 and US-180 in **VALLE**, another twenty miles south. Though in somewhat of a godforsaken spot, with only the Flintstones for company (see opposite), the inn has modern rooms at reasonable prices, a heated outdoor pool, and a standard restaurant open for all meals. The more rudimentary *Grand Canyon Motel*

For regulations governing **backcountry camping** in the park, see p.92.

(**○**), across the highway and open in summer only, is booked through the same office.

Failing either of these, your closest options are in Flagstaff, Williams, and Cameron. The closest hostels to the park are in Flagstaff and outside Williams.

Camping

Tent and RV camping (without hookups) is available at the Park Service's year-round **Mather Campground**, south of the main road through Grand Canyon Village, not far from Market Plaza. Sites for up to two vehicles and six people cost $15 per night between April and November, when reservations (strongly recommended) can be made up to five months in advance either through Spherix (same day ☏928/638-2611, advance 1-800/365-2267 or ☏301/722-1257 from outside the US) or online at ⓦ www.reservations.nps .gov. Between December and March sites are first-come, first-served, and the fee drops to $10 per night. The adjacent **Trailer Village** offers exclusively RV sites with hookups, which run $22 per site per night for two people, plus $2 for each additional adult; reserve through Xanterra (☏303/297-2757 or ⓦ www .grandcanyonlodges.com).

In summer, additional first-come, first-served sites, without hookups, are available 25 miles east of Grand Canyon Village at the NPS-run **Desert View Campground** (mid-May to mid-Oct; no reservations; $10).

Outside the park in **Tusayan** is *Camper Village* (☏928/638-2887, ⓦ www .grandcanyonentrance.com; some RV hookups; $18–23), a commercial campground, while the Kaibab National Forest runs the minimally equipped, first-come, first-served *Ten-X Campground* (mid-April to Sept; no hookups or showers; $10), two miles south of the park. Twenty miles farther south in **Valle**, *Flintstone's Bedrock City* (mid-March to Oct; ☏928/635-2600; $13 tent sites, $17 RV hookups) is a family-oriented commercial campground with a simple store, snack bar, and its own prehistoric theme park based on the popular cartoon series.

Eating and drinking

Although only the gorgeous canyon-rim dining room at *El Tovar* is noteworthy, you'll find a reasonable selection of places to **eat** in Grand Canyon Village, and you certainly won't gain anything by opting for Tusayan instead. It's also possible to buy basic **groceries** at the Canyon Village Marketplace, near *Yavapai Lodge*, or in Tusayan. If you're out exploring, you'll find **snack bars** at Hermits Rest (daily: summer 9am–sunset, otherwise 9am–4pm) and Desert View (daily: summer 8am–7pm, winter 9am–4pm).

Grand Canyon Village

Both *El Tovar* and *Bright Angel Lodge* offer proper **restaurants**, but since their capacity is far too low to meet demand, you'll probably end up eating in the large *Maswik* or *Yavapai* **cafeterias**. For an even quicker meal, the Canyon Village Marketplace runs a pretty good **deli counter** (daily: summer 7am–6pm, otherwise 8am–5pm).

As for **drinking**, *El Tovar* provides a cozy, wood-paneled **cocktail lounge** (daily 11am–11pm), which serves a small menu of appetizers and desserts; at sunset, retreat with your goodies to the lovely and strangely underused outdoor terrace, on the lawn within a few feet of the rim. The lounge at *Bright Angel* (daily 11am–11pm) often features live country music and doubles as a **coffee bar** from 5.30am daily. *Maswik Lodge* hosts a **sports bar** (daily 5–11pm) with big-screen TV.

Arizona Room *Bright Angel Lodge.* Informal, plain, but good-quality restaurant just a few yards from the rim – no views to speak of, but you do get a strong sense of the vast space nearby. The open kitchen serves conventional meat and seafood entrees. Sandwiches, salads, and simple meals cost $8–11 at lunch, while typical dinner prices include a slab of baby back ribs for $24, a 10oz steak for $19, or a roasted quarter-chicken for $11.25. No reservations; your best bet is to nip in a little before sunset, otherwise you may have to wait up to two hours in the bar by the entrance. Daily 11.30am–3pm (summer only) & 4.30–10pm. Closed early Jan to mid-Feb.

Bright Angel Restaurant *Bright Angel Lodge.* Straightforward, windowless diner open for every meal and serving pretty much anything you might want, from snacks, burgers, sandwiches, and salads for under $10 to steaks at around $16. Daily 6.30am–10pm; no reservations.

El Tovar *El Tovar* ☎ 928/638-2631, ext 6432. Very grand, very classy dark-wood dining room, with subdued lighting and lovely big windows that focus all attention outward, especially at sunset – though only the front tier of tables have actual canyon views. Reservations are accepted for dinner only and are often grabbed days, sometimes weeks, in advance. The food itself is rich and expensive, especially at dinner, when almost all entrees, such as braised lamb shank, roast duck, or salmon tostada, cost well over $20. Appetizers are a bit more imaginative, with barbecued sea scallops at $11 and even *Clesan-du-Klish*, or Navajo blue-corn tamales, at $9. Daily 6.30am–11am, 11.30am–2pm & 5–10pm.

Maswik Cafeteria *Maswik Lodge.* Self-service fast food aimed especially at tour groups, with separate Mexican and Italian sections, as well as burgers and standard plate lunches. Breakfast can come in under $5, but lunch and dinner entrees are closer to $10. Offers two spacious seating areas and an adjoining bar. Daily 6am–10pm.

Yavapai Cafeteria *Yavapai Lodge.* Park staff and other locals prefer the *Yavapai's* large cafeteria to the *Maswik's* for its salad bar, fried chicken, and slightly lower prices for burgers and daily specials; visitors are unlikely to spot the difference, and if you're not staying here, it's not worth a special trip. The lines are often long, so if it's the chicken you've come for, head straight for that counter. The central dining area has a dull, canteen-like feel, but there is a nicer glassed-in annex. Summer daily 6am–9pm, spring and fall daily 7am–8pm; shorter hours and occasional closures in low season.

Tusayan

Tusayan's two finest restaurants are, no surprise, in its two fanciest hotels. All other sizable hotels have run-of-the-mill dining rooms, while the town hosts such self-explanatory family restaurants as *We Cook Pizza & Pasta* (☎928/638-2278), *Spaghetti Western* (☎928/638-0331), and *Yippe-Ei-O! Steakhouse* (☎928/638-2780), as well as a *McDonald's*, a *Pizza Hut*, a *Taco Bell*, and a *Wendy's*.

Canyon Star *The Grand Hotel* ☎ 928/638-3333. Large, attractive hotel restaurant, where dinner is a choice between "hardy ranch fare," like $27 steaks or $16 barbecue ribs, or lighter salads and fish dishes at more like $15–17. Lunchtime salads, sandwiches, and Mexican staples mostly cost around $10. The food's nothing special, but the real *raison d'être* is the central dance floor, which hosts "Native American Experience" dances (6.30pm & 8pm nightly), scheduled primarily for tour groups and often featuring hoop dancers. The floor also welcomes live country music. Daily 7–10am, 11am–2pm & 5–9pm.

Coronado Room *Best Western Grand Canyon Squire Inn* ☎ 928/638-2681. The *Squire Inn's* smart dinner-only dining room serves reasonable-quality all-American entrees like prime rib or filet mignon for around $24, as well as such Southwestern fare as chimichangas and fajitas for $17. Its trademark dessert is a white chocolate piano filled with chocolate mousse. Daily 5–10pm.

Jennifer's Bakery & Internet Café ☎928/638-2626. This spacious, comfortable espresso bar across from the IMAX theater does a brisk trade in pastries and sandwiches and also offers Internet access. Daily 7am–8pm in summer; shorter hours in low season.

Listings

Bank The bank in Market Plaza is open Mon–Thurs 9am–5pm & Fri 9am–6pm and has a 24hr ATM machine.

Camping equipment For sale or rent at the Canyon Village Marketplace in Market Plaza (daily: summer 7am–8.30pm, spring & fall 8am–8pm, winter 8am–7pm).

Cinema Grand Canyon IMAX Theater (☎928/638-2203, ⊛www.grandcanyon imaxtheater.com; March–Oct daily 8.30am–8.30pm, Nov–Feb daily 10.30am–6.30pm; $10 adults, $7 under age 12) is Tusayan's sole sightseeing attraction. It features hourly shows, on the half-hour, of *Hidden Secrets of the Grand Canyon*, a 35min big-screen movie that dates from 1984 and centers on a reconstruction of John Wesley Powell's pioneering canyon voyages. While mildly entertaining, it's far from essential viewing.

Disabled travelers The park's comprehensive *Accessibility Guide* is available at all visitor centers and lodges. For more information, see p.31.

Garage service The auto repair garage in the heart of Grand Canyon Village is open daily 8am–noon & 1–5pm; 24hr emergency service also available (☎928/638-2631).

Gas The closest gas stations to the South Rim are in Tusayan and at Desert View.

Internet access Public email stations at *Bright Angel Lodge, Kachina Lodge, Maswik Lodge, Yavapai Lodge*, and Camper Services, as well as at *Jennifer's Bakery* in Tusayan (see above).

Laundromat You'll find a large and inexpensive coin-operated laundry just outside the entrance to *Mather Campground*. Summer daily 6am–11pm, last load 9.45pm; spring and fall daily 7am–9pm, last load 7.45pm; winter daily 8am–6pm, last load 4.45pm.

Medical help Call ☎911 for emergencies; ☎928/638-2551 for the village clinic (daily 8am–6pm; emergencies only at other times); ☎928/638-2460 for the pharmacy; and ☎928/638-2395 for dentist.

Post office In Market Plaza, near *Yavapai Lodge* (Mon–Fri 9am–4.30pm, Sat 11am–1pm; lobby, with stamp machines, daily 5am–10pm).

Showers Coin-op showers, starting at $1 and open to all visitors, are in the laundry building at the entrance to *Mather Campground* (daily: summer 6am–11pm, spring and fall 7am–9pm, winter 8am–6pm).

Weddings Between mid-May and mid-October, the Park Service allows visitors to rent the lovely isolated overlook at Shoshone Point (see p.62) for weddings and other special occasions (☎928/638-7761).

Exploring the South Rim

The first thing every visitor wants to do is to see the canyon. Where you see it for the first time doesn't really matter much; twenty or so named viewpoints line the South Rim, with countless others in between, and none of them can be said to be the "best." The color section in the middle of this book covers the highlights and offers some idea of what to expect. In any case, you don't have to move from place to place to obtain radically different views of the canyon – simply remain in one spot and watch the shifting colors and shadows as the day unfolds.

Contrary to what you might expect, the views from **Grand Canyon Village** itself are not exceptional. To enjoy long-range panoramas, you'll have to venture at least as far as **Maricopa** or **Yavapai** points. Those, and most of the overlooks along the two rim-side sightseeing routes – **Hermit Road** to the west and **Desert View Drive** to the east – make ideal vantage points from which to watch unforgettable **sunrises** and **sunsets**.

Grand Canyon Village and around

For almost a century after the *El Tovar* opened in 1905, at the center of what was to become **Grand Canyon Village**, most South Rim visitors got their first glimpse of the canyon from the rim-edge footpath alongside the hotel. These days, however, thanks to construction of the new information plaza two miles east, your initiation may well come at nearby **Mather Point**.

Mather Point

With its own (albeit small) parking lot just a few hundred yards from the information plaza, busy **Mather Point** centers on a pair of rocky outcrops that jut out just below the rim. When the crowds prove too much, there's always space somewhere along the railed rim trail, with subtly changing views at every step.

For prospective hikers, Mather Point is a perfect introduction to the canyon. Facing roughly northeast, it offers views straight up Bright Angel Canyon, which skewers down from the North Rim. This is the route followed by the **North Kaibab Trail**, which begins near *Grand Canyon Lodge*; a glint of metal halfway down betrays the presence of the footbridge spanning Bright Angel Creek. Two other rim-to-river trails are visible closer in. To the east, the **South Kaibab Trail** zigzags down from Yaki Point, while the westernmost of two visible stretches of the Colorado marks the South Kaibab's intersection with the **Bright Angel Trail**. Below you, nestled alongside the other tiny patch of river, lie the cabins of **Phantom Ranch**, where all those trails lead.

Yavapai Point

About ten minutes west on foot from Mather Point is **Yavapai Point**, the easternmost stop served by Village Route shuttle buses. Yavapai also offers parking for private vehicles, though not enough to meet demand during busy periods. Long-range views from here are similar to those from Mather, encompassing the range of pyramid-shaped buttes, or "temples," that parallel the North Rim. From left to right, you'll see Osiris, Shiva, Isis, Buddha, Manu, Deva, Brahma, Zoroaster, and Vishnu. Two segments of the Colorado are also visible, one of which takes in both Phantom Ranch and the Kaibab Suspension Bridge, or Black Bridge, which spans the river.

Nearby is the **Yavapai Observation Station** (daily: summer 8am–8pm, winter 8am–5pm). If you can tear your eyes away from the views through its tinted bay windows, the station features illuminating displays on how the canyon may have formed. It takes another ten minutes' walk west along the rim before rounding the corner of Grandeur Point brings you within sight of the village proper, and a good ten minutes more beyond that to reach Hopi House and *El Tovar*.

The view from El Tovar

Grand Canyon Village skirts the inner curve of a recess that cuts well back into the South Rim. Geologists refer to such features as **arenas**; this one is also a **swale**, in that the middle is significantly lower than the two sides. As a result, from the paved, railed terrace that traces the rim you can only see straight across the canyon – though by any standard, still a stupendous prospect. Promontories

All hiking trails that descend into the canyon from the South Rim are described in **Chapter Three.**

GRAND CANYON VILLAGE

Feet
8000
6800
5600
4400
3200
0

500 yds

N

Desert View

Phantom Ranch

Hermits Rest

Hopi Point

Powell Point

Maricopa Point

The Battleship

Indian Garden Campground

BRIGHT ANGEL TRAIL

TONTO TRAIL

Grandeur Point

Yavapai Point

Museum

RIM TRAIL

Mather Point

O'Neill Butte

Cedar Mesa

SOUTH KAIBAB TRAIL

Cedar Ridge

Yaki Point

South Kaibab Trailhead

DESERT VIEW DRIVE

Canyon View Information Plaza

Trailer Village

Mather Amphitheater

Park Headquarters

Yavapai Lodge

Mather Campground

Market Plaza

Shrine of the Ages

Laundry/Showers

Clinic

SOUTH ENTRANCE ROAD

MARKET PLAZA RD

Tusayan

Trailview Overlook

Lookout Studio

Kolb Studio

Bright Angel Lodge

Kachina Lodge

El Tovar

Hopi House

Verkamp's Curios

Train Depot

Thunderbird Lodge

CENTER ROAD

Backcountry Information Center

Maswik Transportation Center

Maswik Lodge

ROME WELL ROAD

GRAND CANYON RAILWAY

Sunset and sunrise

Perhaps the single question Grand Canyon park rangers most tire of being asked is, "Where's the best place to watch the sunset?" The answer is, there is no best place, neither for sunset nor for sunrise. How could there be? Each rim of the canyon is almost three hundred miles long, the views change every few yards, and weather and visibility are in constant flux.

That said, the canyon *does* look especially dramatic at the start and end of each day. When the sun is high, the rich colors often bleach out, and heat and dust can diminish visibility. By contrast, when the sun is low, the rich reds and oranges of the sandstone formations emerge in stark contrast to the sharp black shadows, a simply stunning spectacle.

It's well worth seeking out a major viewpoint as sunset approaches and, to a lesser extent, at dawn. On the South Rim, choose a spot away from the village, which because it occupies a low spot on an indentation along the rim does not command long-range views to either east or west. It's best to have both, which means heading somewhere like Hopi, Mohave, or Pima points to the west or Yavapai, Yaki, or Desert View to the east. The most popular spots are Hopi Point at sunset and Yavapai at sunrise, an obvious downside being that often a thousand or more people try to cram into those small patches at the relevant moment. You'd be better off at a relatively quiet overlook where you can wander at will rather than jostle for position. One recommended option is Shoshone Point, which sees few visitors, as it's a twenty-minute walk from the nearest road.

Finally, bear in mind that it's not the sunset that's the spectacle, it's the canyon; if you aim to arrive five minutes before the precise time the sun goes down, you'll see very little. To illuminate anything within the canyon itself, the sun has to be significantly above the horizon, so the finest viewing comes in the final hour or so before sunset, and it comes from looking east, away from the sun and towards those buttes and temples that continue to catch direct sunlight, not west into the shadows. Similarly, it doesn't matter if you miss the moment of dawn; it's the ensuing hour, in which the rising sun picks out the canyon's pinnacles one by one, that will live in your memory.

on either side end at **Grandeur Point** to the east and **Maricopa Point** to the west; the ridge beneath the latter stretches into a sturdy sandstone mesa known picturesquely as **The Battleship**. Directly below, the **Bright Angel Trail** threads through the oasis of **Indian Gardens** before disappearing into a deep crevice, while another long trail leads across the flat, pale-green Tonto Platform to **Plateau Point**.

Glaringly absent in the view from *El Tovar* is the Colorado itself. Although the mighty walls of the Granite Gorge – the chasm that holds the actual river – are visible on the far side, you can't see their full 1300ft depth, so the river rushes by out of sight at the bottom. Thanks to the Bright Angel geologic fault, however, there is a gap in the gorge, where Bright Angel Canyon slices into the **North Rim**. Just to the left atop the rim is *Grand Canyon Lodge* – look for it after dark when the lights come on.

A village walking tour

Grand Canyon Village stretches a lot farther back into the woods than you might imagine and includes a well-hidden residential district for park employees. While those parts hold no interest for sightseers, the rim itself is lined by an attractive assortment of historic buildings.

El Tovar

Designed by Charles F. Whittlesey, the *El Tovar* opened in 1905, two years after Yellowstone's *Old Faithful Inn* had established a taste for this kind of overgrown log cabin. The hotel name was taken from Pedro El Tovar, a member of Coronado's expedition, who was the first European to hear about the canyon but was not among the party who actually came here in 1540 (see p.210).

According to its original brochure, *El Tovar* "combined in admirable proportions the Swiss chalet and the Norway villa," and guests were invited to come in search of "freedom from ultrafashionable restrictions." Back then, each of its four floors held a single bathroom to serve 25 rooms.

While you won't find any historical exhibits or displays, you can get the old-time, unhurried flavor of the place by wandering through the lobby, with its impressive displays of stuffed animal heads, and both its dining room and cocktail lounge are highly recommended (see p.48). Accommodation at *El Tovar* is reviewed on p.45.

Hopi House

The village's most distinctive structure, the triple-tiered **Hopi House** opened on January 1, 1905, just two weeks before its close neighbor the *El Tovar*. Modeled on an actual Hopi dwelling in the village of Oraibi, a hundred miles to the east, it was designed by **Mary Jane Colter** as a place where "the most primitive Indians in America" could both live and display their skills. Early residents included the now venerated Pueblo potter Nampeyo. These days it's neither so overtly educational nor so patronizing; instead, it's a high-class gift

The return of the condor

Of all the awesome spectacles on display along the South Rim, few can match the sight of a full-grown **California condor** soaring past on canyon updrafts. These magnificent birds, with a wingspan over nine feet and a lifespan approaching sixty years, were reintroduced to Arizona in 1996. Visitors now routinely spot them hovering over Grand Canyon Village or perched just below the rim.

Condors were native to the canyon, and indeed to most of North America, for thousands of years, but their population had dwindled long before the first Europeans arrived. The last nesting condor in the canyon region was recorded near Lees Ferry in the 1890s, while a solitary bird was spotted circling Williams in 1924. In the 1980s, researchers trapped the last remaining 22 individual wild condors in California and promptly began a captive breeding program. The birds were first reintroduced in California and subsequently in northern Arizona.

At the Arizona release site, on the Vermilion Cliffs fifty miles northeast of the South Rim, scientists take great pains to minimize contact between condors and humans, so the birds don't learn to associate humans with food. Condors are very inquisitive creatures, however, and to the delight of tourists almost all the Arizona birds spend much of their time in the village vicinity. Project workers and park rangers try to discourage the condors from approaching too close and deposit animal carcasses for them in remote places. These natural scavengers also manage to find carrion by themselves.

Progress has been slow but definite. About fifty free-flying, tagged, and monitored condors now live in the Grand Canyon, and they've started laying eggs, though no baby condor has yet grown to maturity. Nonetheless, hopes are high that a viable population will take hold. For the latest news, call in at park visitor centers or contact the Peregrine Fund (☎928/355-2270, ⊛www.peregrinefund.org).

shop showcasing such Native American crafts as silver jewelry, Navajo rugs, and ceramics. The main store on the ground floor is open daily from 8am until 8pm (9am–5pm in winter), while the more exclusive upstairs gallery is open between 9am and 5pm year-round.

Verkamp's Curios

The easternmost building on the rim is **Verkamp's Curios** (summer daily 9am–8pm, fall and spring daily 9am–7.30pm, winter daily 9am–5pm), a small two-story gift shop that clashes with the prevailing log-cabin style elsewhere in the village. Trader John G. Verkamp first appeared on the South Rim selling souvenirs from a tent in 1898. He returned to erect this store in 1905, and it's remained here ever since, centering on a large fireplace and selling both cheap tat and ultra-expensive Native American crafts.

Bright Angel Lodge

A few hundred yards west of *El Tovar*, beyond the nondescript *Thunderbird* and *Kachina* lodges, **Bright Angel Lodge** was Mary Jane Colter's last major

△ Fireplace at *Bright Angel Lodge*

work at the canyon. Completed in 1935, as tourist numbers picked up after the worst of the Depression, it replaced *Bright Angel Camp*, a ramshackle assortment of cabins and tents. The idea was to provide several cheaper grades of accommodation in a complex of differing but homogenous buildings that resembled an actual village. Two historic structures were incorporated in their entirety: the gable-roofed pioneer **Buckey O'Neill Cabin**, attached to the main lodge, and the separate **Cameron Hotel**, also known as Red Horse Station, which at various times served as a stagecoach station, a hotel, and a US post office.

To the left of the lobby, the lodge's **History Room** features a ten-foot-high fireplace made from all the principal types of rock found in the canyon, arrayed in the correct chronological sequence. It also hosts displays on varying aspects of the canyon's past, particularly the heyday of the Fred Harvey Company. Lodging at *Bright Angel Lodge* is reviewed on p.45, its restaurant on p.48.

Lookout Studio

Lookout Studio appears to sprout organically from a narrow rocky outcrop just west of *Bright Angel Lodge*. Mary Jane Colter built the place for the Fred Harvey Company in 1914 as a "tiny rustic club." The idea was to draw tourists here rather than the rival Kolb Studio to wait out bad weather or simply while away afternoons in solitude. Both the Pueblo-styled building and the view from its open-air terrace are as appealing as ever, though it now holds just another hectic gift shop (daily: summer 8am–sunset, otherwise 9am–5pm).

Kolb Studio

At the head of the Bright Angel Trail, **Kolb Studio** spills over the edge of the canyon, its entrance at rim level and another story down below. This was

---

Mule rides

Joining a **mule train** down the Bright Angel Trail from Grand Canyon Village is a fine old canyon tradition. Places are limited, so it's best to make a reservation (☎928/638-2631) as early as possible; they're accepted up to a year in advance. If you arrive without a reservation, put yourself on the waiting list at the *Bright Angel Lodge* Transportation Desk and turn up there at 6am on the morning you want to ride; there are usually a few last-minute cancellations each day. Riders must be at least four feet seven inches tall (1.38m), speak fluent English, and weigh not more than 200 pounds (91kg); it's not unusual to see would-be mule riders jogging in a desperate attempt to sweat off those last few pounds. While prior experience is unnecessary, take seriously the warnings that you should be afraid neither of large animals nor of great heights.

All rides set off early in the morning on varying schedules throughout the year. **One-day** round-trips as far as Plateau Point cost $136, including lunch, and return to the village by mid-afternoon. **Overnight** trips spend the morning descending the Bright Angel Trail to the riverside **Phantom Ranch**, where you'll spend the day exploring and sleep in two-person cabins. Soon after sunrise the next morning, the mules set off up the South Kaibab Trail. You'll be met by bus at the top and should be back at *Bright Angel Lodge* in time for lunch. Trip costs, including lodgings and all meals, are $366 for one person or $651 for two. **Two-night** rides, available between mid-November and March only, follow the same route but stay another night down at the ranch, at a cost of $514 for one or $865 for two.

The Bright Angel Trail is described in detail on p.96, and the South Kaibab Trail on p.99, while you'll find more about Phantom Ranch on p.107.

Mary Jane Colter

No one has done more to shape and enhance visitors' experiences of the Grand Canyon than the remarkable architect **Mary Jane Colter** (1869–1958). Not only was she largely responsible for crafting the look of Grand Canyon Village, but her handiwork also lines the South Rim – from Hermito Rest in the west to the Watchtower at Desert View in the east – and borders the river on the canyon floor at Phantom Ranch. Indeed, her influence extended all the way from Chicago to LA; she designed the interiors of Union Station in the former and La Grande Station in the latter, as well as numerous hotels and restaurants in between.

△ Mary Jane Colter (right) inspects the plans for *Bright Angel Lodge*, ca 1935

Colter spent fifty years working for both the Santa Fe Railroad and the Fred Harvey Company, in an era when women architects were few and far between. That Fred Harvey, the concessionaire responsible for lodging, dining, and entertaining tourists on the transcontinental railroad, is often said to have "invented the Southwest" is due in large part to her vision.

Born in Pittsburgh in 1869, Mary Colter was raised in St Paul, Minnesota. Trained at the California School of Design in San Francisco, she was heavily influenced by the nascent Arts and Crafts movement. Proponents of Arts and Crafts argued that American architects should seek their inspiration at home, using local materials and looking to indigenous examples, rather than feeling obliged to work in traditional European styles. Colter turned to her lifelong passion for Native American design.

Colter's first Grand Canyon commission produced the Pueblo-influenced **Hopi House**, a showcase for Hopi craft workers, in 1905. Both **Hermits Rest** and **Lookout Studio** followed in 1914, with **Phantom Ranch** appearing in 1922. Her best-loved masterpiece, the **Watchtower** at Desert View, was completed in 1932, and **Bright Angel Lodge** came along three years later. Colter also created such signature Harvey hotels as **El Navajo** in Gallup and the wonderful **La Posada** in Winslow.

Her role went far beyond producing the overall design. Colter would supervise every step of construction, choosing individual rocks and timbers for both authenticity and inherent beauty and tearing apart anything that failed to meet her exacting standards. Her attention to detail was legendary, with the interior design given as much weight as the overall edifice. She was even responsible for the china service used on the *Super Chief* train, which incorporated motifs taken from ancient Mimbres pottery.

Even as Colter was completing her final job in 1949, a cocktail lounge at *La Fonda* hotel in Santa Fe, her various Route 66 landmarks were starting to close down. Having sadly observed, "There's such a thing as living too long," she died in January 1958, bequeathing her extensive collection of Native American jewelry and ceramics to the museum at Mesa Verde National Park. Since her death, however, her unique contribution to the American West has been increasingly recognized, and much of her finest work has been lovingly restored.

Author Frank Waters conjured up a beautifully romantic portrait of Colter in his 1950 book, *Masked Gods*: "For years an incomprehensible woman in pants, she rode horseback through the Four Corners, making sketches of prehistoric Pueblo ruins, studying details of construction. . . . She could teach masons how to lay adobe bricks, plasterers how to mix washes, carpenters how to fix viga joints."

originally the home and workplace of Emery and Ellsworth Kolb, brothers who opened a photographic studio here in 1902. They'd take pictures of each day's contingent of departing mule riders, run down the trail to develop film using the water at Indian Gardens, then run back up to ready the prints for returning riders. In 1911 and 1912, they also shot the first-ever film of a boating expedition along the entire canyon. This became the longest-running movie of all time; Emery presented it here daily from 1915 until just before his death, at age 95, in 1976.

Its photographic days behind it, the studio is now divided between a well-stocked bookstore upstairs and a gallery of changing exhibitions downstairs, which also harbors a nice little bay window offering superb views (daily: summer 8am–8pm, fall and spring 8am–7pm, winter 8am–5pm).

Hermit Road

The eight-mile, dead-end scenic drive officially known as **Hermit Road**, but familiar to many returning visitors as **West Rim Drive**, starts a hundred yards west of *Bright Angel Lodge*, just as Grand Canyon Village peters out. Offering a succession of very different but consistently impressive canyon panoramas, it's the most obvious, and most enjoyable, half-day sightseeing trip from the village. In summer it offers a welcome escape from traffic, as the only vehicles granted access are the Hermits Rest Route **shuttle buses**, the Xanterra tour buses, and those displaying disabled permits; private cars are otherwise permitted only between December and February.

The Santa Fe Railroad forged the original **Hermit Rim Road** between 1910 and 1912 to provide stagecoach excursions for its passengers. At that time, the Bright Angel Trail was privately owned, so the Santa Fe laid out its own Hermit Trail at road's end, which it used for mule rides and overnight trips. The "**Hermit**" name, incidentally, was a piece of harmless mythmaking centered around one Louis Boucher, a white-bearded old prospector who made his home for twenty years at Dripping Spring, just below the trailhead.

For most of its length the road runs within a few yards of the canyon, paralleled by the **Rim Trail**, even closer to the edge. The ideal way to explore this trail is to combine judicious use of the shuttle buses with stretches of **walking** – few bother to walk the entire eight miles. Paved for the first 1.4 miles, as far as Maricopa Point, the trail later becomes an unmarked and not exactly conspicuous dirt path. The trail is rough in spots and occasionally teeters along alarming drop-offs – in which case you can always retreat to the road – but it's not nearly as tiring as the inner canyon trails. So long as you bring a bottle of water, you should have no problems.

Bear in mind that although the buses make eight stops, they do so *only* on the **outward** journey; returning buses only stop at Hermits Rest, Mohave Point, and Hopi Point. If you get off at either of the first three overlooks, you'll need to hike either back to the village or onward as far as Hopi Point. The **hiking** permutations are endless, but recommended routes include the twenty-minute walks between Hopi and Mohave points and between Pima Point and Hermits Rest.

Traveling the length of Hermit Road, out and back, without leaving the bus takes about ninety minutes. To allow time for a couple of short hikes and a stop at Hermits Rest, set aside perhaps three hours. If you prefer to hike, the four-mile round-trip from the village to Hopi Point, for example, takes less than two hours.

Finally, **cycling** is permitted on Hermit Road year-round, though you're expected to dismount every time a shuttle goes past.

Trailview Overlook

The first shuttle stop, **Trailview Overlook**, is in fact a large parking lot that serves two distinct viewpoints, known as **Trailview I** and **II**. Although the road initially makes an extravagant loop inland, this spot is less than three-quarters of a mile from the village, thus the views are similar, albeit from a slightly higher elevation. However, you will find a sweeping prospect of the village itself, staggered along the canyon rim.

As the name suggests, the viewpoints also offer a fine overview of the **Bright Angel Trail**. Prospective hikers can see exactly what they're in for, as every cruel red-dirt switchback is clearly etched against the canyon walls below.

Maricopa Point

After about a mile, the Rim Trail rounds a corner and passes beyond sight of Grand Canyon Village, finally opening up views both west and east. At the second shuttle stop, the railed, rocky overlook at **Maricopa Point** commands just such a sweeping canyon panorama. This is a prime spot to identify the majestic buttes on the far side of the river, including Brahma and Zoroaster temples, each capped with hard red sandstone.

The monumental parade stretches from Isis Temple in the far west to Vishnu Temple in the east, isolated beyond Cape Royal – the last visible point on the North Rim. In the lower foreground stands Cheops Pyramid, layered with what geologists call the Grand Canyon Series of tilted silt, shale, and sandstone, all atop the gnarled schist of the Granite Gorge. Straight below, south of the unseen river, is the broad Battleship promontory.

Powell Point

West of Maricopa Point, both the road and the trail (now unpaved) detour inland around a high fence festooned with solemn radiation warnings. At the

△ Monument to river pioneer John Wesley Powell at Powell Point

heart of this enclosure lurks the hulking headframe of the **Orphan Mine**. From its beginnings in 1893 as a copper mine a thousand feet below the rim, it grew to become America's largest uranium mine by the 1950s. Oddly, the company that owned it also ran an on-site hotel, the *Grand Canyon Inn*, which it even considered expanding in terraces far beneath the rim. Both hotel and mine went out of business in the late 1960s, however, and the park acquired the land in 1988. Significant uranium deposits remain in the vicinity, by no coincidence at all in areas outside the park's protective boundaries.

The headland immediately west of the mine enclosure, a short walk from the shuttle stop, is **Powell Point**, where the park was officially dedicated on April 30, 1920. This was known as Sentinel Point until 1916, when a small Maya-style stepped pyramid was erected as a memorial to the late John Wesley Powell and the crews of his two Colorado River expeditions. From the far side of its paved but rail-less platform, views across the river take in the curious semicircular cliff wall of the **Tower of Set**; shaped something like an opening bracket, it's mirrored by a similar wall on **Isis Temple** to the east.

Hopi Point

Two miles out from Grand Canyon Village is the busiest of the western view-points, **Hopi Point** – an ideal destination for hikers and the closest stop served by buses returning to the village. Its reputation as the perfect place from which to admire the **sunset** rests on the fact that this promontory thrusts farther north than any of its neighbors, granting it a virtual 360-degree canyon prospect, including the vast panoply of temples to the west. That said, thousands of visitors flock here on summer evenings, which can make it uncomfortably crowded.

The shuttle buses stop short of the tip of the large parking lot, enabling you take a short loop stroll around its tiered perimeter, catching assorted glimpses of the Colorado along the way. The most dramatic segment of the river lies immediately below Plateau Point; you can see the last few yards of the trail that leads out to the point, as described on p.98, but there's no possible route down into the gorge. Amazingly enough, the river is 350 feet wide down there, lying at the foot of gnarled and impossibly ancient walls of black schist streaked through with vertical pink faults. To the west, the Colorado threads a tortuous route between interleaved spurs of red rock, and a maze of lesser canyons twists among the mighty buttes.

A plaque at Hopi Point commemorates the Civilian Conservation Corps, a Depression-era labor force set up by Franklin Roosevelt. Nicknamed the President's Tree Army, the corps completed much valuable work in the park between 1933 and 1942. Another plaque highlights Birdseye Point on the North Rim and honors Colonel Claude Hale Birdseye, the onetime US Geological Survey chief topographic engineer who headed a survey expedition through the canyon in 1923.

Mohave Point

West of Hopi Point, the road and trail trace the lip of a lesser basin known as **The Inferno**, curving gracefully for three-quarters of a mile to **Mohave Point**, a large railed promontory unblemished by explanatory placards.

Though the sheer cliffs below Hopi Point largely obscure eastward views, one does gain an appreciation of how truly steep these walls are. The stark sandstone cliffs glow spectacular shades of red toward dusk, while equally impressive cliffs to the west are swept by impenetrable creeping shadows.

Two more stretches of the Colorado are visible, including the foaming white turmoil of **Granite Rapid**.

The Abyss

Pocking the South Rim west of Mohave Point is another large recess, named **The Abyss** in deference to its immense, steep sides. Shuttle buses make their next stop a mile along, at the far end of the **Great Mohave Wall**, which plummets vertically more than 3000ft.

Though the peaks now visible on the western horizon appear to lie farther along the South Rim, they in fact line the far side of the river. Part of the **Uinkaret** range, they include 8026ft **Mount Trumbull**, more than fifty miles distant. Close at hand, four successive parallel sandstone ridges rise like stage scenery in front of Pima Point.

The main reason anyone gets off the bus at The Abyss is to hike in either direction along the vertiginous Rim Trail. While the trail is relatively benign, if the drop starts to bother you, simply walk along the road instead.

Pima Point

Pima Point lies four miles beyond Mohave Point, along a spur road off Hermit Road. It's at the tip of a promontory that separates the basins cut by Monument Creek to the east – responsible for the Abyss – and Hermit Creek to the west. The drop here is so abrupt that the Colorado lies less than two horizontal miles distant, and you can look straight down into the maw of three-quarter-mile **Granite Rapid**. From the far bank, however, it's another twelve labyrinthine miles to the North Rim. Visible to the west is a significant stretch of **Boucher Rapid**, named for the so-called hermit (see p.57).

Below, the **Hermit Trail** traces a conspicuous path across the **Tonto Platform**. In the days when Santa Fe mule trains trod down this trail, tourists would stay overnight at Hermit Camp. Today, few traces survive of the camp or aerial tramway that supplied it from the west side of Pima Point.

From here, only the tiniest notch in the horizon separates Powell Plateau on the North Rim from **Havasupai Point**, the last visible headland on the South Rim – an especially stunning prospect in the early morning. Helpful Park Service displays near the shuttle stop illustrate canyon geology using photos of nearby formations and explain how the canyon structure differs far west beyond road's end.

Hermits Rest

Just over a mile past Pima Point, Hermit Road ends at the **Hermits Rest** way station, laid out by Mary Jane Colter in 1914 as an artful evocation of a canyon prospector's dwelling. Even the soot that blackens the fireplace here is faux. As Colter put it, "You can't imagine what it cost to make this place look old."

A path leads from the parking lot through a deliberately crude archway of stone slabs, decked with a hanging bell found by Colter in an antique store. You'll continue along the canyon rim to what at first glance appears to be no more than a ramshackle pile of rocks stacked against the hillside. Closer inspection reveals a rambling but very inviting structure that centers on the massive domed fireplace and hosts a snack bar and large gift shop (daily: summer 8am–7.30pm, otherwise 9am–sunset).

As Hermits Rest fronts the side canyon shaped by Hermit Creek, it doesn't offer as extensive views as Pima or Maricopa points. Only a tiny patch of the Colorado is visible, though you can gaze up the creek toward its source,

Dripping Spring, where "hermit" Louis Boucher really did make his home. The **Hermit Trail** (see p.112) sets off just past the store. Abandoned by the Santa Fe Railroad in 1931, it remains popular with inner canyon hikers.

Desert View Drive

From Mather Point, **Desert View Drive** runs east 23 miles to Desert View, just inside the park's East Entrance Station. Originally named East Rim Drive, the road was constructed in 1931 to accommodate visiting motorists, who by then outnumbered rail passengers. Today the road bridges AZ-64, which runs north to the park from Williams and extends east to Cameron.

Despite threats to restrict all Desert View Drive parking lots to shuttle and tour buses, only Yaki Point presents any restrictions (see below). For the time being, the drive itself remains open year-round for self-guided driving tours; allow at least two hours for a round-trip from the village. (For information on Xanterra bus tours of the drive, see pp.43–44.) In addition to the formal viewpoints described below, the road skirts the rim in places, and while you're not supposed to stop for picnics and sightseeing, plenty of people do.

Yaki Point

The first of the Desert View Drive lookouts, **Yaki Point** sits at the end of a mile-long spur road just east of the South Entrance Road. Closed to private vehicles between March and November, it's served year-round by shuttle buses from the village (see p.43).

Two miles east of Yavapai Point as the condor flies, Yaki commands much the same perspective as its neighbor. Straight across the river is fluted Zoroaster Temple, while thanks to the curve of the Colorado River, Vishnu Temple stands silhouetted against the eastern horizon. The stark finger of the Watchtower at Desert View is also visible nearly fifteen miles due east.

Although five different **inner canyon trails** are visible from Yaki Point – including the Bright Angel, Plateau Point, and Tonto trails on this side of the river and the Clear Creek Trail on the far side – the river itself remains stubbornly out of view. The fifth trail, the **South Kaibab Trail** (see p.99), is the reason most people take the spur road; it starts its rapid descent to Phantom Ranch from a separate parking lot, just 0.3 mile off Desert View Drive. From the main overlook, you can spot the trail far below, switchbacking down an exposed slope of red-rock scree between two buttes, while rocks beyond the viewpoint offer clearer views down to its principal staging post, O'Neill Butte. Unless you're actually hiking the trail, there's no reason to call in at the trailhead parking lot, which stands alongside the mule corral used by pack trips returning from Phantom Ranch.

Shoshone Point

A couple of miles east of Yaki Point, **Shoshone Point** is the least-known and least-visited of the South Rim viewpoints, for the simple reason that it's only accessible on **foot**, along an easy one-mile trail from Desert View Drive. It's an absolute gem of a place, offering beautiful views and an unparalleled sense of peace and privacy. This hour-long round-trip hike from the road may well be your only chance to be alone with the canyon on the South Rim, at arguably the finest viewpoint on either rim.

The trail to Shoshone Point begins from an unpaved parking lot in the woods on the rim side of Desert View Drive, 1.4 miles east of the turnoff to Yaki Point.

△ Natural stone outcrop at Shoshone Point

You'll know you've found it when you see a yellow metal gate across a dirt road, with a brown park notice reading "Site use by permit only." The sign is there to discourage casual visitors, as the Park Service prefers instead to make the site available for weddings and other private gatherings (mid-May to mid-October; reservations ☏928/638-7761; see p.49). However, rangers at the information plaza keep no record of whether or not the point has been reserved, and permits are not required of casual hikers. Instead, you're simply asked to respect the privacy of any group that may be out there and to refrain from hiking altogether if you notice a lot of cars in the parking lot. Outside the reservation dates (see above), you may hike at will.

At a fairly brisk pace, it takes about fifteen minutes to reach the rim along this pleasant, meandering trail with minimal elevation change. You'll pass through first ponderosa pines and then piñon and juniper, which host plenty of bird and animal life and provide welcome shade in summer.

Beyond a clearing that holds picnic tables, barbecue grills, and a couple of portable toilets, the point stands in splendid isolation, far from the clamor of crowds and traffic. A solitary pale hoodoo, or rock column, marks the tip of its slender neck, which may feel precarious in the absence of the usual railings. The sublime eastward views take in Cape Royal, at the south tip of the Walhalla Plateau, and the crest of Vishnu Temple in mid-canyon. Zoroaster and Brahma temples stand in line directly across the gorge.

Grandview Point

Twelve miles east of the village, or 6.4 miles beyond the Shoshone Point parking lot, a spur road branches north to the year-round parking lot at **Grandview Point**. Among the most dramatic and expansive of all canyon viewpoints, Grandview is thought to mark the general vicinity from which Spanish adventurers first saw the canyon, in 1540. Legend has it their Hopi guides deliberately led them to a spot from which no trails were visible, so the gorge would appear an even more impassable obstacle.

Grandview Point was also the place where **tourism** first took root in the canyon. After discovering rich copper deposits 3000ft below the rim in 1890, prospector Peter Berry forged the **Grandview Trail** down to his **Last Chance** mine in 1892. Five years later he opened the *Grandview Hotel* to accommodate a growing number of visitors. The hotel thrived at first, but within ten years the arrival of the railroad off to the west drove Berry out of business. Traces of the hotel remain, amid the forest about a mile back from the rim.

Railroad or no railroad, the prospect here is inarguably superior to views from the village. There's no need to set foot on the precarious trail to spot the sinuous course of the Colorado, which makes a broad, languorous entrance from the east before disappearing into the stunning sandstone labyrinth. Below are the twin prongs of **Horseshoe Mesa**, home to Berry's copper mine. The left spire points to **Wotans Throne**, detached from the North Rim and a couple of hundred feet higher than Grandview itself; between the prongs stands **Cape Royal**, at the tip of the Walhalla Plateau; and to the right, **Cape Final** juts out at the far east end of the North Rim, above and behind Vishnu Temple.

The overlook is an attractive spot in its own right, nestled amid one of the few pure stands of ponderosa pine on the South Rim and frequented by roaming elk at both sunset and sunrise. Tour buses frequent the point, but you can always escape the hubbub by hiking a short way down the trail.

Grandview Monocline

Three miles beyond Grandview Point, Desert View Drive abruptly descends 300ft **Buggeln Hill**, the most visible feature of the **Grandview Monocline**. In a land of such wonders, this inconspicuous geologic hitch – a small rock fold marked by an unremarkable little hill – hardly merits a second glance, but it may well be responsible for the greatest wonder of all. To this point, the Colorado flows southward, skirting the edge of the Kaibab Plateau as it slices through softer Moenkopi Formation rock. Below Buggeln Hill, however, the Grandview Monocline thrusts a wall of hard Kaibab limestone into the river's path, forcing it west into the plateau and creating the Grand Canyon as we know it.

Moran Point

Just beyond Buggeln Hill lies **Moran Point**, named for nineteenth-century artist Thomas Moran. This overlook faces west toward the heart of the maelstrom. Close at hand, higher than the lookout, an isolated rock fin known as the **Sinking Ship** juts into the canyon from atop the hill, its stratified sandstone layers bearing witness to the Grandview Monocline's angle of tilt.

Tusayan Ruin and Museum

On the south side of the road, four miles past Moran Point, is the parking area for Tusayan Ruin and Museum. Set back in the forest a quarter mile from the rim, **Tusayan Ruin** – not to be confused with the town of Tusayan – is an open-air archeological site centered on the remains of a typical twelfth-century **pueblo**. Built circa AD 1185, the site comprises fifteen separate rooms, including two circular ceremonial chambers, or *kivas*, which suggests it was home to two separate clans. For perhaps a quarter century it sheltered a community of some thirty people with clear cultural connections to modern Pueblo Indians and Arizona's Hopi people in particular. Anthropologists now refer to these ancients as **Ancestral Puebloans**, replacing the older term **Anasazi**.

At a time when Ancestral Puebloans were gradually withdrawing from the canyon region, Tusayan's inhabitants farmed the wash close to their homes and trekked regularly into the canyon along what's now called the Tanner Trail. They seem to have felt some sense of menace or apprehension, however, as fort-like structures found along the rim nearby date from the same era.

Of the original Tusayan complex, only low stone walls remain – much like the other two thousand or so Ancestral Puebloan sites identified in and around the canyon. While it doesn't approach the grand ruins at such places as Canyon de Chelly and Mesa Verde, Tusayan's very existence enabled President Teddy Roosevelt to accord national monument status to the entire canyon (see p.213). A small on-site **museum** (daily 9am–5pm; free) holds displays regarding contemporary Navajo and Hopi peoples, as well as 4000-year-old twig figurines and Ancestral Puebloan pottery found nearby. Park rangers lead **tours** of the ruins daily at 11am and 1.30pm.

Lipan Point

Another couple of miles past Tusayan Ruin, **Lipan Point** ranks in the top tier of South Rim overlooks. While Desert View, a few miles east, offers a similar prospect and better facilities, Lipan is quieter and better positioned to appreciate several pivotal events in the canyon life cycle.

Emerging from Marble Canyon to the north, the Colorado flows into view just past its junction with the Little Colorado, which cuts in from the east through the vast Marble Platform. Flanking the river south of the confluence, the platform's sheer walls are known as the **Palisades of the Desert**. Visible directly below the viewpoint is the **Tanner Trail**, which descends from the parking lot to the mouth of Tanner Canyon. Here, the Colorado makes its dramatic shift to the west.

At first it meanders past the eroded slopes of the Grand Canyon Series, turning an extravagant S-curve at the mouth of **Unkar Creek**. The adjacent Unkar Delta once hosted a large Ancestral Puebloan population, who farmed both down by the river and up north on the Walhalla Plateau. It's a beautiful spot, with distinct sandstone strata that strike maroon, ruby, and raspberry notes at sunset.

Farther west, river runners face their first major white-water challenge, as the river gouges into the Granite Gorge and enters the ferocious mile-long **Hance Rapid**.

Desert View

Twenty-five miles east of Grand Canyon Village, **Desert View** is the last canyon viewpoint along Desert View Drive. From the park boundary, AZ-64 continues another 34 miles to US-89 at Cameron, so Desert View also serves as the *first* canyon overlook for westbound visitors. Few will be disappointed, as this spot offers two staggering panoramas in one.

To the north, four miles distant, the Colorado approaches its sudden westward turn. Flanking its east bank are the stark Palisades of the Desert, above which stretch the pallid plains of the Marble Plateau, beneath an overwhelming sky. Ninety miles northeast, beyond the Vermilion and Echo cliffs, looms the gray bulk of Navajo Mountain. During the Mesozoic era, which ended some 65 million years ago, this vast sweep lay beneath an additional 4000 to 5000ft of sedimentary sandstone. Among the few remaining vestiges of that long-eroded landscape is the reddish mesa of **Cedar Mountain**, a mile or two back from the rim.

Off to the west, by contrast, the river vanishes into the Granite Gorge, engulfed on all sides by buttes and mesas, temples, shrines, and tabernacles. In the morning these present an extraordinary array of colors and shapes. Dawn brings rich golds and reds, which gradually bleach away under the rising sun, while toward dusk the formations weave shadowy interleaving screens devoid of all form and dimension.

What first draws visitors' attention, however, is a remarkable structure perched along the very rim – the **Watchtower**. Melded almost imperceptibly into its sandstone surroundings, this circular tower is the crowning achievement of architect **Mary Jane Colter** (see p.55). Completed in 1932, it was inspired by her study of Ancestral Puebloan remains throughout the Four Corners region. Colter modeled its design on the Round Tower in southwest Colorado's Mesa Verde National Park and its masonry on towers at Hovenweep National Monument in southeast Utah. The Watchtower incorporates petroglyphs found near Ash Fork, timbers from the abandoned *Grandview Hotel*, and even stones from nearby ruins.

Colter's aim was not to replicate an existing Indian structure; she simply wanted to provide a fitting landmark for Fred Harvey's sightseeing tours and to educate tourists about ancient and modern Native American culture. While some consider the building culturally intrusive, it's hard to conceive of a new Park Service structure that displays a fraction of its imagination and flair or sparks such openness and cooperation from Native American groups.

Open daily between 8am and sunset, the ground floor of the Watchtower was laid out as a ceremonial kiva – though that's hard to discern through the clutter of gifts and souvenirs. Still, it's worth a climb to its three upper stories. In the first circular chamber, a mural by Hopi artist Fred Kabotie depicts a tribal snake legend, while the second chamber holds reproduction pictographs and petroglyphs painted by a Fred Harvey employee. The spare uppermost floor, or Eagle's Nest, features panoramic windows. While the roof is off-limits, visitors can access a second-floor open-air terrace, complete with strange 1930s "reflectoscopes," a sort of upside-down, boxed mirror designed to enhance the aesthetic appeal of the views.

Over the years, the Watchtower has welcomed a host of less distinguished though useful neighbors, including an **information center** and **bookstore** (daily: summer 9am–7pm; spring and fall 9am–6pm; winter 9am–5pm), the **Desert View Marketplace** (daily 9am–5pm), a **gas station** (daily; 24hr access with credit card), and the Trading Post gift store and **snack bar** (daily: summer 7.30am–6pm, spring and fall 9am–5pm, winter 9am–4pm), where the ultra-basic menu features a hamburger for $3.50, a cold sandwich for $3.25, and a slice of pie for $2.25. Down a short spur road from the gas station is the **Desert View Campground** (see p.47).

At 7498ft, **Navajo Point** is the highest spot along the South Rim, served by a separate parking lot a few hundred yards west of Desert View. Though it's still 500ft lower than **Cape Final**, eight miles away on the North Rim, you do get a real sense of the forested plateau on the far side.

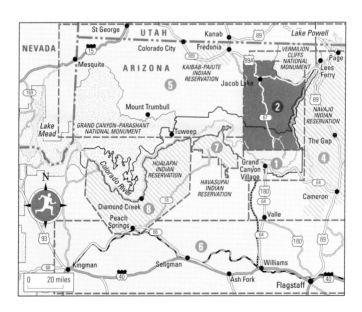

North Rim

CHAPTER 2

Highlights

✱ **Western cabins at Grand Canyon Lodge** What could be finer than a rim-edge cabin at one of the great US national park lodges? See p.73

✱ **Dining Room at Grand Canyon Lodge** Top-quality food, friendly service, and unbeatable views; just be sure to reserve in advance. See p.73

✱ **North Rim Campground** The most spacious and least crowded of the national park campgrounds. See p.73

✱ **Bright Angel Point** Stroll beyond the lodge to the end of this perilous-looking little promontory for magnificent sunrise and sunset views. See p.74

✱ **Point Imperial** The park's highest viewpoint, at the north end of the Walhalla Plateau, enables you to see the canyon in transformation as the river cuts through the Marble Platform. See p.79

✱ **Cape Royal** The perfect vantage point from which to appreciate the overall scope of the canyon. See p.81

✱ **Angels Window** Gaze through this natural window to see the Colorado far below, or walk across the top of it for a dramatic eagle's-eye view. See p.81

✱ **Kaibab National Forest** Drive the gravel roads off either side of the highway to explore lovely woodlands, at their most majestic in early fall. See p.82

✱ **Monument Point** This remote viewpoint abounds in ancient marine fossils. See p.84

△ A view of the Colorado through Angels Window at Cape Royal

North Rim

igher, bleaker, and much more remote than the South Rim, the **North Rim** of the Grand Canyon is only accessible to travelers about half the year. Once winter's first major snowfall blocks **AZ-67**, the sole paved access road, the entire North Rim section of the national park remains closed till the following spring. Although that first snow traditionally arrives toward the end of October, in recent years the area has received a mere fraction of its average annual snowfall of 140 inches, and in 2005, for example, the road did not close until December 19. Regardless, the only park lodging on the North Rim, *Grand Canyon Lodge*, adheres to a fixed schedule, closing on October 15 and opening the second week of May. During the hiatus between its closing and the first snowfall, the park itself remains open, but no food, gas, or lodging other than camping is available, and visitors must be prepared to leave at a moment's notice.

Even in peak season, the North Rim offers a sense of splendid isolation, as its annual quota of between 350,000 and 450,000 visitors is less than a tenth that of the South Rim. While you won't exactly have the place to yourself, you may still feel as though you're venturing into unexplored wilderness. The basic layout is similar to that on the South Rim, centering on a cluster of Park Service buildings at **Bright Angel Point**, where the highway meets the canyon, with a rim road on neighboring **Walhalla Plateau**, to the east, where drivers can savor additional lookouts.

The drive to the North Rim entails a long haul across the forested **Kaibab Plateau**, actually the other half of the South Rim's Coconino Plateau, bisected by the canyon. AZ-67 is a much more attractive road than its South Rim counterpart, however, sweeping past majestic stands of spruce, aspen, and fir and opening on successive appealing, often flower-filled, natural meadows. The canyon, too, is significantly different on this side of the Colorado. Erosion is far more advanced, largely because twice as much rain falls, and it freezes more often. The Kaibab Plateau slopes south, so water flowing toward the rim has cut back twice as far from the river. Thus massive side canyons lace this side of the river, the largest of which, the little-known **Kanab Canyon**, effectively splits it in two. The area known as the North Rim represents just the eastern portion of the canyon's northern rim; its western half, most notably the superb **Toroweap Overlook**, is only accessible from the Arizona Strip and is, therefore, covered in Chapter Five.

Human occupation along the North Rim has always been minimal. Native Americans merely passed through in summer, while Mormons and prospectors seldom ventured this way. In fact, apart from the odd trapper and adventurer, the region remained largely unexplored until geologists, hunters, and even a few tourists began turning up at the start of the twentieth century. Crews forged the

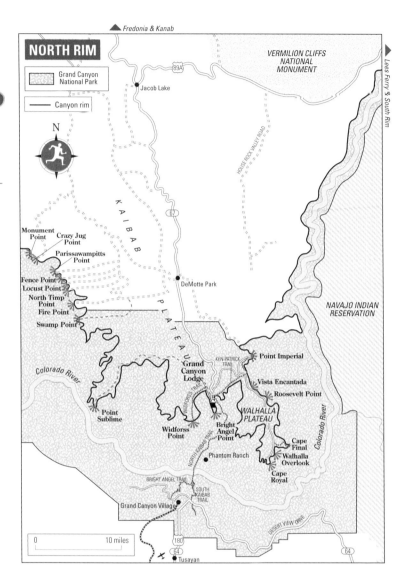

▲ Fredonia & Kanab

NORTH RIM

Grand Canyon
National Park

Canyon rim

N

*VERMILION CLIFFS
NATIONAL
MONUMENT*

Lees Ferry & South Rim

Jacob Lake

89A

HOUSE ROCK VALLEY ROAD

K
A
I
B
A
B

67

Monument
Point   Crazy Jug
Point

Parissawampitts
Point

DeMotte Park

Fence Point
Locust Point
North Timp
Point
Fire Point

Swamp Point

P
L
A
T
E
A
U

*NAVAJO INDIAN
RESERVATION*

Colorado River

KEN PATRICK
TRAIL

Grand
Canyon
Lodge

Point Imperial

Vista Encantada

Roosevelt Point

WIDFORSS TRAIL

Point
Sublime

Widforss
Point

Bright
Angel
Point

*WALHALLA
PLATEAU*

Colorado River

NORTH KAIBAB TRAIL

Phantom Ranch

Cape
Final
Walhalla
Overlook

Cape
Royal

BRIGHT ANGEL TRAIL

SOUTH
KAIBAB
TRAIL

Grand Canyon Village

DESERT VIEW DRIVE

0   10 miles

180

64   64

Tusayan

first dirt road from Kanab, Utah, in 1919, while the opening of Navajo Bridge, near Lees Ferry, in 1929 made driving from the South Rim feasible.

Arrival, information, and getting around

The only paved access to the North Rim is via **AZ-67** (see p.136), which runs south for 44 miles from **Jacob Lake** to Bright Angel Point. En route, it climbs a thousand feet, reaching the high point on the Kaibab Plateau five miles south of **DeMotte Park**. That barely perceptible 9000ft ridge, about twelve miles short of the North Rim, roughly corresponds to the national park boundary. Rangers at the **North Entrance Station** just beyond collect any applicable fees (see p.26) and hand out the park newspaper, *The Guide*, which is published in separate editions for each rim.

The road descends gradually south another six miles to Fuller Canyon Road, the access road to the Walhalla Plateau overlooks (see p.77), then three more miles to road's end, along the way passing turnoffs for the backcountry office, the North Kaibab Trailhead, and the campground. You never quite see the canyon from the highway, which ends at a turnaround in front of *Grand Canyon Lodge*, with several large parking lots off to the left.

Information

Occupying the first building on the left in the lodge complex, the **North Rim Visitor Center** (daily May to mid-Oct 8am–6pm; ☎928/638-7864, ⓦwww.nps.gov/grca) is the main information source. Staff drawn from several public lands agencies can suggest routes and advise you on current conditions for hiking and backcountry road trips. They'll also highlight the day's schedule of free **guided walks** and **ranger talks** – held at the lodge, the campground, and certain Walhalla Plateau viewpoints. A ninety-minute nature walk starts here daily at 8.30am. Sharing the same space, the small Grand Canyon Association **bookstore** stocks maps and trail guides.

Housed in the ranger station a quarter-mile north of the campground, the **North Rim Backcountry Office** (daily 8am–noon & 1–5pm; ☎928/638-7868) issues the permits required of anyone going on an overnight backpacking trip. Day hikers do not need permits.

Transportation and tours

While you won't find any free shuttle buses or organized sightseeing tours at the North Rim, the **Transcanyon Shuttle** (☎602/638-2820) does offer daily van service to the **South Rim**. Leaving from *Grand Canyon Lodge* at 7am, it reaches the South Rim at noon, then departs at 1.30pm for a 6.30pm return to the lodge. Fares run $65 one-way for adults and $50 for children 12 and under, or round-trip for $110/90, respectively; cash only.

There's also a hiker shuttle to the North Kaibab Trailhead, which leaves the lodge at 5.20am and 7.20am daily. It costs $5 for the first person in your group and $2 for each additional passenger.

A desk in the lodge lobby handles reservations for North Rim **mule rides** (☎435/679-8665, ⓦwww.canyonrides.com). A one-hour rim-edge ride costs $30, while two half-day options – either along the rim to Uncle Jim Point or down the North Kaibab as far as the Supai Tunnel – cost $55. A full-day ride down to Roaring Springs and back is $105. There are no overnight trips. The minimum age limit is 7 for the one-hour rides, 8 for the half-day rides, and 12 for the full-day trip.

For more information about backcountry permits and trails from the North Rim, turn to Chapter Three, "Hiking the inner canyon".

Grand Canyon Lodge and around

The rambling, attractive **Grand Canyon Lodge**, a glorified log cabin in the finest national-park tradition, is poised majestically on the promontory that ends at **Bright Angel Point**. Designed by Gilbert Stanley Underwood, it was built in 1928 for the Union Pacific Railroad – not that its trains passed anywhere nearby. Instead, the company would bring excursionists here on bus tours that also visited Zion and Bryce Canyon. After the lodge burned down in 1932, it was rebuilt in 1936 using a bit more stone and a bit less timber. The Park Service took it over in 1971, when Union Pacific closed down.

To the right of the lobby is the lodge's lovely dining room (see opposite), while steps straight ahead descend to the building's best feature, a spacious viewing lounge known as the **Sun Room**, where rows of comfortable armchairs face huge picture windows. The foreground view here is of the side canyon known as **The Transept**; the canyon proper lies beyond, though you don't so much see it as sense the vast void.

Open patios to either side of the Sun Room beckon you to relax and enjoy the spectacle. The smaller patio to the right offers individual reading chairs, while the one to the left holds ranks of long benches, making it an ideal venue for ranger talks; recent seasons have offered daily talks about condors at 2pm and canyon geology at 4pm. Short footpaths lead down to railed overlooks every bit as dramatic as the point itself – and invariably packed at sunset.

Accommodation

Guest rooms at *Grand Canyon Lodge* lie outside the main building, split among a complex of individual cabins and larger motel-style blocks. Almost all are arranged in tiers along the wooded hillside that flanks the main road; as they're across the road from the parking lot, they're usually remarkably quiet. Paved footpaths thread between them, dimly lit at night beneath a sky filled with stars.

△ The terrace at Grand Canyon Lodge

There are three different cabin types. Each of the 51 well-appointed **Western cabins** (Ⓖ) holds two queen beds, with a full-size bathroom and a porch, and can sleep up to four people. Just four cabins stand close enough to the rim to offer **canyon views**, the only North Rim lodging options to do so; they cost $10 extra per night and are often booked as far as thirteen months in advance.

The 83 spartan **Frontier cabins** (Ⓢ) can accommodate three guests each, with one double bed and one single, and have smaller bathrooms, while the 22 similar **Pioneer cabins** (Ⓖ), capable of sleeping five people, comprise two separate bedrooms – one with a double bed and a single bed, the other with two single beds – and a small bathroom.

Farthest from the lodge are a couple of two-story blocks, each of which holds twenty **hotel rooms** (Ⓢ), with queen beds and private bathrooms. Only the Frontier cabins and hotel rooms provide telephones.

As the whole place is usually booked up several months in advance, **reservations** are essential; contact Xanterra Parks & Resorts (same day or to contact guest ☏928/638-2611, advance 303/297-2757 or 1-888/297-2757, Ⓦwww .grandcanyonnorthrim.com). Cancellations are often available at short notice, so keep calling if you'd like to reserve or switch rooms.

Eating and drinking

Meals in the main **Dining Room** (daily 6.30–10am, 11.30am–2.30pm & 4.45–9.30pm) are truly memorable. The room itself, with its soaring timber ceiling, is elegant and impressive, and if you're lucky enough to have a window table (assigned at random, not by reservation), you'll enjoy awesome canyon views. The food, a robust but relatively modern interpretation of American resort cuisine, is of a very high standard as well. For dinner, pasta entrees such as shrimp with feta and pine nuts run $15–18, steaks are more like $22, and specials like Four Corners lime chicken or the substantial roasted pork rancheros cost $16. All include soup or salad. Lunch options, at around $10, center on sandwiches, light grilled specials, and salads, while breakfast can either be a full buffet for around $9 or à la carte. Service is friendly rather than formal, and the staff seems admirably keen to answer the same old canyon queries from every table.

Reservations (☏928/638-2612, ext 160) are accepted only for dinner, when they're essential. In fact, you should book your table as early in the season as possible; trying to do so once you arrive at the North Rim is liable to be way too late. Turn up without a reservation, and you'll eat at 9pm at the earliest, though likely not at all.

Two alternatives anchor either side of the lodge driveway. The **Deli in the Pines**, a little windowless cafeteria, is open daily from 8am until 9pm, serving very ordinary breakfasts, then deli sandwiches or salads for around $6 and pizza either by the slice or whole pie ($12.50–18). Across the way, the **Rough Rider Saloon** (daily 5.30–10.30am & 11.30am–11pm) is a suitably rough-hewn **bar,** stocked with a wide range of beers and liquor, that doubles as an early-morning **espresso bar**, doling out coffee and pastries. **Groceries** are available at a general store by the campground.

Camping

At the end of a spur road off AZ-67, just over a mile north of the lodge, the pleasant *North Rim Campground* offers 87 car-camping sites amid the forest. RV hookups are not available. All sites run $15 per night, except for the four that flank the rim of The Transept, which cost $20. Reservations are managed by Spherix (same day ☎928/638-2611, advance ☎1-800/365-2267 or ☎301/722-1257 from outside the US, ⓦwww.reservations.nps.gov). While sites are often booked in advance, space is always available for backpackers, bicyclists, and others traveling without vehicles ($4 each). No one is allowed to stay at the campground for more than seven nights in a calendar year.

The campground reopens each spring in conjunction with the lodge, but depending on the weather, it may remain open a little longer at the end of the season, perhaps through late October. You'll find the general store, gas station, and coin-operated laundry and showers just outside the gates.

For details about backcountry camping within the park, see Chapter Three. Camping is also available outside park boundaries in the Kaibab National Forest (contact North Rim or Kaibab Plateau visitor centers for details) or in campgrounds at Jacob Lake (see p.136) and DeMotte Park (see p.136).

Listings

Camping equipment and groceries Available at the general store opposite *North Rim Campground* (hours range from 7am–9pm to 8am–7pm).
Gas Chevron station near the campground; limited hours (daily 7am–7pm).
Laundromat and showers Also near campground (daily 7am–9pm; showers $1.25).

Medical help There is no health clinic on the North Rim. Call ☎911 for emergencies.
Post office In *Grand Canyon Lodge* (Mon–Fri 8–11am & 11.30am–4pm, Sat 8am–1pm).
Weather For the latest North Rim weather information, call ☎928/638-7888.

Bright Angel Point

A short paved trail starting to the left of *Grand Canyon Lodge* leads to the very tip of **Bright Angel Point**. While it's an easy walk, the path does rise and fall a bit, with sheer drops to either side in places. This promontory juts between two relatively minor tributary canyons – the deep **Transept** to your right and the mighty red wall of **Roaring Springs Canyon** to your left.

△ Sunset at Bright Angel Point

Four hundred yards along, you'll reach the sanctuary of a railed viewing area, backed by massive boulders that daredevils climb in search of solitude. While the prospect ahead is justly ranked among the great park panoramas, the Grand Canyon proper is all but obscured by long, straight **Bright Angel Canyon**, which cuts at an oblique angle across your entire field of view.

Bright Angel Canyon is so unusually straight because it was formed at least in part by seismic action. It therefore follows the line of the **Bright Angel Fault**, which spawned earthquakes responsible for creating both this and corresponding canyons south of the river (see p.218).

Away to the right, you can just about see where it joins the Grand Canyon proper, but none of the Inner Gorge, let alone the Colorado River, is visible. You may hear the sound of rushing water, but it's coming from **Roaring Springs**, much closer to hand almost 3500 feet below, which supplies all the water used by the park on both rims (see p.102).

Mentally extending the line of Bright Angel Canyon across to the far side reveals the fault continuing up to the South Rim, though it's hard to spot a sign of life at Grand Canyon Village, eleven miles away, until the sun goes down and the lights start to flicker. That simple turn of the head also traces the easiest trans-canyon hiking route – the **North Kaibab Trail**, which drops down to the Colorado on this side via Roaring Springs and Bright Angel canyons, and climbs up via the matching **Bright Angel Trail** across the river. On foot, that's a 24-mile one-way hike.

On a clear day you can see far beyond the South Rim to the **San Francisco Peaks** near Flagstaff. The highest point on the horizon, 12,633ft **Humphreys Peak**, is 62 miles distant. In the canyon below, sandwiched between the far wall of Bright Angel Canyon and the South Rim, are such prominent formations as the neat-capped **Brahma Temple**, framed between the lesser Deva and Zoroaster temples.

Kaibab Plateau trails

If you're reasonably fit and not here on a scorching midsummer day, then even a brief foray down the **North Kaibab Trail** (see p.101) has to be the most satisfying North Rim day hike. However, a number of less demanding trails atop the **Kaibab Plateau** offer the chance to meander through peaceful ponderosa forest to lesser-known canyon perspectives. **Permits** are not required for day hikes on any of the trails described below. All **inner canyon** hiking trails are described in Chapter Three, along with detailed advice on necessary preparations and precautions.

Transept Trail

The 1.5-mile **Transept Trail** is a backwoods route between **Grand Canyon Lodge** and the **campground**. Rather than walking along the highway, you parallel the side canyon known as **The Transept**. Though dwarfed by the canyon proper, the latter still plummets an awesome half-mile below this cliffside path. Starting from the right side of the lodge, the trail skirts the rim, circles the campground, and ends beside the general store. An enjoyable enough walk, it's not so much a hiking trail as a shortcut from A to B – almost no one takes it solely for pleasure.

Uncle Jim Trail

If you're looking for a medium-length day hike on the Kaibab Plateau, the four-mile loop along the **Uncle Jim Trail** is your best option. It sets off from the same parking lot as the North Kaibab Trail (see p.101), beside the highway 1.5 miles north of *Grand Canyon Lodge*.

From the mule corral at the east end of the lot, the trail heads up into the woods. You'll pass several inspiring views down the length of **Roaring Springs Canyon** before the path loses touch with the rim. Half a mile along, the Ken Patrick Trail (see below) forks left, while the Uncle Jim veers right.

Another half-mile farther, a second junction marks the start of the loop. Whichever direction you choose will lead two miles past a couple of stunning overlooks. The closest to **Uncle Jim Point** faces east across the head of Bright Angel Canyon to the Walhalla Plateau, while the other opens up south toward the far rim and west toward the trailhead. Pause at the latter for a superb view of the North Kaibab Trail as it switchbacks into Roaring Springs Canyon.

Ken Patrick Trail

A much longer plateau day hike is possible along the **Ken Patrick Trail**. Branching off the Uncle Jim Trail a half-mile along (see above), the ten-mile trail meets **Cape Royal Road** seven miles from the trailhead, then continues three miles farther to **Point Imperial** (see p.79). Few hikers pass this way, which means route-finding can be difficult, with the occasional fallen tree and large patches of wasteland charred during the ferocious **Outlet Fire** of May 2000, a prescribed burn set by the Forest Service that quickly blew out of control.

The most scenic stretch is the final rim-edge climb from Cape Royal Road to Point Imperial, which offers wonderful prospects of Marble Plateau to the east. If you can arrange to be dropped off along the road and picked up at the point, or vice versa, that section makes a great short hike. It's also possible to

Uncle Jim and his lions

The "Uncle Jim" commemorated by the Uncle Jim Trail was **James T. Owens**, a Forest Service warden credited with shooting 532 **mountain lions** on the North Rim between 1906 and 1918. Teddy Roosevelt wrote approvingly of Owens, "He early hailed with delight the growth of the movement among our people to put a stop to the senseless and wanton destruction of our wildlife." The destruction Roosevelt and Owens deplored was of "good" animals, such as deer, by "bad" predators, such as lions; their solution, to eliminate the lions, had the bonus of leaving plenty of deer for hunters to kill, which they of course perceived as neither senseless nor wanton. That early attempt at wildlife management resulted in an explosion of the deer population, followed by their mass starvation. It also led to a policy change at the Park Service, which no longer attempts to wipe out predators.

Uncle Jim was also responsible for introducing the **buffalo** (see p.134) that roam House Rock Valley, near the Vermilion Cliffs. In 1906, he and Charles Jesse "Buffalo" Jones drove 56 head of buffalo into the valley, where they crossbred the animals with cattle to raise "cattalo." While that venture failed, the thriving herd still carries cattle genes, though the difference is imperceptible to the untrained eye. In recent years the buffalo have ventured in ever-greater numbers onto the North Rim, thus posing another wildlife management problem for the Park Service, which is wary of introducing nonnative species onto the Kaibab Plateau.

continue north from Point Imperial along the **Point Imperial Trail**, which leads a further three miles along the rim, again through a heavily burned area, to Saddle Mountain, where it meets the **Nankoweap Trail** (see p.115) down to the inner canyon.

Widforss Trail

The only route venturing west from the lodge area, the **Widforss Trail** leads to the tip of its eponymous headland. While a relatively easy hike, the out-and-back route entails a ten-mile round-trip likely to take around five hours. Those who reach the point are rewarded with tremendous views, but the latter half of the trail meanders away from the rim through dense forest, so most visitors hike just a short distance and settle for views closer in.

To reach the trailhead, follow the gravel road that heads west from AZ-67 a quarter-mile south of its junction with Fuller Canyon Road, roughly three miles north of *Grand Canyon Lodge*. (Note that the gravel road continues for seventeen miles to **Point Sublime**, as described on p.82, but is only recommended for 4WD vehicles.) A half-mile along the road you'll reach **Harvey Meadow**, where, with luck, a dispenser should hold copies of a Park Service brochure highlighting fourteen numbered points along the first two miles of the trail.

From the meadow, the trail climbs gently to forested rocky outcrops and its first glimpse of the yawning chasm of **The Transept**. Onward, the undulating trail meanders between the rim and the woods for repeated variations on a theme. Just shy of two miles in, you'll reach a broad panorama at the very head of The Transept. To this point, your trusty brochure will have identified notable specimens of ponderosa pine, oak, aspen, and maple, as well as a droning sewage treatment facility concealed beneath the lodge.

From here, the trail plumbs the forest depths for just over two miles. You'll eventually emerge at a stunning overlook that faces due south. While Bright Angel Point is hidden from view farther east, by way of compensation the core of the Grand Canyon lies before you. Straight ahead rise Buddha and Isis temples, beyond which all of Grand Canyon Village and surrounding Coconino Plateau spread out for your delight.

Strictly speaking, you're not quite at **Widforss Point**, which is the stark headland a few hundred yards to your left, but in the absence of a permanent onward trail, you'd do best to settle for what you've got. Both trail and point were named for Gunnar Mauritz Widforss, the so-called "Painter of the National Parks," who was born in Sweden in 1879 and was renowned for his vivid Grand Canyon watercolors.

Walhalla Plateau

Most of the North Rim **canyon overlooks** accessible by paved road line the eastern edge of the **Walhalla Plateau**. This fifteen-mile-long headland east of Bright Angel Point juts into the Grand Canyon where the Colorado makes its colossal sweeping curve from the south to the northwest. As a result, the plateau offers a superb vantage point, with some of the park's finest views, and reveals how the canyon fits into the larger context of the northern Arizona desertscape.

If you've driven as far as the lodge, it would be a mistake not to explore the plateau as well. Be forewarned, however, that aside from a few chemical toilets,

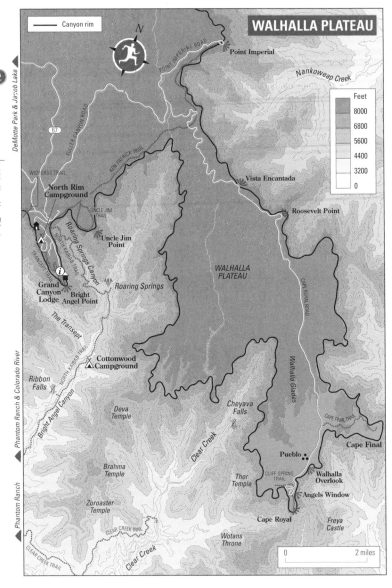

you won't find facilities of any kind. That includes gas stations, so be sure your tank is full enough for a round-trip of at least fifty miles. It takes perhaps half a day to see the whole area thoroughly, and the views are generally best as the afternoon progresses. If you don't mind driving back in the dark, try to schedule your arrival at Cape Royal, the plateau's southern tip, during the hour or so leading up to sunset.

To reach the plateau, start out east along **Fuller Canyon Road**, off AZ-67 three miles north of the lodge. Five miles along, you'll reach a junction where **Point Imperial Road** branches north, while **Cape Royal Road** turns south, crosses the neck of the plateau, and winds through cool, dense woods. The junction still bears scars from the Outlet Fire of May 2000.

Point Imperial

Before or after your exploration of the Walhalla Plateau, it's well worth making the short detour to **Point Imperial**, a gradual three-mile climb from the intersection described above. At 8803ft, this is the highest spot along the entire canyon rim. To reach the viewpoint, you'll have to descend a short distance from the parking lot. Jutting out just below the overlook is a long, sandy red ridge, capped by a stark butte.

Staring down into the dry-as-dust labyrinth, you'll find it virtually impossible to guess which gorge channels the Colorado. In fact, almost everything you see below lies on the near side of the river. While the canyon here is more than nine miles wide, the river is less than a mile from the sheer wall of the **Desert Facade** on the far side.

The landscape beyond the canyon stretches for a phenomenal distance. The vast **Marble Platform** is almost 3000ft lower than Point Imperial, so a huge swathe of the Navajo Indian Reservation lies flat and bare before you. About the only breaks in the monotony are the slight hump of distant Navajo Mountain and the cut created by the Little Colorado River, where it rushes to meet its elder sibling.

An overlook closer to the parking lot, labeled **Northeast View**, provides an even better prospect of the Marble Platform. Through a notch between two minor peaks, you can see Marble Canyon's snakelike path through the rock, flanked by the Vermilion Cliffs to the west and Echo Cliffs to the east. A dot where the two seem to meet marks Lees Ferry.

Vista Encantada

The Walhalla Plateau is narrowest at its northern end, where it clings to the rest of the North Rim by a slender thread. At some point, it will presum-

△ Point Imperial and the distant Marble Platform

ably become a mighty detached mesa; for the moment, however, Cape Royal Road manages to wriggle onto the plateau. Four miles past the neck lies **Vista Encantada**, which faces northeast.

The views here are similar to those from Point Imperial, as both overlook the basin of **Nankoweap Creek**, which continues to wear away the curving rim between the two points. Once again, the Colorado is hidden from view, but the pale green flatlands of the Navajo reservation spread away endlessly into the haze. Picnic tables make this a popular spot for midday breaks.

Roosevelt Point

Formerly called the Painted Desert Overlook, **Roosevelt Point** was renamed in the 1990s in honor of President Theodore Roosevelt – an early champion of the Grand Canyon. It's only two miles from Vista Encantada, so the canyon views are similar, and Navajo Mountain still rises from the northeast horizon, eighty miles distant, but the new perspective opens up additional Navajo Nation panoramas. To the southeast you can catch at least a hint of the **Painted Desert** badlands, which extend southeast from Cameron to the Petrified Forest outside Holbrook. The name change was appropriate, however, as the more colorful desert sands lie well beyond sight.

Roosevelt Point also provides a unique head-on view of the **confluence** of the Colorado and Little Colorado. Oddly, the rivers meet at right angles, the Little Colorado emerging from its own sheer-sided, half-mile-deep gorge. Geologists puzzle over how that came about, some suggesting the Colorado itself once flowed east through the Little Colorado gorge, before being somehow "captured" and set on its present westward course.

Cape Final

For six miles beyond Roosevelt Point, Cape Royal Road keeps to the forest. Your one chance at a canyon view comes toward the end of that stretch, at the trailhead for a four-mile round-trip **hike** to remote **Cape Final**. By now, you're close enough to Cape Royal that there's no great need to add yet another overlook to your itinerary. The reason to pause here is if you just plain like the idea of spending a couple of hours on an easy trail through the woods, away from the crowds and with the bonus of a couple of isolated prospects of the inner canyon.

The **Cape Final Trail** leads uphill from a small clearing, exactly 11.8 miles south of the Point Imperial Road intersection. The parking lot itself is a long way from the rim and offers no views whatsoever. Though you'd never know to look at it, the rudimentary dirt track that meanders away from it through the pines was once a full-fledged park road. It soon levels off, then descends gently, suddenly emerging on the rim at a big northeastward view. Just off to the left, the colossal monoliths **Poston Butte** and **Siegfried Pyre** soar almost to the rim, while the **Chuar Valley** slopes toward the river.

Turning right, away from the rim, the trail thins out. As the ponderosas dwindle, to be replaced by oak and piñon, it crosses to the south side of this minor headland and ends at a south-facing overlook. Below, the Colorado is now clearly visible as it tumbles together with Unkar Creek to create the **Unkar Delta Rapid**, as described below.

Walhalla Overlook

A mile past the Cape Final trailhead, **Walhalla Overlook** is a rim-side parking area that offers another fine view down to the confluence of Unkar Creek and the Colorado, almost exactly a mile below. Boasting some of the canyon's most fertile farming land, the **Unkar Delta** was home to a thriving **Ancestral Puebloan** community around a thousand years ago. They grew corn, squash, and beans on irrigated fields close to the river and terraces at higher, drier elevations.

As the population increased, the group adopted a sophisticated strategy to exploit resources along the rim. With its heavy annual snowfall, most of the North Rim is simply too cold to support agriculture, but the Walhalla Plateau is a unique case. Effectively a peninsula, it is warmed on all sides by rising air from the canyon depths.

More than a hundred ancient farming sites have been identified in the **Walhalla Glades**, near the plateau's southern tip. After wintering on the canyon floor, the Ancestral Puebloans would climb out in early spring along the line of Unkar Creek – there's no trail now, but back then it was a fast, direct route. The group would plant crops where they'd be fed by snowmelt and store snow in jars to water seedlings as they grew. The fall harvest season coincided with the best time to hunt deer and other game.

Across the road from the overlook, a short trail leads through a hundred yards of charred forest to the foundation of a small **pueblo**. Archeologists think that a family of around twenty members occupied the central six-room structure between about 1050 and 1150. In truth, these crude stone piles are hardly a spectacular sight – certainly not for anyone familiar with ancient ruins elsewhere in the Southwest – but they do offer an emotive reminder of the canyon's long human history.

Cliff Spring Trail

A quarter-mile past **Walhalla Overlook**, another minor overlook features views of Cape Royal, in particular Angels Window (see below). The same parking lot serves as the start of the short **Cliff Spring Trail**, which crosses the road and then descends west along a dry, gravelly streambed. Soon after passing a remarkably complete Ancestral Puebloan granary tucked under a boulder, you'll reach a damp, mossy alcove beneath the rim. Seepage from the overhanging Kaibab limestone collects in small pools, but the water is not safe to drink.

A round-trip hike this far is about a mile and takes less than half an hour. Onward as far again, the difficult trail requires some scrambling to reach impressive westward views. Eventually the ledge you're on dwindles to nothing beside a thousand-foot drop, and you're forced to turn back.

Cape Royal

At **Cape Royal**, where the Walhalla Plateau peters out, the promontory extends far into the canyon and is constantly bathed by warm air currents. As a result, the ponderosa disappears, and piñon-juniper woodland predominates.

There's nothing to see from the unremarkable loop parking lot 14.3 miles from the Point Imperial Road junction. However, a level, paved nature trail with identifying labels leads to the two principal overlooks. A round-trip **hike** of roughly half a mile, it's just long enough to warrant wearing proper shoes and carrying drinking water.

You'll first reach **Angels Window**, a wedge-shaped natural arch that perfectly frames a segment of the Colorado River. Unless you're especially afraid of heights, turn left off the main trail onto a brief spur that crosses the window on an extremely narrow railed path. It ends atop an equally vertiginous railed slab with views across the Navajo flatlands. Two broad, green-trimmed stretches of river lie below, including foamy Unkar Creek Rapid.

A couple of hundred yards farther along the main trail, Cape Royal offers broad westward views that range nearly the full 360 degrees, though an intervening ridge obscures Bright Angel Point. This is the only Walhalla viewpoint overlooking the central portion of the Grand Canyon, including such major landmarks as **Wotans Throne** and **Vishnu Temple** straight ahead and **Brahma** and **Zoroaster** temples off to the right.

As the crow flies, the canyon here is roughly eight miles wide. In theory, most of the best-known **South Rim viewpoints** should be visible, including Desert View (backed by flat-topped Cedar Mountain), as well as Yaki, Yavapai, Hopi, and Pima points. Without strong binoculars, however, it's hard to distinguish one from the next, though the Watchtower at Desert View stands out if you know where to look. It's tempting to leave the path and ledge-hop even closer to the rim, but bear in mind that this site is notorious for fatal falls from its crumbling stone slabs.

Western Kaibab Plateau

North Rim visitors are often frustrated that such a vast area seems to hold so few roads. You can't help feeling that a wealth of spectacular scenery lies just out of reach. In fact, get hold of a good map – ideally the *North Kaibab Ranger District*, published by the Kaibab National Forest, or the BLM Arizona Strip Field Office's *Visitor Map*, though *not* AAA's otherwise reliable *Indian Country* – and you'll soon realize there are plenty of minor roads out there. The trouble is, all are gravel or dirt, and while the overall picture has improved considerably in recent years, many remain accessible only to **high-clearance 4WD vehicles**.

The most rewarding routes run **west** of Bright Angel Point and AZ-67, largely within the **Kaibab National Forest**. In this "land of many uses," the roads are maintained for logging trucks and the like and thus are often passable in standard vehicles. However, the canyon rim lies inside national park boundaries, and it's often those final stretches along Park Service roads to the viewpoints that require 4WD.

Before driving anywhere, it's absolutely essential to **ask for advice** at either the USFS Kaibab Plateau Visitor Center in Jacob Lake (see p.136) or the North Rim Visitor Center. Rangers can provide you with excellent maps and suggest the best roads, which may well entail a convoluted route rather than the shortest. Road closures can vary from day to day, depending on such factors as weather and where any prescribed or natural fires might be burning. Don't follow your whims or underestimate how much time it may take – visiting more than one overlook may well require an hour or more of backtracking. While on the better roads it's often possible to drive about forty miles per hour, expect to average more like twenty miles per hour.

The pick of literally dozens of possibilities, routes described below lead to notable trailheads and exceptional viewpoints. These roads are seldom less than ravishing, particularly in September and early October, when fall colors are in full swing.

Point Sublime

In the estimation of Clarence Dutton, the pioneer surveyor who named it in 1882, **Point Sublime** is perhaps the finest of all Grand Canyon viewpoints.

Although the magnificent Toroweap Overlook is technically on the North Rim, it's only accessible from the Arizona Strip and is therefore covered in Chapter Five.

Unfortunately for less hardy modern visitors, it stands at the end of a seventeen-mile dirt road that's usually restricted to 4WD vehicles. If you have one, drive three miles north of *Grand Canyon Lodge* on AZ-67, then turn west on the gravel road that leads to the Widforss Trail (see p.77). A half-mile past the trailhead, follow the curve of the road to the left.

The prospect at road's end is absolutely colossal, extending both east and west and incorporating a glorious fifty-mile stretch of the inner canyon. Point Sublime is closer to the Colorado than any other North Rim viewpoint, and the **Boucher Rapid** rushes by in full view below the overlook. Rhapsodizing that "the infinity of sharply defined detail is amazing," Dutton was especially struck by the isolated mesa he called **Shiva Temple**. In 1937, the American Museum of Natural History sent an expedition to this "lost world," hoping that its flat 275-acre summit might hold species unknown to science. All they discovered was that large mammals somehow manage to visit the summit regularly, as did Ancestral Puebloans.

Below and to the east of Point Sublime, **Tuna Creek** was the scene of a dramatic rescue in June 1944. Three airmen who parachuted from a bomber after its engines failed during a training run were stranded down there for ten days before park rangers were able to plot a route and reach them on foot.

Swamp Point

West of Point Sublime, both the Colorado and canyon rim curve northward. While the next major promontory, the **Powell Plateau**, rises higher than the rest of the North Rim and approaches within two miles of the river, it is detached from the rim and offers no accessible vistas. The closest vantage, **Swamp Point**, sits just above **Muav Saddle**, the short span a thousand feet below the rim that leads to the plateau.

As well as overlooking the plateau – which, though it holds no permanent water, sustained a sizable Ancestral Puebloan population – Swamp Point commands a fine northwest prospect, centering on **Tapeats Amphitheater**. Even so, few visitors drive here just to enjoy the view. Most come to access trailheads for the grueling, advanced **North Bass Trail** (see p.116) and shorter **Powell Saddle Trail**, a five-mile hike onto the Powell Plateau.

Once again, 4WD is essential, and even that won't help you before early June, as the previous winter's fallen trees often block the way. Once rangers give the all clear, drive less than a mile south of DeMotte Park on AZ-67 and turn right on Forest Development Road (FDR) 22, which climbs due west. After 2.1 miles, turn left on FDR 270 and drive 2.3 miles, then turn right on FDR 223 (signed Fire Point). After 5.8 miles, turn left on FDR 268 and follow the signs, which after 0.3 mile should lead you through a left turn onto FDR 268B. Just over a mile farther, you'll enter the park, where road conditions deteriorate over the remaining 7.8 miles to the point.

Fire Point

Little more than a mile north of Swamp Point, but more likely accessible in a standard vehicle, **Fire Point** is another spectacular overlook that faces **Great Thumb Mesa** on the South Rim and provides a dramatic side view of striated Powell Plateau.

To reach it, start by following the directions to Swamp Point, above, but stay straight on FDR 223 rather than turning left on FDR 268. The point lies six miles past that junction, or sixteen miles from AZ-67. While the route is usually passable in summer, if you're driving a non-4WD vehicle, err on the side of caution – pull over a half-mile within the park boundary and tackle the final half-mile stretch on foot.

Parissawampitts Point

The eighteen-mile **Rainbow Rim Trail** links a cluster of five points on separate fingerlike promontories north of Fire Point. The North Rim's closest equivalent to the Rim Trail, this demanding, little-used route dips repeatedly into steep side canyons between the successive differing overlooks. The northernmost of the five, **Parissawampitts Point**, is the easiest to reach by road.

Once again, drive less than a mile south of DeMotte Park on AZ-67 and turn right on FDR 22. Follow that for 10.9 miles, then turn left on FDR 206 and drive 3.7 miles. At FDR 214 turn right and follow the distinctly worse track west for eight miles past lovely, secluded potential camping sites. Park in the clearing at road's end, but as you descend toward the rim, don't go straight, the intuitive choice – instead turn left. You'll soon reach clearings that command huge vistas across **Tapeats Amphitheater** to the Granite Gorge, where the unseen Colorado winds westward toward Mount Trumbull.

Each of the four points south of Parissawampitts – from north to south, **Fence**, **Locust**, **North Timp**, and **Timp** – is accessible along a separate spur road off FDR 206, so you could leave a shuttle vehicle at one of those, then drive to Parissawampitts and hike the Rainbow Rim Trail in one direction. It strays so far inland between each viewpoint, however, that it's probably simpler just to hike out and back from Parissawampitts. While this offers a more varied forest hike than you'd get on the South Rim, in all honesty the views aren't in the same league.

Crazy Jug Point

Of the many western Kaibab Plateau viewpoints, the one most readily accessible in a standard vehicle is usually **Crazy Jug Point**. That said, it lies a full 27 miles from the highway along gravel and dirt roads, a trip that in good conditions takes just under an hour each way. The reward is a colossal panorama of the Granite Gorge (though not the Colorado itself) between the Powell Plateau and Great Thumb Mesa, with **Tapeats Amphitheater** spread out below.

As before, head south about a mile on AZ-67 from DeMotte Park and turn right on FDR 22; the latter runs all the way to Fredonia, so you could approach from that direction. After 10.9 miles, turn right on FDR 206, drive 7.4 miles, then turn left on FDR 425.

Monument Point

If you've ventured as far as Crazy Jug Point, it's well worth driving another 1.5 miles west to the **Monument Point** parking area, despite the steadily deteriorating road surface. You may be surprised at the number of vehicles parked in such a remote spot; most visitors are here to access the trailhead for the challenging backcountry **Bill Hall Trail**, which after 3.4 miles meets the **Thunder River Trail** and descends to the Colorado via Tapeats Creek.

Monument Point stands atop a small hill just under a mile from the parking area. If you're short on time, there's an equally impressive viewpoint closer in, at the head of Tapeats Amphitheater. As you walk, look for ancient marine fossils embedded in limestone along the canyon rim – a stark reminder of how this landscape has transformed over the eons.

Hiking the inner canyon

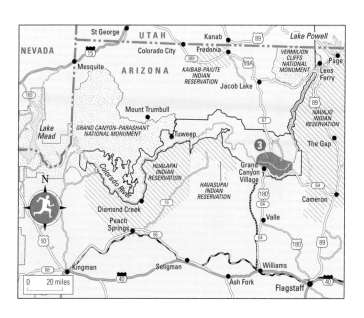

CHAPTER 3   # Highlights

✳ **Bright Angel Trail** Deservedly the park's most popular hiking trail and a superb introduction to life below the rim. **See p.96**

✳ **South Kaibab Trail** This dramatic, exposed descent to the canyon floor offers the best day hikes in the park. **See p.99**

✳ **North Kaibab Trail** The North Rim's finest trail passes superb waterfalls and stupendous scenery on its two-day, fourteen-mile drop to the Colorado River. **See p.101**

✳ **Phantom Ranch** Rest your feet from all that hiking with an overnight stay at this rustic lodging on the canyon floor. **See p.107**

✳ **Grandview Trail** A great day hike on a challenging but rewarding – and skillfully engineered – trail. **See p.111**

✳ **Day hike to Santa Maria Spring** Escape the crowds with a peaceful and relatively easy day hike that abounds in canyon wildlife and vegetation. **See p.112**

△ Switchbacking up the North Kaibab Trail, above the Redwall Bridge

Hiking the inner canyon

What seemed to be easy from above was not so, but instead very hard and difficult.
– Don García López de Cárdenas, 1540

Undertaking a **hike** below the rim, into the very maw of the canyon, may well be both the most challenging, and most rewarding, thing you do in Grand Canyon National Park – or, for that matter, in your entire life. It's essential not to underestimate how difficult hiking in the canyon can be. The mere fact that the easier part, the descent, comes before the much harder slog back to the rim is enough to confuse and exhaust the hardiest mountain hikers, while the summer heat, along with the high altitude and thin air of the Colorado Plateau, can turn even the shortest hike into a grueling trek. You'll find an overview of the issues involved in planning a Grand Canyon expedition, as well as summaries of highly recommended day hikes, in the color section **at the center of this book.**

Above all, park rangers have one simple message for all would-be hikers: **Don't try to hike to the river and back in one day**. It's hard to stress quite how important that advice is. It might not look far on the map, but completing a round-trip day hike to the canyon floor, which involves a total walk of at least fourteen miles and an elevation change of one mile in each direction, is harder than running a marathon. That's the plain, unadorned truth, even though you

Hiking along the rim

This chapter deals exclusively with hikes that descend below the rim. However, there are plenty of good, and much less physically demanding, trails at rim level. Here's a selection of the finest, which are described in detail elsewhere in this book:

Shoshone Point	South Rim	2 miles round-trip	p.61
Rim Trail	South Rim	8 miles one-way	p.57
Uncle Jim Trail	North Rim	4-mile loop	p.76
Widforss Trail	North Rim	10 miles round-trip	p.77
Cape Final Trail	North Rim	4 miles round-trip	p.80
Cliff Spring Trail	North Rim	2 miles round-trip	p.81

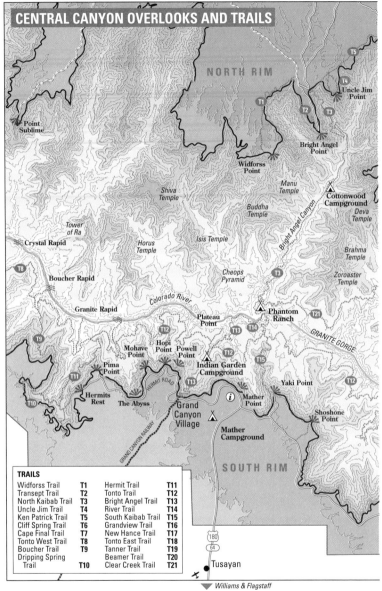

CENTRAL CANYON OVERLOOKS AND TRAILS

▲ Jacob Lake

NORTH RIM

Uncle Jim Point
T5
T4
T1
T2
T3

Point Sublime

Bright Angel Point

Widforss Point

Manu Temple

Shiva Temple

Buddha Temple

Cottonwood Campground

Deva Temple

Tower of Ra

Crystal Rapid

Horus Temple

Isis Temple

Brahma Temple

T8

Boucher Rapid

Cheops Pyramid

Zoroaster Temple

T3

Colorado River

Granite Rapid

Plateau Point

Phantom Ranch

T21

GRANITE GORGE

T9

T12

Hopi Point

T13

T14

Mohave Point

Powell Point

T12

T15

Pima Point

Indian Garden Campground

T11

Yaki Point

T12

Hermits Rest

T13

HERMIT ROAD

The Abyss

i

Mather Point

T10

Grand Canyon Village

GRAND CANYON RAILWAY

Mather Campground

Shoshone Point

SOUTH RIM

TRAILS			
Widforss Trail	**T1**	Hermit Trail	**T11**
Transept Trail	**T2**	Tonto Trail	**T12**
North Kaibab Trail	**T3**	Bright Angel Trail	**T13**
Uncle Jim Trail	**T4**	River Trail	**T14**
Ken Patrick Trail	**T5**	South Kaibab Trail	**T15**
Cliff Spring Trail	**T6**	Grandview Trail	**T16**
Cape Final Trail	**T7**	New Hance Trail	**T17**
Tonto West Trail	**T8**	Tonto East Trail	**T18**
Boucher Trail	**T9**	Tanner Trail	**T19**
Dripping Spring		Beamer Trail	**T20**
Trail	**T10**	Clear Creek Trail	**T21**

180
64

● Tusayan

▼ Williams & Flagstaff

may well meet people on the trail who are doing it, and there are plenty of canyon obsessives who not only perform greater feats of endurance than that, but also make sure everyone knows about it.

The point is, the Grand Canyon is an extreme arena that attracts extreme athletes; unless you know exactly what you're doing, which means at the very least that you've already hiked extensively in the canyon, it's a mistake to think you can match them. While it won't necessarily be you who dies – if you're lucky, on a cool overcast day in April or October, you might even find it straightforward – several hikers do die each year in the attempt, and several hundred more receive emergency medical treatment. Casualties regularly include fit, healthy young people. For example, a 24-year-old woman died hiking in 2004 within months of completing the Boston Marathon.

Choosing a trail and other hiking practicalities

All hiking should be on designated **trails**. Grand Canyon National Park offers about five hundred miles of such routes, on terrain divided into four official zones of difficulty – not to say that any of it is easy.

First-time hikers are advised to restrict themselves to the **corridor zone**, which comprises the 33 miles of trail regularly maintained by park rangers and is, thanks to two footbridges, the only area in which it's possible for hikers to cross the Colorado River. The Bright Angel, South Kaibab, and North Kaibab trails here are regularly patrolled and offer facilities such as emergency phones and piped water.

Almost all other trails reviewed in this chapter lie within the **threshold zone**, where trails are often rough underfoot, harder to follow, and liable to lack water, toilets, and formal campgrounds. A few pass wholly or partly through the **primitive zone**, where trails are not maintained, facilities are nonexistent, and you may well need route-finding skills to stay on course. Only backcountry experts should venture into the **wild zone**, which holds virtually no formal trails or water sources. The Park Service recommends against entering the primitive or wild zones in summer.

It's best not to be too ambitious on your first canyon hike. Even if you're sure you want to go as far as the river at some point during your stay, you won't regret having a practice **day hike** before the main event. On the South Rim, most first-timers opt for the **Bright Angel** or **South Kaibab** trails, though both the **Grandview** and **Hermit** also offer good short trips. On the North Rim, the **North Kaibab** is the only sensible option.

Die-hard wilderness enthusiasts often grumble that the sheer mass of hikers in summer, especially on the trails to and from Phantom Ranch, diminishes their enjoyment. If that strikes a chord with you, then you may prefer to hike one of the lesser-known trails, though of course such trails can be brutal in summer. For most casual visitors, however, the traffic on the corridor trails is not a problem – it's not *that* bad, and it provides a greater sense of companionship and solidarity.

Hiking safety

The secret to successful hiking is to **plan ahead**. Follow rangers' advice and allow twice as long to climb back out of the canyon as you take to hike down. That takes a bit of getting used to, but basically, if you set off at 8am and want to be back on the rim at 5pm, you should start your ascent at 11am.

Assuming you're adequately equipped with water and other supplies, as outlined below, the best way to guarantee your safety is never to leave the trail. If you imagine you've spotted a shortcut, you're wrong; leaving the trail will make you much harder to find in an emergency. That's especially true for solo hikers, who form a large proportion of canyon casualties. Ideally, you shouldn't hike alone; if you must, stick to the busier trails and, preferably, day hikes.

On a more general note, try to walk slowly, so you're never out of breath. If you're having trouble maintaining an ordinary conversation, you're walking too fast. And take at least one five-minute break every hour, ideally lying down with legs raised above the level of your heart.

Water and food

The sheer quantity of **water** you have to carry – and drink – while hiking in the Grand Canyon almost defies belief. In typical summer temperatures exceeding 100°F, your body loses a phenomenal four pints of fluid every hour spent on the trail. To keep up with that sort of demand, drink a minimum of **one gallon** a day in summer and perhaps half that in cooler conditions.

Find out whether water will be available on your chosen trail – rangers keep abreast of the latest conditions – and carry at least two pints with you at all times, even if you expect to refill en route. Only the Bright Angel and North Kaibab trails provide piped drinking water, and even that can be unexpectedly cut off if the pipeline breaks. On other trails where water is to be had, you'll have to **treat** it first, either by boiling it for at least five minutes or cleansing it with iodine-based purifying tablets or a *Giardia*-rated filter, available from any camping or sporting goods store.

Pre-hydrate before a big hike, by drinking large amounts the night before. Once you set off, drink regularly, even if you don't feel thirsty. There's a limit to how much liquid your body can actually absorb at any one time – around one quart per hour – so you need to be drinking steadily; hydration systems such as those made by CamelBak, in which a mouthpiece and tube connects to a water pouch in your backpack, are highly recommended.

Early symptoms of **heat exhaustion** include loss of both appetite and thirst, so it's possible to become seriously dehydrated without feeling thirsty. Other warning signs include nausea, dizziness, headache, cramps, and strangely cool skin. The best indicator of whether you're drinking enough is your **urine**; its frequency and quantity should be the same as normal, and it should remain clear rather than discolored. (On that note, incidentally, if there's no restroom nearby, the official line is that you should try to urinate on bare rock or sand, away from water sources, rather than on plants or soil.) Just to confuse things, there's also the risk of **hyponatremia**, or **water intoxication**, which in its first stages closely resembles heat exhaustion and happens if you drink too much without eating.

As hikers can burn up to a thousand calories per hour – not just from walking, but also in the energy it takes to keep cool – expect to eat at least twice as much **food** as normal, both before and during your hike. Eat every time you drink. Salty snacks such as cookies, crackers, and trail mix are recommended, as well as jerky or salami and ready-made dehydrated meals. **Electrolyte replacement** drinks, which you can buy either prepared or in powder form, are a great help; many hikers carry two hydration packs, one filled with water and one with Gatorade or a similar product. Avoid salt tablets, as taking salt on its own can do more harm than good.

In addition, whenever you come to a water source within the canyon, **soak yourself** – your head, your hair, your clothing, everything. That will keep you much cooler as you hike on.

Finally, it's easy to forget that at the end of a long hike there may be no facilities at the trailhead. Be sure to leave some food and water in your vehicle as well.

Snakes and creepy crawlies

No one is known to have died in the Grand Canyon from being bitten or stung by a snake, scorpion, or indeed any other form of reptile, insect, or spider.

Although the canyon is home to several species of **snake**, including three kinds of rattlesnake, bites are extremely rare and almost invariably the result of misguided attempts at handling. If you do get bitten, current medical thinking rejects the concept of cutting yourself open and attempting to suck out the venom; in most cases, in fact, no venom is injected. You'd do better to stay calm, apply a cold compress to the wound, constrict the area with a tourniquet, drink lots of water, rest in a shady place, and send for help.

Scorpion stings, especially from bark scorpions, are more common. Their poison is nasty, but causes nausea rather than serious illness or death. When camping, be sure to shake out your shoes, clothing, and bedding before use.

To avoid painful bites from **red ants**, tidy up any crumbs or spillages after you eat and don't sit or sleep on the same spot afterward.

Security precautions

Though it issues permits to all backcountry hikers, the Park Service doesn't formally keep track of what happens to each group. There is no official check-in or checkout, so no one will necessarily notice if you fail to return. It's therefore essential to leave details of your planned itinerary with family, friends, or coworkers and arrange to call them when you've emerged safely from the canyon. If you fail to do so, they can raise the alarm by calling the Park Service at ⓣ928/638-2477. Stick to your itinerary – you'll be held liable for the cost of any search and rescue operation, which can run into the thousands of dollars, especially if helicopter evacuation becomes necessary.

Note that cell phones are very unlikely to work, as most areas, both along the rim and down in the canyon, are too remote to get a signal. Satellite phones are somewhat more reliable, but often fail in the gorge.

Backcountry camping

To restrict numbers, **backcountry camping** within Grand Canyon National Park – as opposed to camping in the developed *Mather Campground* and *Desert View* sites on the South Rim and the *North Rim Campground* near Bright Angel Point – is by **permit** only. Demand is very high, and more than half of all applications are turned down. Anyone overnighting in the canyon without a permit, other than guests in the cabins or dorms at Phantom Ranch, is subject to a heavy fine.

Permits cost a flat fee of $10, plus an additional $5 per person per night for sites below the rim or $5 per group per night for undeveloped campsites on the rim. Applications are accepted **in person**, by **mail** (PO Box 129, Grand Canyon, AZ 86023), or by **fax** (ⓕ928/638-2125), but not by email or phone. Full details, including the relevant form, are available online at ⓦwww.nps .gov/grca/backcountry or in the park's free *Backcountry Trip Planner*, available at all visitor centers.

All applications must specify an exact **itinerary**, with precise details of where you'll spend each night; depending on where you're hiking, this will be either named campgrounds or the wide-ranging "use areas" listed on official park maps (also available online). Between March and mid-November, there's a limit on the most popular trails of two nights per party per campsite, whether or not those nights are consecutive. Applicants can suggest up to three alternative dates and routes. You'll also be asked for the number in your group – which can't exceed eleven – and even your vehicle license plate numbers. The fee is payable in advance, by credit card or check, and is nonrefundable. Frequent Hiker Membership ($25 per year) spares you paying the $10 fee each time, but confers no other benefits.

Mailed or **faxed** applications are accepted for dates through the end of the fourth complete month after they're submitted. Thus in January you can apply for nothing later than the end of May, while if you're planning a trip in the peak month of July, you'd better mail your application on March 1. Both mail and fax applications are responded to by mail.

To apply **in person**, turn up at either the **Backcountry Information Center** (daily 8am–noon & 1–5pm; ☎928/638-7875), near *Maswik Lodge* in Grand Canyon Village on the South Rim, or at the **North Rim Backcountry Office** (daily 8am–noon & 1–5pm; ☎928/638-7868), a quarter-mile north of the *North Rim Campground*.

While both offices accept advance applications, and turning up in person does jump you ahead of all unprocessed applicants, most hikers who visit the offices are hoping for a **last-minute cancellation**. Even in peak season, your chances of being able to hike within a day or two are pretty good, especially if you're flexible as to which trail you'd like to explore. Your name will be added to a waiting list, and each morning at 8am that day's cancellations are reassigned – though you must be present to get one.

Where to camp

The most popular campgrounds within the canyon are the three along the rim-to-rim corridor trails – *Indian Garden* on the Bright Angel Trail, *Bright Angel Campground* near the river, and *Cottonwood Campground* on the North Kaibab Trail. Sites elsewhere vary between similar permanent campgrounds, designated campsites – specified by the Park Service, though they hold no facilities – and wilderness camping. Wherever you camp, minimize your impact on the canyon. Camp where someone else has camped before and make no additional physical changes.

No **fires** are permitted within the canyon, except in emergencies, though camping stoves are allowed. Human waste should be buried from four to six inches deep at least 200ft from the nearest water supply, while all trash, including toilet paper, should be packed out. Never use soap in or near a water source.

Flash floods, which can appear from nowhere, are most likely in July and August. Fatalities are rare, but they have occurred over the last decade on both the Bright Angel and North Kaibab trails. Survivors often report having had just a few minutes' warning, in the form of a loud rumble heading downstream along the nearest watercourse. The most important precaution you can take is always to camp well above the bed of even the driest-seeming wash. If you hear any ominous noise, head immediately for high ground, and don't attempt to cross flooded areas until the water has receded.

What to take

Exactly what **equipment** you'll need depends on which trail you're taking, for how long, and in what season. Bear in mind that it's usually around 30°F warmer beside the river than it is up at the rim; be prepared for extremes of both hot and cold.

For a **day hike**, essentials include dependable **hiking boots** that you've already broken in, worn for blister protection either with designated hiking **socks** or two pairs of ordinary socks, thick on the outside and thinner within; a **long-sleeved shirt** and **pants** for sun protection, together with a wide-brimmed **hat**, **sunblock**, and **sunglasses**; containers for carrying up to a gallon of **water**, plus, if necessary, a water purification system; substantial **food**; a **pocket knife**; a **flashlight**; and a **signal mirror** and/or **whistle** for emergencies. On trails without pit toilets, you'll also need **toilet paper** and **Ziploc bags** in which to store that and other waste.

All hikers should carry a **first-aid kit**, at its most basic including bandages and moleskin for blisters, painkillers and anti-inflammatories such as Advil, and knee and ankle wraps. A great deal of hikers' lore surrounds feet in particular; many people swear by duct tape as additional precaution against blisters, and everyone agrees that you should trim your **toenails** as much as possible before a downhill hike. A hiking **stick** or pair of trekking poles can be invaluable on knee-jarring downhill stretches.

While you're unlikely to lose your way on the main trails, a good **map** will greatly improve your sense of where you are. Earthwalk Press's *Bright Angel Trail* (1:24,000), which covers the three corridor trails, and Trails Illustrated's wider-ranging *Grand Canyon National Park* (1:73,530) are both recommended.

The major decision for **backpackers** is whether to bring a **tent**. While it's certainly necessary in winter, protection against cold is not a factor in summer. However, rain is always a possibility, in July and August especially, and you may also prefer to be sealed away from the desert wildlife, so a **rain fly** or waterproof **bivvy sack** may suit you. A **sleeping bag** is always recommended – though in summer it could simply be a light cotton sleeping sack – as are a foam pad or air mattress and a ground cloth beneath it all. As for a cooking **stove**, hot food may be more bother than it's worth in summer, but it's a lifesaver in winter. **Sandals** are a welcome indulgence for camp use.

Equipment rental

Outfitters the world over should sell any specialized equipment you need, and you'll find several good stores in nearby **Flagstaff** (see p.156). The **General Store** beside the *North Rim Campground* (see p.74) stocks a fairly limited range, while the **Canyon Village Marketplace** on the South Rim (formerly known as Babbitt's; see p.49) has a very good selection. The latter also **rents** equipment, including day packs and backpacks, stoves, sleeping bags, and tents; typical rates for a tent would be $15 for the first day and $9 each subsequent day. Rental reservations are only accepted between one and five days in advance (☏928/638-2262).

Grand Canyon Field Institute

The perfect way for novice hikers to get a first taste of the canyon, or for more experienced ones to improve their skills, is to join one of the many expeditions led each year by the **Grand Canyon Field Institute**. Cosponsored by the Grand Canyon Association and the National Park Service, this friendly, enthusiastic organization offers an extensive program of well-priced, expert-led **guided tours and hikes** in and around the canyon. All participants receive detailed advice on how to prepare and what to bring.

Different tours, some of which are restricted to women only, specialize in geology, history, natural history, photography, wilderness techniques, and other topics. Most involve camping and backpacking, while others include lodge stays or even llama trekking; all are graded according to the difficulty of any hiking involved, and your acceptance is subject to completion of a detailed health questionnaire. Typical prices include $375 for a three-night hike down to Indian Garden; $535 for a four-night rim-to-rim backpack, including shuttle service; and $495 for a six-night off-trail adventure in the wilderness of the western canyon.

For full details, visit ⊛www.grandcanyon.org/fieldinstitute or write to PO Box 399, Grand Canyon, AZ 86023 (☏928/638-2485 or 1-866/471-4435, ℗928/638-2484).

The corridor trails

The only continuous routes between the South and North rims, the three **corridor trails** – the **Bright Angel**, **South Kaibab**, and **North Kaibab** – are deservedly the most popular hiking trails within the park. All provide **backpackers** with a wonderful inner canyon baptism – featuring well-equipped campgrounds

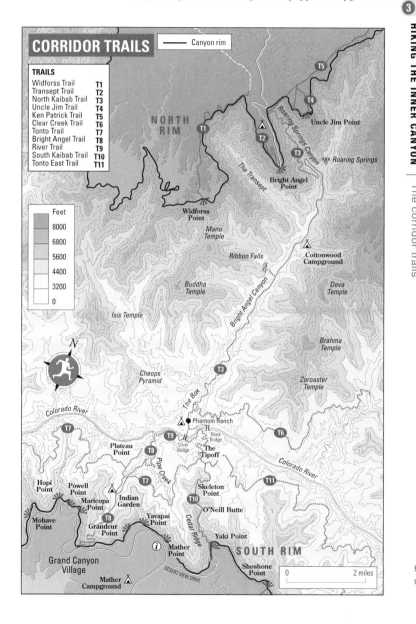

CORRIDOR TRAILS — Canyon rim

TRAILS

Widforss Trail	T1
Transept Trail	T2
North Kaibab Trail	T3
Uncle Jim Trail	T4
Ken Patrick Trail	T5
Clear Creek Trail	T6
Tonto Trail	T7
Bright Angel Trail	T8
River Trail	T9
South Kaibab Trail	T10
Tonto East Trail	T11

Feet

8000
6800
5600
4400
3200
0

NORTH RIM

Uncle Jim Point

Roaring Springs Canyon

Roaring Springs

The Transept

Bright Angel Point

Widforss Point

Manu Temple

Ribbon Falls

Cottonwood Campground

Buddha Temple

Deva Temple

Isis Temple

Bright Angel Canyon

Brahma Temple

Cheops Pyramid

Zoroaster Temple

The Box

Colorado River

Phantom Ranch

Black Bridge

Plateau Point

Silver Bridge

The Tipoff

Colorado River

Hopi Point

Powell Point

Maricopa Point

Indian Garden

Pipe Creek

Skeleton Point

O'Neill Butte

Mohave Point

Grandeur Point

Yavapai Point

Cedar Ridge

Yaki Point

Grand Canyon Village

Mather Point

SOUTH RIM

Shoshone Point

DESERT VIEW DRIVE

Mather Campground

0   2 miles

en route and the lure of **Phantom Ranch** down by the river – while also offering good, short **day hikes** for novice canyoneers who lack either the time or the energy to complete the entire routes. Again, as previously explained, it's crucial not to try to hike down to the river and back up again in a single day.

Because most hikers want to start from and finish at the South Rim, the most common itinerary is to hike **down the South Kaibab**, spend a night or two by the river, then return **up the Bright Angel**. That's certainly better than doing it the other way round, as the climb up the South Kaibab is a real killer. The reason more people don't do the **rim-to-rim** hike, from the South Rim to the North or vice versa, is largely because it's longer – the North Kaibab alone takes at least two days – and also because you end up more than two hundred driving miles from where you began. However, the **Transcanyon Shuttle** ($65 one-way; see p.119) does offer daily van service between the rims.

Finally, the corridor trails are also the only ones on which **mules** are allowed; for details on mule trips, see p.55 (South Rim) and p.71 (North Rim). Hikers are expected always to give way to mule trains, by standing still and quietly beside the trail.

⊕ Bright Angel Trail

By far the busiest inner canyon hiking route, the **Bright Angel Trail** starts in Grand Canyon Village, beside the wooden shack that once served as the Kolb photographic studio (see p.55). Although the side canyon immediately below the village makes access to the Tonto Platform relatively straightforward, it's still a long hard climb, with **water** available in the topmost 4.6 miles between May and September only. Most **day hikers** content themselves with walking to either of the two resthouses in the first three miles, but with an early start you should be able to manage the round-trip of nine miles to **Indian Garden**, or even the eleven miles to **Plateau Point**. Just don't consider hiking to the Colorado and back in a single day, and only try to reach the river if you've reserved lodgings there for the night.

The "Bright Angel" name, first ascribed by John Wesley Powell to the tributary stream that flows down from the North Rim, is so ubiquitous in the Grand Canyon that it's easy to get confused. The Bright Angel Trail doesn't start from Bright Angel Point, which lies on the North Rim, and it doesn't quite reach, let alone follow, Bright Angel Creek. Technically, it ends where it meets the Colorado, 7.8 miles from the rim, and the 1.8-mile hike from there to Phantom Ranch, beside the creek, is on the separate **River Trail**. The Bright Angel Trail does, however, launch itself into the canyon a couple of hundred yards west of *Bright Angel Lodge*, and most pertinent, it owes its existence to **Bright Angel Fault**, the geologic fault line that makes rim-to-river access possible at this point.

Trailhead Grand Canyon Village (6860ft)
Water Mile-and-a-Half Resthouse (May–Sept)
Three-Mile Resthouse (May–Sept)
Indian Garden
Stream water (treat before use)

Day hike to Indian Garden (3800ft)
Difficulty Difficult
Distance 9.2 miles round-trip
Estimated time 5–7hr

Day hike to Plateau Point (3665ft)
Difficulty Very strenuous
Distance 11.2 miles round-trip
Estimated time 8–10hr

Phantom Ranch (2486ft)
Difficulty Strenuous
Distance 9.6 miles one-way
Estimated time 5–6hr descent, 7–9hr ascent

As one of the "easiest" natural routes into the canyon, the trail down to Indian Garden was known to Ancestral Puebloans a thousand years ago and was still in use by the **Havasupai** when prospectors Pete Berry and Niles and Ralph Cameron improved it in 1890. Ralph took it over in 1903, exploiting spurious mining claims to charge riders a toll of $1 each. It was finally passed over to the park in 1928.

△ Resting at Indian Garden, on the Bright Angel Trail

Initial descent
There's no gentle introduction to the Bright Angel Trail, which hurtles straight into a long, exposed set of switchbacks down the dry rocky hillside. Two short **tunnels** within the first mile mark transitions between geologic layers, the first from Kaibab limestone to the Toroweap Formation, the second on to Coconino sandstone.

Soon after dropping down that steep, dark cliff, you reach **Mile-and-a-Half Resthouse**, a basic way station that offers water (May–Sept), restrooms, and emergency phones. By now, wildlife is much more abundant, including pesky squirrels and ravens. A similar onward haul, past first Hermit shale and then the Supai Formation – watch for Ancestral Puebloan **pictographs**, all but obscured by graffiti – brings you to the equally self-explanatory **Three-Mile Resthouse**, which has water (again in summer only) and phones but not restrooms.

As is readily apparent from its sweeping canyon views, Three-Mile Resthouse marks the final boundary between forest and desert. Below it lies the precipitous **Redwall limestone**, the major obstacle to inner canyon access throughout the park, breached here thanks to the Bright Angel Fault. Even so, it takes the forty tight switchbacks of **Jacob's Ladder** – the most murderous stretch of the return journey – to carry you down to the gently sloping bed of Garden Creek.

Indian Garden
Though you'll almost certainly have spotted it from the rim, the verdant green strip of **Garden Creek** still makes a welcome surprise at the foot of those baking-hot switchbacks. Just past a patch of prickly pears and other yellow- and red-blossomed cacti, you hear the astonishing sound of trickling water. The streambed is lined with dazzling green cottonwood trees.

Native peoples really did grow crops at **Indian Garden**, 4.6 miles from the rim. As well as the creek, there's also a perennial **spring**, where seepage from the more porous rock layers above collects atop the impervious Bright Angel shale. Originally planted in prehistoric times, the "garden" was continuously used by the Havasupai from around 1300 until the modern era; early tourists admired the ancient stone granaries. In 1905, Theodore Roosevelt is said to have curtly instructed the Havasupai chief to "get your people out"; they were eventually evicted in 1928, by which time they were no longer farmers but dependent on the tourist trade.

These days this unexpected little oasis holds a year-round water supply, a ranger station, restrooms, separate **camping** and day-use areas, and a staging post for mules. Forever busy with hikers, backpackers, and mule riders, it's not exactly pristine wilderness, but it's such a well-shaded and attractive staging post for weary trail users that no one's complaining.

Plateau Point

The Bright Angel Trail continues its descent to the river from Indian Garden, as described below. However, if you turn left across Garden Creek at Indian Garden and head west three-quarters of a mile on the **Tonto Trail** (see p.114), you'll reach an obvious spur trail to the right. This spur threads its way out 0.8 mile to **Plateau Point**, a superb overlook above the Granite Gorge, from which it's not possible to descend any farther.

Forged to allow day-tripping mule riders a glimpse of the river, the **Plateau Point Trail** also makes an ideal route for hikers. However, although it involves almost no additional elevation change, the round-trip still adds three very exposed miles to any day hike. For that reason, it's not recommended between June and August. At other times, allow at least eight hours to get to Plateau Point and back from the rim.

Barren even by inner canyon standards, the Tonto Platform landscape is spectacular, with agave and yucca plants shooting up from the sandy soil and the mighty red buttes and mesas now framed against the blue sky. Shortly after you get your first awesome glimpse of the gorge's sheer black walls, the trail dead-ends at a precarious perch atop rocky outcrops. Below you tumbles a long stretch of the dark-green Colorado, though both the bridges and Phantom Ranch lie out of sight around the next promontory to the east. With binoculars, you can just make out buildings atop the South Rim.

Devils Corkscrew and the Colorado River

Flowing down from Indian Garden, Garden Creek has cut a narrow cleft into the Tapeats sandstone below. With the Bright Angel Trail alongside, it swiftly enters a secluded little gorge known as the **Tapeats Narrows**. This is among the most delightful segments of any inner canyon trail – if you could somehow arrive here without having hiked down, you'd never imagine you were deep in the Grand Canyon. The temptation to linger beside the babbling stream is irresistible, but don't drink from it – you've just seen where it's been, beside the mule pen.

At the lower end of the narrows, Garden Creek veers into a tangle of rocks as it rushes to meet **Pipe Creek**. Humans, however, have to take the slow way down, along one last searing set of switchbacks, the **Devils Corkscrew**, which were hacked into the rock as a shortcut to the river during the 1930s. (Before that, river-bound Bright Angel hikers took the Tonto Trail 4.1 miles east from Indian Garden to join the South Kaibab Trail at The Tipoff.) Beyond the **Columbine Spring** waterfall at the bottom, the gradient eases, and you crisscross Pipe Creek repeatedly as it meanders down its own pleasant side canyon to reach the Colorado at **Pipe Creek Beach**, 3.2 miles from Indian Garden. Nearby is the small **River Resthouse**, with a phone but no water or restrooms.

It's a breathtaking moment when you first find yourself in the **Granite Gorge**, with thousand-foot walls of gnarled gray **Vishnu schist** soaring over either side of the river. Only here at its very bottom, the rims obscured from sight and only the occasional butte or temple rearing its head above the inner walls, can the Grand Canyon ever feel at all gloomy or oppressive, though a more common response among hikers is exhilaration at finally being down in the ancient depths of the planet. It takes a good ten-minute walk along the **River Trail**, undulating over rocky debris slopes, before you round a corner and see a bridge in the distance, and another mile or so through sandy dunes before you reach it.

The slender, see-through **Bright Angel Suspension Bridge**, also known as the **Silver Bridge**, was built in the 1960s to carry the **pipeline** from Roaring Springs, high on the North Kaibab Trail (see p.101), by which the South Rim receives all its water. Mules quite sensibly balk at the way both pipeline and river are clearly visible between the slats and how the whole bridge bounces at every step. Thus, mule trains continue east less than a mile along the River Trail to the South Kaibab Trail. Hikers invariably cross here, eager to reach **Phantom Ranch** on the far side.

⑫ South Kaibab Trail

The **South Kaibab Trail** – the most direct route from the South Rim to Phantom Ranch – is the only major park trail never to have been used by the canyon's ancient inhabitants. Rangers hacked it out of the bare rock in 1924, when it looked as though they'd never wrest control of the Bright Angel Trail away from Ralph Cameron (see p.97). Whereas all Ancestral Puebloan trails follow natural drainage channels into the canyon, the South Kaibab stays atop narrow, exposed **Cedar Ridge**. Sure, the views are fabulous, but the pitiless lack of shade and water en route make this a grueling trek; the Park Service recommends that no one should try to ascend it in summer. It's used principally by backpackers who descend this way and return via the Bright Angel Trail; mule riders who climb back out after spending the night at Phantom Ranch; and day hikers who venture a short way

Trailhead Yaki Point (7200ft)
Water None
Day hike to Cedar Mesa (6060ft)
Difficulty Strenuous
Distance 3 miles round-trip
Estimated time 2–4hr
Day hike to Skeleton Point (5160ft)
Difficulty Very strenuous
Distance 6 miles round-trip
Estimated time 4–6hr
Phantom Ranch (2486ft)
Difficulty Strenuous
Distance 7.1 miles one-way
Estimated time 4–6hr descent (ascent not recommended)

down to enjoy those views. On all but the very shortest day hikes, plan to carry a gallon of water per person.

You can only drive to the trailhead at **Yaki Point**, four miles east of Grand Canyon Village, between December and February. Year-round, however, you can get there by cab (p.44) or on the free park shuttle buses – either the **Kaibab Trail Route** or, ideally, the early-morning **Hikers' Express**, both of which are detailed on p.43.

Although avoiding the midday sun is advisable in summer, it's a shame to start down the trail much before dawn; the views as the sun rises are superb. Starting from the Yaki Point mule corral – not the main overlook – the trail drops down the western flank of the promontory, negotiating the off-white Kaibab limestone layer via a long but not too steep switchback. This first stretch is easy going underfoot, on a graded path lined with neat boulders. Three-quarters of a mile along, it reaches the tip of the promontory, where for the first time massive views open to the east as well as the west. The Park Service has recently taken to calling this **Ooh Aah Point**; it's a dramatic enough spot, but the name was bestowed partly to give day hikers the sense of having reached an important destination.

Turn back now, and you've had a satisfying glimpse of the canyon from the inside. Otherwise, the scale of the onward task is readily apparent. Reaching the level plateau of **Cedar Mesa** below involves a sharp, three-quarter-mile zigzag descent of the red Coconino sandstone layer. Allowing an hour to get there from the trailhead, and two hours to climb back up again, that makes a good half-day hike. The views from this scraggy, exposed russet mesa – which holds pit toilets but no other facilities – are tremendous. As well as seeing thirty miles up the canyon in either direction and straight up Bright Angel Canyon to the North Rim, you can gaze down on the Tonto Trail, snaking across the Tonto Platform, and the Devils Corkscrew on the Bright Angel Trail to the west. To cap it off, it's also a popular hangout for **condors**.

Although the Park Service discourages day hikers from continuing beyond Cedar Mesa, the next segment of the trail, as it drops off the mesa's east side, is relatively mild. After a forty-minute traverse along the flank of the mesa, which skirts 6071ft **O'Neill Butte**, it levels out on another small plateau dotted with towering agave.

Just after you plummet off **Skeleton Point**, the tip of this little plateau, you'll get your first glimpse of the Colorado. A succession of major switchbacks, interspersed with a brief saddle or two where you can catch your breath, now cuts down through a notch in the Redwall. After perhaps three hours of hiking from the trailhead, a distance of 4.4 miles, you emerge on the **Tonto Platform**, the **Tonto Trail** a short distance ahead.

While hardy backpackers can connect with the Grandview Trail (see p.111) by hiking 18.5 miles **east** along the Tonto Trail, the obvious way to go is **west**. Were you to continue for four miles, you'd reach **Indian Garden** (see p.97), where you could join the Bright Angel Trail and follow it back up to the village. At this point, you're more likely heading for the river. It's now less than two miles away, but the most hair-raising section of the South Kaibab Trail lies ahead.

The launch pad for Granite Gorge hikers is a spot known as **The Tipoff**, a cleft in the rock just beyond a set of pit toilets; it's equipped with an emergency phone. Turn right off the Tonto Trail here, descend a couple of gray switchbacks, and you're suddenly confronted by a long, alarmingly vertiginous traverse, where the trail seems barely scraped into the red dust of the Hakatai shale as it curves above an abysmal drop. Here and there, a few mighty blocks of blackened Tapeats sandstone teeter above your head. Walking this stretch is not quite as bad as it looks, but then little here could be. Attaining the haven of the broad promontory at the far end, you're rewarded with a prospect of the full majesty of the **Granite Gorge**, with Phantom Ranch spread out invitingly below.

Further steep switchbacks fly by during the final descent, which culminates first with a rendezvous with the **River Trail** (which connects with the Bright Angel Trail, as described on p.96) and then with the forty-yard tunnel that brings you to the broad, green Colorado itself. Hanging from eight 1.5-inch-thick cables, the slender 400ft **Kaibab Suspension Bridge**, also known as the **Black Bridge**, was erected in 1928 to replace a makeshift cable car. Each cable weighs more than a ton and was carried down the Kaibab Trail

△ Stairway above Cedar Mesa, on the South Kaibab Trail

on the shoulders of 42 Havasupai. The bridge of choice for the canyon's skittish mules, who prefer its rubberized, non-see-through floor, it stands 78 feet above the water and makes a great vantage point for spotting exhilarated river runners as they round the last curve before Phantom Ranch.

⑱ North Kaibab Trail

Some version of the **North Kaibab Trail**, which follows **Bright Angel Creek** from the North Rim to the Colorado, has been in use for more than a thousand years. At one time, the Park Service trail started several miles east of Bright Angel Point and traced the creek's entire course to the river; the present route, which begins with a descent through **Roaring Springs Canyon**, was established in the late 1920s to improve access from the North Rim tourism hub and to shorten the trail's overall length. Old and new

Trailhead North Kaibab Trailhead (8250ft)
Water Supai Tunnel (May–Oct)
Cottonwood Campground (May–Oct)
Stream water (treat before use)

Day hike to Supai Tunnel (6840ft)
Difficulty Strenuous
Distance 4 miles round-trip
Estimated time 3–5hr

Day hike to Roaring Springs (5040ft)
Difficulty Very strenuous
Distance 9.4 miles round-trip
Estimated time 7–9hr

Day 1: to Cottonwood Campground (4040ft)
Difficulty Strenuous
Distance 6.9 miles one-way
Estimated time 4–5hr descent, 6–8hr ascent

Day 2: Cottonwood Campground to Phantom Ranch (2486ft)
Difficulty Moderate
Distance 7.1 miles one-way
Estimated time 4–5hr each way

routes combine at the actual **Roaring Springs**, almost five miles down, the farthest you should venture on a day hike. In fact, as the first few miles are the steepest, it's more realistic to settle for a four-mile round-trip as far as the Supai Tunnel. Be aware that the trail does not necessarily open when the North Rim itself opens for the season, in mid-May; it can take rangers a few weeks to clear away winter rockslides and fallen trees.

The trail starts from a wooded parking lot at a curve in AZ-67 less than two miles north of *Grand Canyon Lodge* (see p.72). When the lot fills early on busy summer days, many hikers simply leave their vehicles along the roadside. Even that alternative is soon exhausted, however, in which case you'll have to park at the lodge or campground and walk from there. A limited, early-morning **hiker shuttle** leaves *Grand Canyon Lodge* at 5.20am and 7.20am daily (see p.102). Notices at the trailhead, filled with somber advice about heat and water, recommend all hikers set off by 6am.

The trail sets out through the pines on a dusty track that zigzags steadily down past the Kaibab limestone layer. Views here center on Roaring Springs Canyon, the product of its own geologic fault.

Many people settle for reaching the **Coconino Overlook**, a rock slab just off the trail 0.7 mile down. Marking the bottom of the Toroweap Formation and the top of the Coconino sandstone layer, this prominence overlooks the junction of Roaring Springs and Bright Angel canyons. Just over a mile farther, about an hour from the top, you'll reach a clearing beneath magnificent Coconino cliffs coated with dark desert varnish. Equipped with a summer-only water tap and pit toilets, this is the turnaround point for mule trains on half-day trips (see p.71).

Immediately around the corner lies the short **Supai Tunnel**, bored through the sandstone in the 1930s. Though less than twenty yards long, it leads to a seemingly different world of long, exposed switchbacks. These take roughly half an hour to descend past the red Supai sandstone layer to the **Redwall Bridge**. After a flash flood destroyed much of the trail here in 1966, the bridge was built to provide safe passage across Roaring Springs Creek.

Once across the bridge, you'll come to a gentle but consistently spectacular traverse of the Redwall limestone, following a manmade ledge carved halfway up a mighty cliff with a sheer drop-off to your left. The scenery in this area, with its bizarre limestone outcrops, calls to mind some strange, sacred Chinese mountain and is best enjoyed from a huge fern-bedecked alcove farther along. It takes about an hour to reach **Roaring Springs**, the tallest of several waterfalls that cascade down the opposite wall of Roaring Springs Canyon. A worthwhile quarter-mile detour to the left of the trail leads down to the lovely streamside oasis fed by all this water, where you'll find several picnic tables and a mule corral. No drinking water is available, and the pools are only deep enough to cool your toes, but this makes a welcome rest stop and is the ideal turnaround point on a long day hike.

Supplying the lodges and amenities on both rims of the canyon, the water from Roaring Springs is pumped straight up to *Grand Canyon Lodge* on the North Rim and piped down to the river and up to the South Rim. The pump house is such an essential facility that the Park Service employee responsible for its upkeep lives down in the canyon, a minute or two away. Since 1973, that employee has been painter Bruce Aiken, whose resplendently glowing canyon canvases sell for as much as $60,000 (Ⓦ www.bruceaiken.com).

Not far on, Roaring Springs Creek flows into the more substantial Bright Angel Creek. The trail flanks the latter's west bank through the slender Tapeats Narrows, then crosses to the east bank just past its confluence with the lesser Manzanita Creek.

Cottonwood Campground, 1.4 miles past that bridge and 2.5 miles beyond the springs, is a major overnight destination for trans-canyon hikers. Laid out in the 1930s by the Civilian Conservation Corps, it's an attractive spot, occupying a broad swath of the canyon floor directly beneath Bright Angel Point. It provides a summer-only water faucet and restrooms, but only the ranger station benefits from the shade of the eponymous Fremont cottonwoods; the actual campsites stand amid rather sandy scrub.

The highlight of the final seven-mile stretch to Phantom Ranch is lacy **Ribbon Falls**, 1.5 miles below the campground and 0.3 mile west up a spur trail into a side canyon. Two paths lead across the creek to the falls, but only the first – at an obvious junction along the main trail, just shy of a short hill – is recommended. That one crosses a footbridge, while the other requires a risky fording of the water. Ribbon Falls is a beautiful double cascade that tumbles about a hundred feet down shiny, moss-stained cliffs wreathed in rich vegetation. Small wonder that a clan of the Zuni people, who now live two hundred miles southeast in New Mexico, proudly traces its origins here.

Below the falls, the North Kaibab Trail finally enters the Granite Gorge through **The Box**, a narrow, muddy four-mile passage between twin thousand-foot walls of the ancient black Vishnu schist. Four footbridges cross the water before The Box opens a mile or so short of Phantom Ranch. A level, sandy stroll beside the delightful babbling creek leads to the sudden reappearance of dramatic cottonwood trees, your first intimation of the ranch ahead.

△ Prickly pear cactus on the North Kaibab Trail

After the North Rim closes in winter (see p.69), it's still possible to walk *up* the North Kaibab from Phantom Ranch. Just be prepared to turn back – heavy snow and ice are common above Roaring Springs, and ill-equipped hikers who have climbed too high on this trail have died from hypothermia.

H4 Clear Creek Trail

Inner canyon trails are few and far between north of the Colorado, and fewer still offer the chance to parallel the river rather than simply head to or from the rim. Thus the **Clear Creek Trail**, which branches east off the North Kaibab Trail less than a half-mile north of Phantom Ranch, is a popular side trip among backpackers based at or near the ranch.

Trailhead Off North Kaibab Trail, 0.5 mile north of Phantom Ranch (2640ft)	
Water Stream water after 8.5 miles (treat before use)	
Difficulty Strenuous	
Distance 8.7 miles one-way	
Estimated time 5hr each way (at least two days)	
Elevation gain 1600ft	

Not that it's an easy option: It starts with a stiff thousand-foot climb from the Granite Gorge to the Tonto Platform and meanders eastward nearly nine miles beneath Brahma and Zoroaster temples. The views are superb, both down into the gorge and across the vast inner canyon.

The Civilian Conservation Corps forged the trail in 1933 to provide access to the canyon's highest free-falling waterfall, **Cheyava Falls**, which cascades off the Walhalla Plateau and achieves peak flow in late spring. However, the falls lie another four miles of fierce scrambling up the bed of Clear Creek from trail's end, a 26-mile round-trip from Phantom Ranch. To reach them would entail a multi-day wilderness expedition.

Phantom Ranch area

Phantom Ranch marks the only spot on the canyon floor where hikers and mule riders can not only cross the Colorado River, but also camp and even sleep in a real bed. Here at the river's confluence with **Bright Angel Creek**, the Bright Angel, South Kaibab, and North Kaibab trails intersect. This venerable Park Service lodge with an on-site restaurant provides private and dormitory-style lodging in log cabins. In addition, up to 92 campers per night can sleep at the creekside **Bright Angel Campground**.

Although **Bright Angel Creek**, which flows down Bright Angel Canyon from the North Rim, is usually only a few feet wide by the time it meets the Colorado, the sandy deposits around its mouth stretch a few hundred yards in either direction. The journals of John Wesley Powell, who spotted it on August 15, 1869, record, "We discover a stream entering from the north, a clear beautiful creek coming down through a gorgeous red canyon." He named it Bright Angel to contrast with the muddy Dirty Devil River, upstream in Utah.

Hikers who arrive on the North Kaibab Trail will be prepared for the rich riparian habitat; if you've descended the South Kaibab, it will feel like an amazing oasis. Majestic willows and cottonwoods offer welcome shade, and small animals scurry amid the dense undergrowth. However, this **ecosystem** is both threatened and changing. Before Glen Canyon Dam was completed in the mid-1960s, the Colorado carried an average 380,000 tons of earth and rock past Phantom Ranch each day. On a single day in 1921, 27 million tons went hurtling by. Now it carries more like 40,000 tons per day, mostly from rivers that meet the Colorado below the dam, including the Little Colorado. Trees

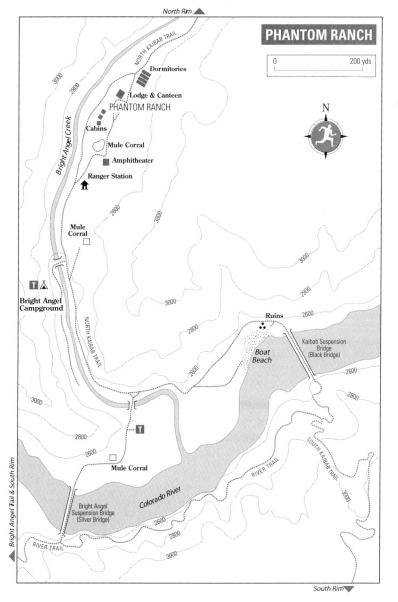

that previously would have been swept away are establishing themselves, while fish adapted to muddy waters are becoming extinct.

Be forewarned that while it's always a relief to reach the river, it's often too **hot** to do very much of anything down here. Temperatures at river level average around 20°F higher than on the South Rim, and perhaps 30°F higher than on the North Rim. Between mid-May and late September the mercury often pushes past 100°F. Cooling off in the shallow waters of Bright Angel Creek is a popular pastime, but don't venture into the Colorado itself. Thanks to the dam, it stays at an icy 45°F year-round; if the currents don't kill you, hypothermia may.

The riverbank

The most interesting section of the riverbank near Phantom Ranch lies just across the **Kaibab Suspension Bridge**, at the foot of the South Kaibab Trail. Immediately west of the bridge, it's still possible to discern the outline of a small **Ancestral Puebloan settlement**, first described by John Wesley Powell in 1869. Consisting of five linked rooms and a ceremonial kiva, it was home to perhaps three or four families for a forty-year period sometime between 1060 and 1150 AD. Just beyond it lies the **Boat Beach**, where canyon rafting expeditions let off and pick up passengers following the 87-mile run from Lees Ferry.

Just downriver, the **Bright Angel Suspension Bridge** lies at the foot of the Bright Angel Trail. Beyond the bridge, a short spur leads past Park Service facilities, including ranger housing, a small mule corral, and public restrooms. Crossing Bright Angel Creek on a small footbridge, you'll join the trail from the Kaibab bridge and follow the creek's east bank toward the campground and ranch.

Bright Angel Campground

A quarter-mile up from the confluence, another small footbridge crosses to the west bank of Bright Angel Creek just north of **Bright Angel Campground**. Flanking the creek amid the cottonwoods, the camp provides 32 sites, each with its own picnic table, as well as central restrooms with running water. Camping at this beautiful spot is by **permit** only (see p.92). Do not hike down without a reservation.

△ The Kaibab Suspension Bridge, at the foot of the South Kaibab Trail

The site was established in 1933 as a base for Civilian Conservation Corps workers, who were improving the park's trail network. They even built a swimming pool down here, though it was later filled in.

Phantom Ranch

A quarter-mile north of the campground, half a mile back from the river, **Phantom Ranch** is the only accommodation option other than camping within the canyon. Clustered around a central lodge, its various cabins, corrals, and outbuildings stand amid huge cottonwoods and fruit orchards, planted here in the early twentieth century to shade a group of tents known as Rust's Camp. Renamed Roosevelt's Camp after a visit by Teddy Roosevelt in 1913, the site was in turn replaced by Phantom Ranch in 1922. Designed by Mary Jane Colter (see box, p.56) as something of a dude ranch for the Fred Harvey Company, the lodge incorporates uncut river stone and natural timbers to blend in with the surroundings. Colter added more buildings over the succeeding years until the complex reached its present size.

First pick of Phantom's fully equipped private **cabins** (④) goes to riders on Fred Harvey **mule trips** (see p.55 for full details, including prices). When demand eases, particularly in winter, they're often available to hikers, as well as rafters staying here before or after a river trip. You can also get a bed in one of four ten-bunk, single-sex **dormitories** (②) – two for men and two for women – which include bedding, showers, towels, and soap.

Reservations, as for South Rim and North Rim lodges, are handled by Xanterra Parks & Resorts, PO Box 699, Grand Canyon, AZ 86023 (☎303/297-2757 or 1-888/297-2757, ⓦwww.grandcanyonlodges.com). Once again, you must not hike down without a reservation; even if you do have one, it's essential to **reconfirm** between one and three days in advance of your stay, either in person at the *Bright Angel Lodge* transportation desk or by calling ☎928/638-3283.

As a rule, Phantom Ranch books up well in advance, but if you're spending a few days at the canyon, it's worth inquiring about **cancellations** for dorm beds and, conceivably, cabins. These are handed out first-come, first-served at *Bright Angel Lodge* early each morning. The night before, check what time the desk will open – it can be as early as 6am.

Phantom's main lodge building serves as a **dining room**, **bar**, and **store**. Meals are served communally at long tables and at set times. These must be reserved in advance, ideally at the time you book your accommodation; they're also available to campers. All supplies get here the same way you do, so food is expensive. The price for **dinner** depends on your main course and includes vegetables, salad, dessert, and coffee for $20–32. The 5pm sitting offers either a 12oz steak for just over $30 or a vegetarian alternative with lentil loaf for just over $20; beef stew is served at 6.30pm, again for just over $20. **Breakfast**, served in two separate sittings well before dawn, includes eggs, pancakes, and bacon for about $17.50, and you can pick up a **sack lunch** to go for about $10. Note that the lodge closes between breakfast sittings, so if you've ordered a sack lunch, arrange a pickup time in advance.

Outside mealtimes, the counter in the lodge sells simple snacks, like trail mix and cookies; drinks, including beer and wine; first-aid supplies such as bandages and sunblock; and such accessories as camera film, batteries, flashlights, and hats (daily: April–Oct 8am–4pm & 8–10pm, Nov–March 8.30am–4pm & 8–10pm). Be sure to ask about the daily program of canyon-themed **ranger talks**, mostly held on the grounds. You'll also find an outdoor payphone, for credit card and calling card calls only.

Finally, you can arrange to have some unfortunate mule tote a large bag in or out of the canyon for you – though you'll still have to carry your own food and water. So-called **duffel service** costs $56 each way.

Other South Rim trails

While the two corridor routes, the Bright Angel and the South Kaibab, are always the busiest South Rim trails, plenty of appealing alternatives exist, even for first-time hikers. Listed in order from east to west, the following trails are unmaintained, which means they can be hard to follow and may be blocked altogether by rockfalls. They're inarguably more demanding, especially on sweltering summer days, which is unfortunately when you'll most likely want to escape the crowds that throng the busier trails. Don't be too deterred, however. These trails do see regular traffic, particularly from day hikers in their upper reaches, so you're unlikely to run into trouble. The two most obvious day hikes are as far as **Santa Maria Spring** along the **Hermit Trail** and down to **Horseshoe Mesa** on the **Grandview Trail**.

ⓗ⓹ Tanner Trail

Easternmost of the South Rim's inner canyon trails, the **Tanner Trail** follows a former Hopi route that was improved by prospector Seth Tanner (see p.121) in the 1880s to better access his copper-mining claims. Fortune seekers in search of John D. Lee's supposed hidden gold mines also passed this way, and it's said that rustlers and bandits combined it with the Nankoweap Trail on the far side to make the self-explanatory Horse-thief Trail. Today, as an unmaintained park trail, it's in pretty poor condition and entails a steep haul. With no water and precious little shade en route, it's used almost exclusively by hardened canyon backpackers.

From the trailhead at **Lipan Point** (see p.64), the path swiftly descends the eastern flank of the promontory. Numerous rockfalls make it easy to lose your way here, and even at its clearest the path is very uneven, but there are no dangerous drop-offs in this first stretch. (It's actually easier going up than coming down, or at least it would be were it not for the extreme fatigue.)

> **Trailhead** Lipan Point (7360ft)
> **Water** None
>
> **Day hike to Seventy-Five-Mile Saddle** (5600ft)
> **Difficulty** Strenuous
> **Distance** 3.8 miles round-trip
> **Estimated time** 4–5hr
>
> **Day hike to the Redwall** (5600ft)
> **Difficulty** Very strenuous
> **Distance** 7 miles round-trip
> **Estimated time** 6–8hr
>
> **Colorado River** (2700ft)
> **Difficulty** Very strenuous
> **Distance** 7.6 miles one-way
> **Estimated time** 5–6hr descent, 7–9hr ascent

Once the terrain starts to level out, after an hour of stiff switchbacks, be sure to keep to the west (left) side of Tanner Creek, rather than follow, let alone cross, the streambed. A rough traverse soon leads to the **Seventy-Five-Mile Saddle**, named for nearby Seventy-Five-Mile Creek, which meets the Colorado just past river mile 75.

While the trail proper doesn't lead along the red sandstone neck that stretches out toward 6536ft **Escalante Butte**, the crumbling, eroded spur that does is a must for day hikers and the ideal turnaround point on a half-day trek. Stroll out

△ A rocky stretch of the Tanner Trail

a few hundred yards to enjoy superb views west, from the towering ruddy walls that frame Seventy-Five-Mile Creek to the Granite Gorge of the Colorado. To the east, you should be able to see the rim-side Watchtower at Desert View and even hear the gleeful cries of tour groups.

The Tanner Trail continues east. Aside from an initial drop, there's little elevation change for the next 1.6 miles, as it skirts the bases of first Escalante Butte and then **Cardenas Butte** (6281ft) – the latter named for Don García López de Cárdenas, the would-be conquistador credited with first setting eyes on the canyon (see p.210). Grassy depressions beside both buttes make ideal campsites for backpackers on the long climb out of the canyon. Hardy day hikers press on as far the top of the **Redwall**, just beyond Cardenas Butte. While the seven-mile round-trip makes a brutal trek in the heat of summer, you'll be rewarded with magnificent views down to where the river makes its crucial westward bend at **Tanner Rapid**.

For onward hikers, the most difficult stretch lies ahead, as the trail plummets down a crack in the crumbling Redwall limestone. The river is four miles down, and the gradient barely relents. At the bottom, sandy, dune-fringed **Tanner Beach** is a popular campsite for both hikers and rafters. It also marks the start of a twenty-mile round-trip hike to the north along the **Beamer Trail**, which runs parallel to the Colorado and leads to the mouth of the Little Colorado River.

ⓗ New Hance Trail

The most demanding of all South Rim trails, the **New Hance Trail** was named for one of the canyon's great characters, **Captain John Hance**, who looked the very picture of the eccentric white-bearded prospector and spent his old age as a treasured Fred Harvey employee, spinning tall tales of his adventures for any tourists who would listen. In 1883, he created the Old Hance Trail to access his asbestos mine across the river; building a cabin at the trailhead, he became the canyon's first white resident. He went on to guide pioneer sightseers down his trail, though by the turn of the century it had eroded and collapsed so completely that not a trace remains.

Trailhead Near Moran Point (7040ft)
Water Seasonal streams after 5.1 miles (treat before use)

Day hike to Coronado Butte Saddle (5900ft)
Difficulty Strenuous
Distance 2.4 miles round-trip
Estimated time 3–4hr

Day hike to the Redwall (4850ft)
Difficulty Very strenuous
Distance 5.8 miles round-trip
Estimated time 6–8hr

Colorado River (2600ft)
Difficulty Very strenuous
Distance 7.6 miles one-way
Estimated time 5–6hr descent, 7–9hr ascent

By all accounts, the old trail was exceptionally steep and dangerous; Hance's replacement, originally known as the Red Canyon Trail but now named for its creator, remains extremely difficult. Some of its switchbacks have crumbled away, and you often have to scramble over minor rockfalls. It's not a hike to undertake lightly, and if you're using it as part of a longer itinerary – say, an expedition along the Tonto Trail – save it for your ascent.

Parking is prohibited at the unmarked New Hance trailhead, which sits a quarter-mile off the highway along a disused road. Leave your vehicle either at Moran Point, and walk the 1.6 miles southwest from there, or at the Buggeln Picnic Area, another mile southwest. As with the Tanner Trail, the route consists of two distinct sets of fierce switchbacks – one down to the saddle below **Coronado Butte**, the other two miles farther, where it drops off the **Redwall**. This time, though, the stretch between the two is equally demanding, so even a day hike to the brink of the Redwall is far from easy. The final couple of miles to the river, beside the verdant Red Canyon Wash, are the most attractive part of the hike, though even those involve some difficult scrambling. The roiling waters of **Hance Rapid** await at trail's end.

⑰ Grandview Trail

The **Grandview Trail** leads out onto double-pointed **Horseshoe Mesa**, providing a rare opportunity to explore one of the many wooded mesas that dot the inner canyon. Although you could connect with other trails to reach the Tonto Platform and eventually find your way down to the Colorado, this is not a rim-to-river route. Involving a shorter trek and less elevation change than other major South Rim routes, the Grandview is one of the most popular **day hikes** in the park. That said, the trail itself is in

Trailhead Grandview Point (7406ft)	
Water None	
Day hike to Horseshoe Mesa (4932ft)	
Difficulty Strenuous	
Distance 6.4 miles round-trip	
Estimated time 5–7hr	

worse condition than you might expect if you've only tackled the corridor trails, and the climb back out is tough by any standards. Allow about six hours for the round-trip.

Pete Berry first improved this trail in 1892 to ease access to his Last Chance copper mine out on **Horseshoe Mesa**. He made enough money to finance construction of the rim-side *Grandview Hotel*, which lasted a little longer than the copper but was eventually bankrupted by the arrival of the railroad to the west. Evidence of Berry's work is still visible. He built many of its switchbacks by inserting metal rods deep into the canyon wall, then covering them with juniper logs, stones, and dirt. While the trail is no longer maintained, everything remains surprisingly sturdy, though its upper sections had to be reconstructed in 2005, following landslides. At times a little hair-raising, the trail is nevertheless easier than both the New Hance and Tanner trails.

As described on p.63, the best views lie at and just below the trailhead, beside the parking lot at Grandview Point. Farther down, narrow cobbled switchbacks cling to the Kaibab limestone cliffs, with steep drop-offs toward the canyon. It takes less than an hour to reach the refuge of the **Coconino Saddle**, a spur between Grapevine Canyon to the west and Hance Canyon to the east, where the trees offer welcome shade. Onward, the switchbacks narrow, and you're faced with long, exposed traverses along the red Supai sandstone layer, where the path dwindles to just a couple of feet wide and gravel skitters over the edge at every step.

Three miles from the rim, another saddle leads onto Horseshoe Mesa, with one last short drop before you reach the pit toilets (but no water) that mark the fringes of the former mining area. The ruddy soil is scattered with mineral-rich flecks and outcrops of copper ore, and the ruins of miners' cabins are everywhere you look. Makeshift trails meander across the plateau, passing abandoned workings and mysterious caves; investigating any of these is officially forbidden and would be an extremely perilous undertaking.

If you're planning to backpack farther into the canyon, the best route down from the mesa – signed to Cottonwood Creek – heads off to the left (west) near the restrooms. Below on the Tonto Platform, a seven-mile **loop** around the foot of Horseshoe Mesa rejoins the Grandview Trail a few hundred yards higher up. Alternatively, you could take the **Tonto Trail** and head either seven miles east to the New Hance Trail, down by the Colorado, or twenty miles west to the South Kaibab Trail.

⊞ Hermit Trail

Appealing to both day hikers and long-distance backpackers, the **Hermit Trail** is another unmaintained route that dates from the days when the obstreperous Ralph Cameron controlled access to most of the prime rim-edge sites (see p.213). First dubbed the El Tovar Trail, the trail was used from 1912 onward by Fred Harvey Company mule excursions. It was soon renamed in honor of reclusive French-Canadian prospector Louis Boucher, the "hermit" who made his home at Dripping Spring (see opposite).

Trailhead Hermits Rest (6640ft)
Water Santa Maria Spring (treat before use)
Year-round stream at 7.7 miles (treat before use)

Day hike to Santa Maria Spring (5000ft)
Difficulty Moderate
Distance 4.6 miles round-trip
Estimated time 3–4hr

Colorado River (2400ft)
Difficulty Strenuous
Distance 8.7 miles one-way
Estimated time 6–7hr descent, 7–9hr ascent

Though abandoned in 1931, the trail remains largely in good shape and makes a good alternative to the often-overcrowded Bright Angel and South Kaibab trails, even if the views are seldom as spectacular. The major appeal is wildlife, particularly birds, butterflies, and, in spring and fall, abundant wildflowers. The best **day hikes** lead to Santa Maria Spring on the main trail (4.6 miles round-trip) and Dripping Spring on the side trails described below (6.5 miles round-trip). Water from both is drinkable if treated.

The trail begins from Hermits Rest, at the west end of Hermit Road (see p.57); in winter, when shuttle buses aren't running, trail users can drive to a parking lot beyond the shuttle stop. Initially rough and rocky underfoot, the trail switchbacks down the eastern flank of Hermit Basin, feeling far removed from the central canyon as it gradually descends a high rock wall above Hermit Creek. Upheavals in the cobbled pathway and rockfalls make for slow progress at first, but the trail eventually levels out on a sandy floor. After 1.5 miles, it meets the seldom-used **Waldron Trail** – mapped out in 1896 as the original route into Hermit Basin – then passes the spur trail to **Dripping Spring** a quarter-mile farther on.

Keep to the trail beyond the Dripping Spring turnoff; the streambed leads over a waterfall. A half-mile farther, after descending a crumbling red ledge, you'll reach **Santa Maria Spring**. Though it seldom amounts to much more than a steady drip from a standpipe into an unattractive manmade trough, the spring is enough to support a delightful oasis of flowering plants. You'll find welcome shade in the gorgeous resthouse, with a comfortable rocking bench and an open facade all but smothered in creeping vines. Day hikers should turn back here; while gentle over the next mile, the onward trail then tackles further steep switchbacks and a tricky downward scramble amid fallen rocks. It eventually hurtles down the Redwall below Pima Point by means of the cramped **Cathedral Stairs** switchbacks and meets the Tonto Trail 6.4 miles from the trailhead.

Between 1913 and 1931, mule riders would spend the night deep in the inner canyon at the permanent **Hermit Camp**, a mile west of the Tonto Trail junction, which was provisioned by cable car from Pima Point. Only the outline of its sturdy stone walls remain, however, so backpackers now congregate at **Hermit Creek Campground**, a few hundred yards beyond. Though a flash flood destroyed its much-loved natural swimming pool in 1996, the site is still spectacular, offering dramatic views of cliffs that soar to the rim.

The most direct route to the Colorado from the Hermit Trail follows Hermit Creek, which you can access either just before Hermit Camp or from the campground. Either way, you'll reach the river in a little over a mile, at a rocky beach just short of **Hermit Rapid**, whose wavelike surge can rise more than twenty feet.

⒣ Dripping Spring Trail

The delightful and none-too-strenuous expedition to **Dripping Spring** ranks among the best mid-length day hikes in the canyon. The spring itself, which was home to the "hermit" Louis Boucher between 1891 and 1912, sits only a few hundred yards beneath the rim, but the nearest road-accessible trailhead is at **Hermits Rest**, and it's necessary to approach the spring from below, so it remains a round-trip of 6.5 miles.

Turn left at the spur junction described opposite, almost two miles down the Hermit Trail, and follow the narrow path as it negotiates a high sweeping curve barely scraped into a steep cliff of red Hermit shale – anyone

> **Trailhead** Hermits Rest (6640ft)
> **Water** Dripping Spring (treat before use)
>
> **Day hike to Dripping Spring** (5800ft)
> **Difficulty** Moderate, with high drop-offs
> **Distance** 6.5 miles round-trip
> **Estimated time** 3–5hr

with a fear of heights would do better to turn back and instead visit Santa Maria Spring (see opposite). A mile along the spur, past two successive wooded amphitheaters, you'll turn left on the **Boucher Trail**, which ascends toward the rim. Not far up, Dripping Spring cascades from the ceiling of a large alcove in the Coconino sandstone wall, amid lush ferns and tiny blossoms. Boucher used this perennial water supply to irrigate gardens and orchards along the creek.

⒣ Boucher Trail

The **Boucher Trail**, which runs a mile or so west of and roughly parallels the Hermit Trail, was once Louis Boucher's Silver Bell Trail, the most direct route to his Dripping Spring home. Strictly speaking, it begins at a remote trailhead above the spring. Today, however, access is so much easier from Hermits Rest that the trail is used almost invariably as part of longer, multi-trail itineraries, most often entailing a descent to the river via the Boucher Trail, followed by an ascent along the Hermit.

Particularly in its early stages, the Boucher Trail is not a hike for canyon novices. Soon after you turn right onto

> **Trailhead** Hermits Rest (6640ft)
> **Water** Dripping Spring (treat before use)
> Boucher Creek at 8.5 miles (treat before use)
>
> **Colorado River** (2325ft)
> **Difficulty** Very strenuous
> **Distance** 10.8 miles one-way
> **Estimated time** 7–9hr descent, 9–11hr ascent

the trail, three miles into the Dripping Spring itinerary described above, you're obliged to teeter along the brink of a sheer drop. In icy winter conditions, this traverse along the west wall of **Hermit Basin** is truly terrifying. Conditions improve when you round the headland beneath **Yuma Point** at the far end, but you still have to negotiate long, difficult scrambling descents before you reach the **Tonto Trail**.

Half a mile farther, turn right and pick your way along the boulder-strewn Boucher Creek streambed to reach the river near **Boucher Rapid**. Alternatively, a 4.5-mile eastward hike on the Tonto Trail leads to **Hermit Creek Campground** on the Hermit Trail (see p.112).

ⓖ South Bass Trail

More than a century ago, the **Bass Trail** was the preeminent trans-canyon hiking route. Now, far west of the village tourist hub and all but reverted to wilderness, it no longer even crosses the canyon. Its early promoter, former cowboy **William Bass**, set up the long-defunct **Bass Camp** tent village near **Havasupai Point** in 1885 and soon instigated regular stagecoach service from Williams. He would lead intrepid visitors down the ancient Indian trail he had improved to reach his copper and asbestos mines and ferry them across the river either by boat, when the water was low, or via cable car.

> **Trailhead** Bass Camp (6646ft)
> **Water** None
>
> **Colorado River** (2200ft)
> **Difficulty** Strenuous
> **Distance** 8 miles one-way
> **Estimated time** 5–6hr descent,
> 6–8hr ascent

Bass went out of business after the railroad reached the South Rim, but his trail remains in reasonable condition for experienced inner canyon hikers who have the route-finding abilities to negotiate the occasional obscured segment. Many still do complete the rim-to-rim trip by hitching a ride with the river runners they chance upon down on the Colorado. However, that route is generally regarded as two separate hikes – the **South Bass Trail**, described here, and the **North Bass Trail**, as outlined on p.116.

The main obstacle to hiking the South Bass is not the absence of water anywhere above the river, but the sheer remoteness of the trailhead. When you ask about current trail conditions at the park visitor center, have a ranger describe the access route in detail. It's a thirty-mile drive off US-180/AZ-64, the first 26 miles of which are on Forest Service road 328, which heads west from Tusayan just south of the abandoned *Moqui Lodge*. The final four miles north from Pasture Wash are so rough that a **high-clearance 4WD** vehicle is essential.

Havasupai Point, two miles east of the trailhead, is reachable via an equally problematic dirt road that branches off to the right shortly before Bass Camp. It marks a natural boundary between the eastern Grand Canyon, characterized by massive amphitheaters, isolated buttes, and generally tangled topography, and the western canyon, which encompasses a much simpler, broad valley known as the **Esplanade**, with the deep **Granite Gorge** still at its core. The ridge immediately east of the trailhead is known as the **Grand Scenic Divide**.

The trail zigzags down through the woods almost three miles to the edge of the Esplanade, alongside towering **Mount Huethawali**. This spot offers the first and best views of the vast canyon sweep, bringing home how abruptly the mesas and buttes disappear as the river flows west. Below, the trail plunges deep into **Bass Canyon**, emerging three miles down on the Tonto Trail. The bed of the often dry wash descends two miles to a lovely little riverside **beach**, often used by passing rafters for overnight stays.

Tonto Trail

The **Tonto Trail** is an exception to the other South Rim trails described here, in that it has no contact with the canyon rim. Neither, over its vast length, does it approach the river. Instead it runs parallel to both rim and river, meandering along the Tonto Platform at a typical elevation of around 4000ft. That means it remains mostly on the parched, cactus-strewn Bright Angel shale layer, which spreads out below the Redwall and Mauv limestone strata and above the Tapeats sandstone layer and the Granite Gorge. This is no easy route, however. Where successive streams and earthquake faults slash down toward the Colorado, the Tonto Trail is forced to traverse lesser gorges and detour around amphitheaters. Water is scarce and facilities nonexistent.

As the trail stretches a phenomenal 92 miles, almost no one walks its full length. Most hikers simply cross it at some point en route to or from the river or at best take a small connecting stretch between two major trails. There's no trailhead as such, but technically it begins at the foot of the New Hance Trail as the **Tonto East Trail**, leading west to the Grandview Trail in seven miles and the South Kaibab twenty miles after that. The **central section**, known simply as the Tonto Trail, runs from The Tipoff on the South Kaibab four miles to Indian Garden on the Bright Angel; thirteen more miles to the Hermit; and six miles beyond that to the Boucher. The **Tonto West Trail** then takes up the baton, running a full thirty miles to the South Bass and another twelve miles to Garnet Canyon, where it meets the Royal Arch Route for the lengthy ascent.

Other North Rim trails

While the **North Kaibab Trail** is by far the most popular inner canyon trail to start from the North Rim, two others lie within reach of seasoned hikers eager to experience greater solitude – and a tougher physical challenge. Both the **Nankoweap Trail** and the **North Bass Trail** demand considerable confidence and self-sufficiency and are best left to backpackers planning multi-day itineraries. Be sure to ask about current conditions when you pick up your permit.

Ⓗ⑫ Nankoweap Trail

Far north of all other Grand Canyon trails, the dramatic **Nankoweap Trail** is unique in not only providing access to the canyon's seldom-visited upper reaches, but also offering tremendous panoramas across the Marble Platform and upstream toward Lees Ferry. With its hair's-breadth ledges and sickeningly high drop-offs, however, it's not recommended for anyone with even the slightest fear of heights. **Charles Doolittle Walcott**, who with John Wesley Powell improved the trail during their geologic expedition of 1882, called it "utterly frightful," and its early stages remain every bit as terrifying. Only true canyon veterans should even consider attempting it.

> **Trailhead** Saddle Mountain (8848ft)
> **Water** Nankoweap Creek at 10.6 miles (treat before use)
>
> **Colorado River** (2800ft)
> **Difficulty** Very strenuous, with high drop-offs
> **Distance** 13.9 miles one-way
> **Estimated time** 9–12hr descent, 12–14hr ascent

Though the **trailhead** lies less than three miles north of Point Imperial (see p.79), and you could hike from there, it is accessible by car if you drive fifteen miles along the graveled Forest Service road 610, which heads east from AZ-67 a mile south of *Kaibab Lodge* (see p.136); the route is normally passable in ordinary vehicles. It takes a mile for the trail itself to begin in earnest; first you have to negotiate a steep little hill, which involves a brisk climb. Then comes the hard part, a heart-stopping sidle along a narrow exposed ledge of Esplanade sandstone. A brief respite at **Marion Ridge**, a campsite overlooked by striking misshapen rock pillars, is followed by more tremulous ledge work as far as **Tilted Mesa**, 6.8 miles down at the outer limit of the Redwall.

Beyond Tilted Mesa, a very steep set of switchbacks – which at least are in good condition – brings you down onto the terrace, where at length you meet the verdant **Nankoweap Creek**, 10.6 miles from the trailhead. Three more miles down the trackless but mostly gentle streambed, at broad, sandy Nankoweap Delta, you arrive at the Colorado itself, flanked by the towering eastern wall of Marble Canyon on the far side. Minor trails lead downstream along the river for around a mile, but ultimately you have to turn around and climb back the way you came. Note that there are no designated campsites along the trail; instead you're free to select your own site in the wilderness.

⑬ North Bass Trail

The North Rim counterpart to William Bass's South Bass Trail (see p.114), the **North Bass Trail**, starts from the overlook at **Swamp Point** (see p.83), accessed via a twenty-mile dirt road west of AZ-67 that's only suitable for 4WD vehicles. As with the South Bass, this trail is recommended for veteran inner canyon hikers only – in many places, the trail is liable to have vanished completely, so you'll need route-finding skills, considerable energy for scrambling down talus slopes and through thick brush, and a head for heights.

Trailhead Swamp Point (7520ft)
Water Muav Saddle Spring at 1.2 miles (treat before use)
Seasonal streams (treat before use)

Colorado River (2200ft)
Difficulty Very strenuous
Distance 13.5 miles one-way
Estimated time 8–10hr descent, 2-day ascent

From Swamp Point, a mile of comparatively well-maintained switchbacks drop down to the **Muav Saddle**, where a long-abandoned Park Service cabin dating from 1925 is still used by overnighting backpackers. A minor dead-end trail leads up from the cabin onto **Powell Plateau** (see p.116), but the main route now descends **Muav Canyon** in earnest, along the rocky bed of **White Creek**.

Once you've covered the almost five miles to the top of the **Redwall**, you've cleared the most difficult section – though several short *uphill* stretches won't have improved your mood. Superb inner canyon views are your reward. Swift switchbacks then carry you down the Redwall to rejoin White Creek. In theory the trail strays away from the creek onto the nearby plateau, but it's much easier simply to follow the streambed all the way to **Shinumo Creek**, five miles below. William Bass planted melons, corn, and squash down here, along with peach orchards, at a spot he found by tracing ancient Indian irrigation ditches; in his day, intact cliff dwellings and granaries were still visible nearby.

Access to the Colorado is via a final steep descent, which ends at a sheltered riverside grove frequented by rafters. Both here and along the trail, there are no officially designated campsites, so follow usual wilderness-camping protocols.

The road between the rims

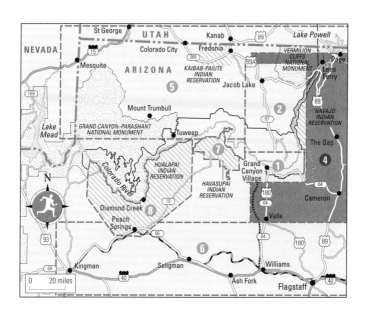

CHAPTER 4   # Highlights

✳ **Cameron Trading Post** This historic Navajo trading post offers lodgings of a surprisingly high standard. See p.122

✳ **Antelope Canyon** Arizona's most famous slot canyon gets very crowded with tour groups, but remains extraordinarily beautiful. See p.124

✳ **Horseshoe Bend** A high, windswept overlook offers a rare glimpse of the Colorado as it makes an amazing 180-degree turn, just before entering the Grand Canyon. See p.125

✳ **Glen Canyon Dam** Visit the massive and controversial dam that stopped the Colorado River, drowned Glen Canyon, and transformed the Grand Canyon. See p.128

✳ **Marble Canyon Lodge** This attractive roadside stop enables weary drivers to spend the night in the heart of the desert. See p.130

✳ **Lees Ferry** Haunting Wild West ruins overlook the exact spot where the Grand Canyon begins. See p.130

✳ **Lonely Dell Ranch** A lovely little agricultural oasis established by Mormon ferryman and convicted killer John Doyle Lee. See p.133

✳ **Vermilion Cliffs** This towering escarpment glows an unearthly red as the sun rises over the Grand Canyon. See p.134

✳ **DeMotte Park** Just shy of the canyon's North Rim, this spectacular forest clearing holds appealing lodging and camping options. See p.136

△ Highway sign on US-89

The road between the rims

Although the South and North rims of the Grand Canyon stand just eleven miles apart, the impossibility of constructing a road across the gorge means that the shortest driving route between the two runs 215 miles and takes at least four hours. Starting from Grand Canyon Village, you follow first Desert View Drive and then AZ-64 east to US-89 at **Cameron**. From there you head north, cross **Marble Canyon** on Navajo Bridge, then double back west to **Jacob Lake**, where you pick up 44-mile AZ-67 south to the North Rim.

Spectacular scenery makes up for the lack of towns, while several lodges and motels, scattered in splendid isolation, make for memorable overnight stays en route. Highlights include the twin escarpments that blaze into sight on either side of the Colorado River as it emerges from Glen Canyon – the **Echo Cliffs** to the east and **Vermilion Cliffs** to the west. A short detour northeast of the Echo Cliffs leads up to **Page**, a humdrum town that's nonetheless close to such compelling natural wonders as **Antelope Canyon** and **Horseshoe Bend**, not to mention manmade **Glen Canyon Dam**, responsible for stopping the Colorado in its tracks and creating the unearthly **Lake Powell**. Just downriver, back on the most direct route, lies the fascinating historical site of **Lees Ferry**, which also marks the official start of the Grand Canyon.

The first explorers to attempt a Colorado crossing in this region were two Spanish friars, padres **Domínguez and Escalante**, who did so back in 1776. However, the route only began to see regular traffic a century later, with the establishment of the **Mormon Trail**, which linked Mormon settlements in

Transcanyon Shuttle

Transcanyon Shuttle (☎602/638-2820) offers daily van service along the route described in this chapter. Departing the North Rim from *Grand Canyon Lodge* at 7am, it calls at *Marble Canyon Lodge* at 9am and reaches the South Rim at noon. The return trip departs the South Rim at 1.30pm, stops at *Marble Canyon Lodge* at 4.15pm and arrives back on the North Rim at 6.30pm. Fares run $65 one-way for adults and $50 for children 12 and under, or round-trip for $110/90, respectively; cash only.

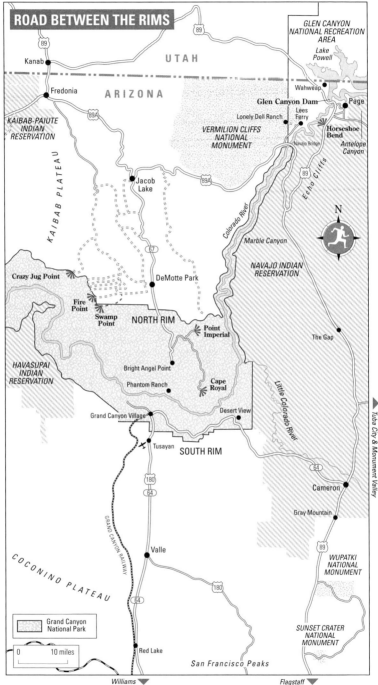

Utah with new, largely unsuccessful colonies in Arizona. The trail was kept busy in part by Mormon newlyweds, who, following civil marriage ceremonies in Arizona, would head up to the nearest temple, in St George, Utah, to seal their vows. Hence its alternate name – the **Honeymoon Trail**.

Little Colorado River Gorge

In its 34-mile run between Desert View on the South Rim (described on p.65) and its junction with US-89 just south of Cameron, AZ-64 descends more than 3000ft. Beyond the first dozen miles, which lie within the pine forests of the Coconino Plateau, vast views open up across the Painted Desert to the northeast. Closer at hand, a seam in the flatlands betrays the presence of the **Little Colorado River**, snaking north along the floor of its own deep canyon to meet its big sister.

Ten miles outside Cameron, between mile markers 285 and 286 – by which time both road and river are running parallel east to west – the **Little Colorado River Gorge Navajo Tribal Park** gives visitors their best chance to catch a glimpse of the river. Though there's no admission charge, per se, you can only reach the end of the promontory that offers the finest views by running the gauntlet of several dozen **Navajo crafts stalls**, mostly selling good-quality jewelry and trinkets.

The drop into the chasm here measures around 1200ft, although the cliffs are so sheer, it's hard to lean out far enough to see the river itself. In any case, for several months of the year – especially in spring and early summer – the Little Colorado is liable to dry up altogether. At other times, however, it's capable of powerful flash floods. The fact that the river remains undammed, despite repeated early Mormon attempts, has acquired an added significance since completion of the **Glen Canyon Dam** in 1963. Now that the Colorado itself carries almost no sediment into the Grand Canyon, certain river species, such as the humpback chub, can only breed in the muddy waters of the Little Colorado.

The Little Colorado also continues to play a crucial role in **Hopi** cosmology. From their mesas sixty miles east, modern Hopi follow in the footsteps of their ancestors along the ancient **Salt Trail**, which skirts the Little Colorado into the Grand Canyon. Not far upriver from its confluence with the Colorado proper lies the legendary *sipapu*, the hole through which the Hopi believe human beings first entered this, the Third World. You won't find this natural domed hot spring marked on any map; only the Hopi are allowed access.

Back on the highway, further crafts stalls, some at lesser overlooks, dot the roadside the rest of the way down to Cameron.

Cameron

Tiny **CAMERON**, which amounts to little more than a handful of buildings, lies a mile or so north of the intersection of AZ-64 and US-89. The Mormon Trail originally crossed the Little Colorado River at a rocky ford six miles upstream. That became known as **Tanner's Crossing**, in honor of Seth Tanner, a Mormon prospector from Tuba City who built a house nearby in the 1870s. He later expanded his operations into the Grand Canyon area, where he also gave his name to the Tanner Trail.

After the danger from quicksand and flooding at Tanner's Crossing led to construction of the first **suspension bridge** across the gorge in 1911, Cameron – named for another legendary canyon prospector, Ralph Cameron – sprang into being on the south side of the span. The original one-lane bridge is still there, but now it only carries an oil pipeline, having been superseded by a broader modern highway bridge.

Cameron Trading Post

Clustered beside the two bridges, the ever-expanding **Cameron Trading Post** remains at heart what it started out as in 1916 – a trading center for the Navajo Nation. Reservation residents still flock in to stock up on wool, flour, and other supplies, catch up with friends, fill up their gas tanks, and pick up their mail, and some trading post business is still conducted by barter.

A brisk **tourist** trade now rubs elbows with those Old West traditions. A large **motel** complex (PO Box 339, Cameron, AZ 86020 ☎602/679-2231 or 1-877/221-6090, ⓦwww.camerontradingpost.com; March–May ❹, June to mid-Oct ❺, mid-Oct to Feb ❸), which perhaps surprisingly offers some of the highest standard accommodations in the region, sits amid beautifully landscaped gardens that slope toward the river. Rooms on upper floors feature large balconies that look out across the Little Colorado to the open desert. **RV** parking is also available, for $15.

Centered on a massive fireplace in the main building, a tin-roofed **dining room** (daily: summer 6am–10pm, otherwise 7am–9.30pm) serves all meals. As its principal customers are tour groups in a hurry to be somewhere else, the food's OK but nothing special – the Navajo taco is probably your best bet, for a filling lunch – and here on the reservation **no alcohol** is served. The adjoining **souvenir store** stocks a huge array of Southwest arts and crafts, both authentic and mass-produced, but for a real treat it's worth crossing to the nearby **gallery**, which stocks such Native American pieces as genuine Hopi *kachinas* and museum–quality Navajo rugs. Even a small rug from the 1890s can cost up to $20,000.

Gray Mountain

When there's no room at Cameron, the nearest alternative lodging is nine miles south on US-89, in the even smaller community of **GRAY MOUNTAIN** (population 68). Just outside the reservation, it's a lonely desert outpost, attractive in its own desolate way, consisting almost entirely of the *Anasazi Inn* (PO Box 29100, Gray Mountain, AZ 86020 ☎928/679-2214 or 1-800/678-2214, ⓦwww.anasaziinn.com; ❸). This complex boasts three separate **motel** blocks – the rooms are of reasonable standard, with prices that vary according to your proximity to the pool – plus the *Gray Mountain Restaurant* across the highway, which serves Mexican specialties and Navajo tacos, as well as steaks.

Echo Cliffs

Driving north from Cameron on US-89 is a delight, with unfolding views of the unearthly, multicolored Painted Desert marred only by rows of mighty electricity pylons marching across the plateau from the Navajo Generating Station at Page. Though it's far from fertile country, much of this is open ranchland, so watch out for cattle if you're driving at night.

Fifteen miles north of Cameron, US-160 climbs away northeast via **Tuba City** toward Monument Valley and Colorado. Continuing north, US-89 passes through **Hidden Springs** in another five miles, the home of a small group of **San Juan Southern Paiute**, who were recognized as a separate tribe in 1990.

By now, the rich orange **Echo Cliffs** – the visible face of the Echo Cliffs Monocline – have started their rise east of the road. Over the next fifty miles, they reach well over 2000ft above the Colorado. The cliffs were named by members of John Wesley Powell's second expedition in 1871, who fired a shot at the river from the top of the ridge and heard the echo come back 24 seconds later.

The one natural break in the cliffs, ten miles past Hidden Springs, is logically enough called **The Gap**, though sadly its small trading post (daily 7am–9pm) cannot claim to have spawned the multinational clothing chain. A dirt road climbs up through the notch, leading to a defunct copper mine and, eventually, Page, but it's not recommended for ordinary vehicles.

Page

US-89 eventually veers to the right at **Antelope Pass**, twenty empty miles beyond The Gap, and heads another 25 miles across an all but barren mesa to the town of **PAGE**, Arizona. Before Glen Canyon Dam was constructed four miles west, from 1956 onward, this area belonged to the Navajo Nation. Thanks to a small spring, however, the mesa made the best site to house the dam's workforce. The Navajo agreed to swap it for a similar-sized chunk of desert between Bluff and Hatch in Utah, road crews blasted the route through the Echo Cliffs now followed by US-89, and Page was born on Thanksgiving Day 1958.

While Page is home to almost ten thousand people, making it the largest community in a 720-mile stretch of the Colorado River, it's a dull, unattractive little place that nonetheless makes a convenient base for visitors to Lake Powell. It originally seemed destined to wither away once the dam was completed. Ironically, it gained a new lease on life when Congress decided that instead of building more dams, the Southwest could meet its power needs by burning coal instead. The **Navajo Generating Station**, which creates electricity using coal from Black Mesa and pumps water from Lake Powell to Phoenix, went up four miles southeast of town and has kept Page at work ever since.

Arrival and information

The helpful staff at Page's **visitor center**, 608 Elm St (Mon–Fri 8am–5pm; ☎928/645-2741 or 1-888/261-7243, Ⓦwww.pagelakepowellchamber.org), offer advice on local amenities and attractions, while brochures are also available at the Powell Memorial Museum (see p.124). Several other offices in town that purport to be information centers are in fact tour operators offering trips to Antelope Canyon (see p.124).

No scheduled buses or flights serve Page, though charter airlines do occasionally fly into the local **airport**, a mile east of town on AZ-98. Grand Circle Shuttle (☎928/645-6806, Ⓦwww.grandcircleshuttle.com) runs a local **taxi** and shuttle service, charging $50 per person for the ride to or from Flagstaff.

Accommodation

While no one would choose to spend much time in Page itself, Lake Powell is enough of an attraction to keep its **motels** busy for most of the year and allow them to hike their rates higher than you might expect.

Best Western Arizonainn 716 Rim View Drive ℡928/645-2466 or 1-800/826-2718, ⓦwww .bestwestern.com. Standard upmarket motel on the outskirts of Page, commanding a massive desert panorama from the poolside. ❺

Best Western at Lake Powell 208 N Lake Powell Blvd ℡928/645-5988 or 1-888/794-2888, ⓦwww.bestwestern.com. Large, good-value motel perched above downtown Page, with a pool. ❹

Courtyard by Marriott 600 Clubhouse Drive ℡928/645-5000 or 1-800/851-3855, ⓦwww .courtyard.com/pgacy. Page's most incongruous splash of luxury – a 153-room resort, complete

with golf course – is below the mesa in view of the dam. ❺

Holiday Inn Express 751 S Navajo Drive ℡928/645-9000 or 1-800/465-4329, ⓦwww .holiday-inn.com. Good quality chain motel, with a pool and free continental breakfast. ❺

Uncle Bill's Place 117 Eighth Ave ℡928/645 1224 or 1-888/359-0945, ⓦwww.canyon-country .com/unclebill. This small, friendly, old-fashioned motel in Page's original residential district offers B&B suites, with one- and two-bedroom en suite options as well as kitchenette apartments that share a bathroom, at very reasonable prices. ❷–❻

Downtown Page

The view as you descend toward Page is utterly surreal. The five power plant chimneys stand silhouetted amid sandstone outcrops, while lines of pylons march off across the desert and the misty hump of Navajo Mountain rises in the distance. As you approach, the waters of Lake Powell emerge from the haze, with drowned buttes poking their heads here and there above the surface.

Page itself, on the other hand, resembles a dull suburban mall writ large; if it has a redeeming feature, you'll have a hard time finding it. Permanent structures have replaced most of its original trailer homes, but the only sight of any interest is the **John Wesley Powell Memorial Museum**, 6 N Lake Powell Blvd (Mon–Sat 9am–5pm; $5; ⓦwww.powellmuseum.org). In addition to charting the exploits of the first man to raft down the Colorado (see p.211), the museum celebrates later river runners and also recounts Page's own brief history. It also holds a locally excavated plesiosaur fossil and an amazing collection of fluorescent rocks.

Antelope Canyon

A couple of miles southeast of Page on AZ-98, mile marker 299 marks the trailhead for **Antelope Canyon**, Arizona's most famous **slot canyon**. The canyon actually comprises two separate sections, on either side of the highway, and both are on Navajo land.

Immediately north of the highway, **Lower Antelope Canyon** achieved worldwide notoriety in 1997, when the tragic deaths of eleven hikers in a flash flood proved just how dangerous such places can be. Nevertheless, they're also irresistibly, astonishingly beautiful. In the last few years, the Navajo have realized what an invaluable tourism asset Antelope Canyon represents, and they now control all access (May–Oct daily 8am–5pm; ℡928/698-3347, ⓦwww .navajonationparks.org/htm/antelopecanyon.htm).

In summer, tourists can visit both sections of the canyon simply by turning up at the parking lot. However, not only is there a $6 entry fee, but you also have to pay an outrageous $13 for a "guide" service that consists either of pointing you to the entrance of Lower Antelope or driving you in a shuttle van down to **Upper Antelope Canyon**, a matter of perhaps two miles.

You're deposited just outside a slender, unprepossessing crack in a red sandstone wall. Stepping inside is like entering both a cathedral, in that you find yourself in a majestic chamber adorned with delicate glowing colors, and a pinball machine, in that you can just imagine that any second some mighty and unavoidable boulder will come thundering down the narrow passageway.

△ The Colorado River at Horseshoe Bend, near Page

Walking the full length of the canyon and back takes barely twenty minutes, even with frequent pauses to admire the interlacing fins of multihued rock that swirl overhead, in places to a height of 120ft. A flash flood is capable of filling the slot to the brim with water and spilling over the top; once such a flood recedes, on the other hand, it leaves the canyon floor scrubbed bare of its usual eight-foot layer of fine soft sand.

Be warned that while Antelope Canyon is every bit as beautiful as photos suggest, it offers little of the wilderness feel of other desert highlights. It's both short and narrow enough to feel *very* crowded at busy times, and as the main priority for all visitors is to take photographs, there's seldom space or time to simply relax and enjoy the place.

Given the high cost of an unaccompanied visit, you may prefer to join a guided **tour** from Page, which typically costs about $25 for a one-hour trip and up to $35 for a longer photography tour. Several competing companies have offices in central Page. Highly recommended for his personalized small-group excursions is the affable, self-styled Chief Tsosie of Grand Circle Adventures, 48 S Lake Powell Blvd (☎928/645-5594, ⓦ www.antelopeslotcanyontours.com), who also leads day trips to lesser-known canyons and overlooks, while Overland Canyon Tours, 697 N Navajo Drive (☎928/608-4072 or 1-800/684-4072, ⓦ www.overlandcanyontours.com), offers extended trips into the backcountry.

Horseshoe Bend

An easy self-guided hike not far south of Page leads to an amazing view of **Horseshoe Bend**, where the Colorado River makes an extravagant 180-degree turn in the depths of Marble Canyon, roughly halfway through its short course between Glen Canyon Dam and the official start of the Grand Canyon at Lees Ferry.

To reach the overlook, drive south on US-89 and turn west on the dirt road just past mile marker 545, exactly 2.6 miles south of the Wal-Mart in Page. The road leads to a parking lot at the foot of a small sandy hill. Climb the railed

The western half of the United States would sustain a population greater than that of our whole country today if the waters that now run to waste were saved and used for irrigation.

– President Theodore Roosevelt, State of the Union address, 1901

The growth of the American West in the twentieth century is largely the story of the "taming" of the **Colorado River**. If the river were to run dry, Los Angeles, Las Vegas, and Phoenix would shrivel up, and the exodus from the Southwest would dwarf anything from the Dust Bowl era.

While the Colorado does not rank among the top 25 rivers in the US in terms of volume, the sheer aggression with which it hurtles from 13,000ft up in the Rockies makes it the fastest and fiercest of them all. That power is what created so many magnificent canyons; it's also why civil engineers can't bear to leave the river alone. They yearn to harness its energy with hydroelectric dams and divert its flow to irrigate the desert instead of rushing uselessly to the sea.

Early in the twentieth century, the sparsely populated Southwestern states began to fear that Southern California's ever-increasing thirst might one day drain them dry. The **Colorado River Compact**, signed in 1922, divided the river between an **Upper Basin**, consisting of Colorado, New Mexico, Utah, and Wyoming, and a **Lower Basin**, comprising Arizona, Nevada, and California. Each basin was to receive 7.5 million acre-feet of the estimated annual flow of 16.8 million, leaving the dregs for Mexico. This was the first of fifteen such agreements in fifty years, largely because the annual flow estimates were wrong; the correct figure is more like 13.9 million acre-feet.

The task of distributing the water fell to the **Bureau of Reclamation**, a new federal agency, and the main tool at its disposal was the **dam**. Its engineers set out on a mission to "reclaim" the West, to reshape it the way it ought to be. They began in 1935 by damming Black Canyon, on California's doorstep, with what came to be known as the **Hoover Dam**. That project sparked a dam-building spree, in the US and worldwide. Though critics argued the American dams were supplying far more hydroelectric power than the nation could possibly use, it was all absorbed soon enough to feed the war effort and fuel the economic boom of the 1950s. According to the Bureau of Reclamation, still more dams were required. Proposals included damming the Green River in northwest Colorado, the San Juan in New Mexico, and the Colorado itself in both Arizona's Bridge Canyon and Utah's Glen Canyon.

Almost a century earlier, in 1869, John Wesley Powell had been entranced by the idyllic canyon that lay below the confluence of the Green and Colorado rivers: "A curious ensemble of wonderful features – carved walls, royal arches, glens, alcove gulches, mounds, and monuments. ... We decide to call it **Glen Canyon**." The few river runners who had seen it in the interim knew it as a cool, tranquil haven, bursting with luxuriant vegetation and desert wildlife – a far cry from the cataract-filled canyons both up- and downstream. Theirs were lone voices in the wilderness, however. Too little known to have earned federal protection, Glen Canyon's remoteness was to work against it.

The environmental movement was in its infancy in the 1950s, and its strategy focused on defending national parks at all costs. As the Green River damsite lay within Dinosaur National Monument, **David Brower**, the executive director of the Sierra Club, argued before a Congressional committee that damming Glen Canyon was a far better idea – in fact, he originally endorsed construction of a dam in the Grand Canyon *on condition* that a dam was built in Glen Canyon as well. Brower felt that only if the Glen Canyon dam were built could he be sure the one in Dinosaur never would be. Conservationists prided themselves on a job well done when the decision was made to dam the Green River *outside* Dinosaur, at Flaming Gorge to the northwest, and to proceed with damming Glen Canyon. The one concession to "the abominable nature lovers," as one Utah senator termed them, was that water would not be allowed to encroach upon Rainbow Bridge National Monument.

On a signal from President Eisenhower, crews detonated the first blast at the damsite in September 1956. Meanwhile, with Glen Canyon doomed but not yet drowned, archeologists, artists, and photographers set out to chronicle such disappearing treasures as the glowing, fern-fringed alcove known as the **Cathedral in the Desert** and the **Crossing of the Fathers**, where Spanish friars Domínguez and Escalante forded the river in 1776.

The Colorado River was brought to a halt on January 21, 1963. That same day, President Kennedy's Secretary of the Interior, Stewart Udall – the great-grandson of John D. Lee, of Lees Ferry – announced plans to build two more dams within the Grand Canyon. By now, the Sierra Club had realized its mistake; and it promptly made another. This time it argued for building coal-burning power plants instead of hydroelectric dams. The Navajo Nation, imagining that nuclear power might soon render its mineral resources worthless, decided to cash in by permitting strip-mining on Black Mesa and construction of the Navajo Generating Station outside Page.

It took seventeen more years and $300 million – and a Supreme Court decision that Congress could ignore its own previous rulings and allow the lake to lap against Rainbow Bridge – before Lake Powell reached its brim, on June 22, 1980. At its maximum depth, the lake is 561ft deep at the dam and holds enough water to cover all of Arizona five inches deep. The water backs up 186 miles on the Colorado River and 72 miles on the San Juan River, as well as inundating 96 side canyons formed by rivers such as the Escalante and the Dirty Devil. Its total shoreline of 1960 miles is longer than the entire US Pacific coast. Despite the searing sun, the lake only loses an estimated 2.5 percent of its volume each year to evaporation.

Although many people consider the lake a loathsome abomination, many more see it as a thing of beauty, and Lake Powell has become Utah's number one tourist attraction, drawing around four million visitors per year. It is, undeniably, an extraordinary spectacle, its turquoise waters rippling against a stark red-rock rim and cradling islands that once were buttes and mesas. No one could ever mistake this for a natural landscape, however, and you don't have to be an out-and-out environmentalist to be disturbed by the transformation of America's last great wilderness into a playground.

By the time David Brower left the Sierra Club to found Friends of the Earth in 1969, he was describing his support for Glen Canyon Dam as "the greatest sin I have ever committed." Shortly before his death, in 2000, the 87-year-old "Archdruid" hosted a Day of Action Against Dams at the damsite, during which he called once again for Lake Powell to be drained so the canyon could regenerate: "Watching Nature heal the Glen will be one of the great dramas on Earth." One of the original arguments for the dam had been that the Colorado's phenomenal load of silt would otherwise fill Lake Mead, behind Hoover Dam, within a few years; Brower argued that the floodgates at Glen Canyon should remain open until that really does happen, perhaps two hundred years from now. Other activists would go much further. The central fantasy of Edward Abbey's *The Monkey Wrench Gang* involved dynamiting the dam, and Abbey was among the demonstrators who in 1981 signaled the birth of the **Earth First** movement by suspending a 300ft strip of plastic down the face of the dam to simulate an almighty crack.

Environmental activists found solace in the droughts of the early twenty-first century, which saw the lake level drop to 146ft below capacity by early 2005 and even exposed such long-submerged features as the Cathedral in the Desert. Since then, however, the rains have returned, and at the time this book went to press, the waters had risen more than 50ft. To some extent, though, the argument has been won; no major dam has been built since the 1960s, and the general consensus is that Glen Canyon Dam will be the last.

path to the top of that hill, then down another 0.4 mile to the lip of the gorge. The river itself is only visible from the very edge, which is unrailed, windy, and pretty hair-raising. The huge curving sweep far below barely fits into the widest-angled lens. Be sure to carry water and allow about an hour for the exposed round-trip hike.

Eating

With the arguable exception of a couple of anodyne hotel dining rooms, Page offers a pretty poor choice of restaurants; a *KFC* across from the visitor center is as good a bet as anything else. In Dam Plaza, *Beans Gourmet Coffee House*, 644 N Navajo Drive (℡928-645-6858), serves espressos and light snacks, while the adjacent *Gunsmoke Saloon* offers beer and live country music nightly.

Bella Napoli 809 N Navajo Drive ℡928/645-2706. All-you-can-eat Italian buffets (soup, salad, pizza, and pasta) for lunch ($7) and dinner ($10), plus a full menu. Daily 11am–2pm & 5pm onward.

Dam Bar & Grille 644 N Navajo Drive ℡928/645-2161. Themed diner and bar, appealingly designed to echo the days when Page was populated solely by dam-building hard hats. Steak and pasta entrées for around $15. Daily 3–11pm.

Peppers Restaurant *Courtyard by Marriott*, 600 Clubhouse Drive ℡928/645-5000. Upscale but not especially expensive hotel restaurant on the way to town as you approach from the dam. Varied if not wildly exciting menu ranges through salads, pasta, sandwiches, and dinner specials. Open daily for all meals.

Glen Canyon Dam

Glen Canyon Dam plugs **Marble Canyon** not at its narrowest point, but at its northern end, just downstream from Wahweap Creek. Where US-89 crosses Glen Canyon Bridge, four miles outside of Page, the vast curve of the dam lies to the north, while Marble Canyon drops 700ft below you.

There's no stopping on the bridge, so if you want a better look, call in at the ultramodern **Carl Hayden Visitor Center** (daily: Oct–April 8am–5pm, May–Sept 8am–6pm; ℡928/608-6404, ✇www.nps.gov/glca) on the west bank, which doubles as the main source of information on the **Glen Canyon National Recreational Area**. Security concerns have led to suspension of the **free tours** for most of the time since September 11, 2001. If they're running when you turn up, allow half an hour to drop via two elevators first to the walkway along the top, then a further 500ft to the generating station at the bottom. Beneath the roar of the 1.3-million-kilowatt turbines, a digital counter steadily ticks off the billions of dollars so far earned by the sale of power.

A spur road just before the bridge on the east bank tunnels down through the cliffs to the river; rafters use it as an access point for the gloriously lazy fifteen-mile **float trip** down to Lees Ferry. There's no white water along the way, and strictly speaking you never enter the Grand Canyon, but it's still a very pleasant drift between imposing high-canyon cliffs. For more details, see p.204 or contact Wilderness River Adventures, 57 S Lake Powell Blvd, Page (℡928/645-3296 or 1-800/992-8022, ✇www.riveradventures.com; $62 adults, $52 under age 13).

Wahweap

Unlike Page, **WAHWEAP**, a couple of miles west of Glen Canyon Dam, has yet to become a town. Lake Powell's principal **marina** has, however, grown

Grand Canyon
trails

If there's one sure remedy for the oft-voiced complaint that it's hard to appreciate or even comprehend the Grand Canyon from the rim, it's to hike down into it. A descent along any of the park's five hundred miles of magnificent trails is rewarded with much more than just another view of the same thing. Instead, one passes through a sequence of utterly different landscapes, each with its own distinct topography, climate, and wildlife. But while the canyon is certainly a sublime, enticing wilderness, it can also be a hostile, unforgiving environment, grueling even for expert hikers

▲ North Kaibab Trail

What makes the canyon unique

Whatever experience you may have gained elsewhere, the Grand Canyon is different. Most hikers are far more familiar with walking *up* hills and mountains, when it's the initial climb that's most demanding, and if your energy levels start to flag, you can simply turn around and walk back to base. Canyon hiking is deceptively seductive. The descent seems easy, and your progress quick. There's always another great view a little farther on, and the lure of the river beckons you forward. Eventually, however, you have to pay; start your ascent when you're already tired, and the midday heat of the inner canyon has set in, and you're in for a murderously long haul. With the South Rim rising 7000ft above sea level, and the North Rim 8000ft, the altitude alone is fatiguing.

As a rule of thumb, most people spend twice as much time climbing back up as it took to hike down. That means turning back after a third of your allotted time; if you plan a six-hour hike, allow two hours to hike down and four hours to hike up. Rangers say the average speed is two miles per hour on the way down and just one on the way up.

▲ Grandview Trail

Trail topography

The main trails from the South Rim are broadly similar, involving a seven- to ten-mile descent to the Colorado. An initial burst of steep switchbacks culminates in **dramatic overlooks** from atop the Coconino sandstone layer, about 1.5 miles along the trail. The Tonto Platform presents another way station about three miles down. The trails continue a couple of miles to the edge of this platform, for views of the Granite Gorge, before taking the **final plunge** to the river. Almost all are drainage trails, which descend along existing watercourses and thus offer only intermittent views; the exception is the South Kaibab, which follows the crest of a high ridge, with views most of the way down.

As the North Rim is set back farther from the river, trails from it are proportionately longer, averaging around fourteen miles, and thus require at least one overnight stop en route if you're headed all the way to the Colorado.

When to hike

The best hiking seasons are **spring** and **fall**, when temperatures are cooler, the trails less crowded, and water is more available. Summer, on the other hand, offers far from ideal conditions, though of course that's when most people visit. At that time of year especially, avoid hiking in the middle of the day. Set off very **early** in the morning – well before 7am if you're heading down, and before 5am if you're climbing out.

Inner canyon wildlife

Below the rim, the Grand Canyon is far from the lifeless desert it might appear from above. One of the great joys of hiking the inner canyon is the chance to experience the **flora** and **fauna** of this unique wilderness ecosystem. As you descend toward the river, the surrounding vegetation progressively changes from spruce and fir to dense ponderosa woodlands and piñon-juniper "pygmy forest," followed by cacti, yucca, and mesquite. Though the lush banks of the Colorado are rich with wildlife, the river itself is such an impassable barrier that separate

▲ South Kaibab Trail

species of animals have evolved on either side. Thus reddish Abert's squirrels pester picnicking hikers on the Bright Angel Trail, while grayer Kaibab squirrels scavenge along the North Kaibab Trail across the river. Similarly, different kinds of rattlesnake inhabit the two rims – none of which has ever seriously harmed human visitors.

Among the best trails for **wildlife enthusiasts** are the Hermit Trail, which is rich in birds and butterflies, and the South Kaibab Trail, which is popular with soaring California condors, especially in the early morning.

▲ Abert squirrel, Bright Angel Trail

Recommended day hikes

The most important piece of advice for would-be hikers is **don't try to hike to the Colorado River and back in one day**. Several hikers each year die from exhaustion in the attempt. The only safe way to approach the river is as part of a multi-day expedition, as described in chapter three.

However, plenty of satisfying day hikes are possible within the canyon. The following six round-trips are highly recommended – well worth taking in their own right and useful experience for anyone planning a longer backpacking trip. While it's always tempting to venture that little bit farther, especially on your first canyon hike, only do so if you're absolutely sure of your stamina and supplies.

South Kaibab Trail to Cedar Mesa (3-mile round-trip): Perhaps the most instantly rewarding of all Grand Canyon hikes, this stark, exposed trail sets off from Yaki Point, not far east of Grand Canyon Village on the South Rim. The views are especially sublime if you set off at dawn, but in summer the heat farther down can be oppressive.

North Kaibab Trail to Supai Tunnel (4-mile round-trip): The North Rim's best-loved trail is demanding from the word go; unless you're especially fit, it's best only to go as far as the dramatic viewpoint atop the Redwall.

Hermit Trail to Santa Maria Spring (4.6-mile round-trip): The peaceful, seldom busy Hermit Trail leaves the South Rim from the far west end of Hermit Road, descending through some of the canyon's most verdant scenery to a lovely little oasis that offers great views.

Bright Angel Trail to Three-Mile Resthouse (6-mile round-trip): The canyon's oldest and busiest trail descends steep switchbacks from the heart of Grand Canyon Village, with fabulous new panoramas opening up at every twist.

Grandview Trail to Horseshoe Mesa (6.4-mile round-trip): One of the few major trails not to descend all the way to the Colorado River, the superbly engineered Grandview Trail nonetheless offers some of the South Rim's finest hiking.

North Kaibab Trail to Roaring Springs (9.4-mile round-trip): It takes a major physical effort to hike to and from this stunning North Rim waterfall in a single day, but the scenery along the way is utterly breathtaking.

▼ The Bright Angel Trail through Indian Garden and the onward trail to Plateau Point

steadily since it was established in 1963, coordinating most of the boat rental and tour business and also offering several hundred motel rooms.

The first man to appreciate Wahweap's potential did so long before the dam was ever built. Art Greene, owner of the *Marble Canyon Lodge* (see p.130), ran boat trips upriver to Rainbow Bridge from the 1940s onward; when he got wind of plans to dam Glen Canyon, he shrewdly leased the land at the mouth of Wahweap Creek at a bargain rate. Knowing it made the perfect site for a marina, Greene refused to budge and wound up making a killing as official concessionaire.

Boat tours from Wahweap

The prime draw at Wahweap, if you have time, is a boat tour fifty miles north to stunning **Rainbow Bridge National Monument**, where the world's largest natural bridge spans beautiful Forbidden Canyon. The length of your trip depends on the level of the lake; what used to be a half-day trip has become an eight-hour one in recent years. For details and the current schedule, contact Lake Powell Resort on the number below ($115 adults, $80 under age 13). The resort also runs shorter treks from Wahweap, ranging from a one-hour paddle wheeler trip (daily June to early Sept; $15 adults, $12 under age 13) to ninety-minute Antelope Canyon excursions ($33 adults, $26 under age 12) and a dinner cruise (daily May–Sept; $67).

Practicalities

Only half the rooms at plush *Lake Powell Resort* (☎928/645-2433 or 1-800/528-6154, Ⓦwww.lakepowell.com; Nov–April ❺, May–Oct ❼) overlook Lake Powell. Its *Rainbow Room* restaurant, however, provides huge lakeside windows and serves good food daily for all meals, with prices kept relatively low to cater to the many tour groups that pass through. The same management also operates an adjacent first-come, first-served **campground** ($18), as well as an **RV park** (April–Oct $26, Nov–March $18).

Marble Canyon

On the route north along US-89 from Cameron toward Page (see p.123), forking left instead at Antelope Pass takes you onto **US-89A**, which presses on for another fifteen miles at the foot of the Echo Cliffs before finally dropping down to reach Navajo Bridge. Although the spot where US-89A finally crosses the Colorado is often loosely referred to as **Lees Ferry**, the highway bridge actually stands six miles downstream from the ferry crossing it superseded.

By this point, the Grand Canyon has officially begun and is already almost 500ft deep. John Wesley Powell named this segment of the gorge **Marble Canyon**, on account of its highly polished walls, indented with caverns and carvings that appear almost architectural. Marble Canyon stretches 61.5 miles from Lees Ferry to the river's confluence with the Little Colorado, but it's another fifty miles from the bridge before the chasm reaches a mile deep. Here, near its starting point, it makes such narrow impression in the vast flatland of the **Marble Platform** that you barely discern it until you're right on top of it.

Navajo Bridge

Even though Prohibition meant the newly built **Navajo Bridge** could only be baptized with ginger ale and not champagne, its opening in 1929, as the world's highest steel arch bridge, marked a turning point in Arizona history. Until then, no bridge spanned the Colorado between Searchlight, Nevada, and northern Utah, while the nearby ferry crossing was so dangerous it had been abandoned altogether. When a crucial piece of equipment needed to finish Navajo Bridge was stranded on the wrong side of the river, the only way to get it across was to take it eight hundred miles by road, via Las Vegas.

Nowadays, the nearest bridge to Navajo Bridge is a mere fifty yards away. The original span was joined by a modern replica – all but identical, but at 44ft more than twice as wide – in 1995. The old bridge is reserved for pedestrians, so you can walk out to the middle and gaze 470ft down to the Colorado, green with algae, at the bottom of Marble Canyon. To add to the spectacle, this spot is also popular with **condors**.

Land ownership here is extraordinarily convoluted, incidentally. The top of the west bank belongs to the Glen Canyon National Recreation Area, though Bureau of Land Management holdings start not far beyond; the top of the east bank belongs to the Navajo Nation; and both bridge and river are in Grand Canyon National Park.

On the west bank, the **Navajo Bridge Interpretive Center** (daily April–Sept 8am–5pm, closed Oct–March; restrooms always open; ☎928/608-6404, ⓦwww.nps.gov/glca) holds hair-raising photos of Navajo steelworkers erecting the 1995 bridge, plus displays and literature about the Glen Canyon region. The large outside viewing area is festooned with all sorts of plaques, including the one honoring John Doyle Lee that's mentioned on p.132.

Marble Canyon Lodge

Not far west of Navajo Bridge, just past the turnoff for Lees Ferry, the **Marble Canyon Lodge** (☎928/355-2225 or 1-800/726-1789; ④) provides more than fifty conventional motel-style units, with TVs but no phones, in low-slung buildings at the foot of the cliffs. The central lodge holds a gift store with the feel of a trading post, which sells Navajo rugs and other Native American crafts, and an adequate but unexciting **restaurant** that's open for all meals daily. Dinner entrees cost $8–14, with a Navajo taco salad for $9 and inexpensive house wine. While the lodge as a whole can be a little slapdash, it's a romantic enough overnight stop, featuring a spectacular desert setting where roadrunners scurry across the sands.

Marble Canyon Lodge has always catered to adventurers here for rafting and fishing trips on the Colorado, and it gears up at 6am each day to meet the needs of river rats. An array of plaques and monuments across the highway honors river pioneers, from the 1776 Domínguez and Escalante expedition (see p.135) onward.

Lees Ferry

Reached via a gently sloping six-mile spur road that branches right from US-89A just beyond Navajo Bridge, **LEES FERRY** is little more than a dot on the map; it's not a town and has a population of zero. Nonetheless, it boasts the geographic distinction of being the official starting point of the Grand Canyon and even greater hydrologic significance as the boundary between the upper and lower basins of the Colorado River. That's actually a political nuance; broadly speaking, under the Colorado River Compact of 1922, half the water in the river "belongs" to the states upstream from Lees Ferry, the other half to those downstream. The complications and contradictions concealed within that simple formula are far too convoluted to go into here, though you'll notice that none of the river is thereby left in peace to flow into the ocean.

The practical importance of Lees Ferry stems from the fact that it's the only place within hundreds of miles that offers easy land access to both banks of the Colorado. That's because it stands at the river's confluence with the **Paria River**, which flows southeastward from southern Utah.

A Paiute named Naraguts guided Mormon elder Jacob Hamblin to this remote spot in 1858, while John Doyle Lee's eponymous **ferry** service (see box p.132) was instigated in 1871. After Lee's death, his wife Emma remained in the area, but sold the ferry back to the Mormons for $3000 worth of cattle. Always a hazardous operation, with the boats in constant danger of being swept downstream, the ferry was finally abandoned after an accident in June 1928, in which three lives, plus a Model T Ford, were lost.

Four miles down from Marble Canyon, the road passes the fairly basic **Lees Ferry Campground**, which lies within Glen Canyon National Recreation Area and offers water and toilets but not showers ($10 per night; ☎928/355-2334). A few hundred yards farther on, it crosses the Paria River to a large parking lot and launch ramp on the Colorado. The concrete gauging station on the far bank marks the exact start – **Mile 0** – of the Grand Canyon. This is where **white-water rafting** expeditions set off into the canyon; passengers can leave the river at Phantom Ranch, five or six days downriver, but the first point at which the boats can be taken out again is Diamond Creek, around twelve days away by muscle power.

Some boat trips do, however, end here. As detailed on p.128, commercial operators based in Page run half-day **smooth-water** float trips to Lees Ferry from just below Glen Canyon Dam. That 15.8-mile stretch, fed by cold, clear water released from the dam – and not yet muddied by the influx from the Paria – has became famous for its **trout fishing**. All local lodges, including Lees Ferry Anglers at *Cliff Dweller's Lodge* (☎928/355-2261 or 1-800/962-9755, ⓦwww .leesferry.com), organize guided fishing expeditions at varying prices. The official daily catch limit is two trout per person.

Lees Ferry trails

Rudimentary trails from the far end of the parking lot lead a couple of hundred yards to an assortment of buildings left over from the ferry era. Largely constructed of slabs of red sandstone, they include a small post office and the sturdy **Lees Ferry Fort**, erected in 1874 as a stronghold against Navajo attacks that never materialized.

The most prominent remains, however, date from an abortive experiment by **Charles H. Spencer**, who set out in 1910 to mine **gold** from the exposed Chinle shale on the slopes above Lees Ferry. Spencer's elaborate scheme, in which he'd sluice the shale down the hillside using pressurized hoses, required him to haul coal to the site, which he attempted both by **mule train** over the Echo Cliffs and by **steamboat** along the river. While the boiler of his abandoned boat lies rusting in the Colorado, his precipitous **Spencer Trail** is still there, switchbacking up the cliffs – though not regularly maintained, it's open to hikers and offers a grueling 1700ft climb. What ultimately stymied Spencer's endeavor was that something kept clogging his amalgamators, rendering them inoperative. Only fifty years later did he find out the problem was caused by **rhenium**, a metal unknown to science back in 1912. Incredibly, he returned to Lees Ferry, now aged over 90, and embarked on another unsuccessful mining venture, this time in pursuit of rhenium itself.

Travelers who read the plaque at Navajo Bridge that hails **John Doyle Lee** as "a man of good faith, sound judgment, and indomitable courage" might never realize that the man who put the Lee in Lees Ferry was also a prime mover in one of the most notorious episodes in Western history. While the precise truth remains in dispute, the generally accepted story runs something like this:

In 1847, Mormons fleeing persecution in Illinois ventured west beyond the United States and founded Salt Lake City. Almost immediately, however, the US extended its boundaries to the Pacific, and California-bound pioneers began to stream through Mormon territory. By 1857, tensions were such that a "Mormon War" was seen as inevitable.

That August, finding that no one would sell them supplies, a wagon train of settlers from Arkansas and Missouri resorted to raiding Mormon farms. Camping at **Mountain Meadows** in southern Utah, the settlers were ambushed by warriors dressed as Native Americans. Whether the attackers were genuine Utes or white Mormons in disguise – as Mark Twain reported in *Roughing It* – is still open to question. Clearly, however, local Mormons saw the wagon train as a threat to be eliminated. Their commander, John Lee, rode up to the beleaguered Gentiles on September 11, claiming to have negotiated a truce with the "Indians," and stated that if they laid down their guns, they would be allowed to proceed west in peace.

Desperately short of ammunition, the migrants agreed. Each was assigned a Mormon escort, and together they set off west. Within a mile, Lee called the order "**Halt! Do your duty!**," whereupon the Mormon militiamen, possibly with assistance from Native Americans, killed the entire group, amounting to 120 unarmed men, women, and children.

When reports of the massacre reached the rest of the country, it was widely believed to have been carried out on the orders of Mormon President **Brigham Young**. No serious legal investigation ever took place, however, and most of the perpetrators lay low in remote desert outposts. In due course, Young bowed to national pressure; Lee was excommunicated in 1870, arrested in 1874, and **executed** by firing squad in Mountain Meadows on March 23, 1877.

Lee's version of events was quite different. He claimed to have acted as a loyal servant of the Church; not to have actually killed anyone; to have given Brigham Young the names of all involved; and to have been made a scapegoat.

It was during his years on the run, albeit in answer to a request from Brigham Young, that Lee set up the first **ferry** service across the Colorado. He arrived here in 1871, with just two of his eighteen wives still standing by him. Lee initially utilized three boats abandoned by John Wesley Powell before building his own boat, *Colorado*, big enough to carry four wagons. The boat was swept across the river in both directions by the current and then towed back upstream to its starting point; the fare was $3 per wagon, 75¢ per animal.

Many legends surround Lee's years in the Grand Canyon. Tales that he planted the peach orchards of the Havasupai are untrue – though he did visit them in his wanderings – while persistent stories of **lost gold mines** have never been proved. He's said to have been in the habit of disappearing for days at a time and returning with cans filled with gold nuggets. His wife Emma believed he'd struck it lucky, but none of the prospectors who followed her suggestions ever found a thing.

Haunting photos of Lee on the day he died show a gaunt old man sitting on his coffin, waiting for the firing squad – hidden beneath a blanket to prevent reprisals.

Keep walking beyond Spencer's employee bunkhouse and more derelict machinery, and after about a mile you'll come to the actual launch point of Lee's famous ferry. It's a hard, thirsty hike, however, with little reward at the far end.

△ John Doyle Lee's Lonely Dell Ranch at Lees Ferry

Lonely Dell Ranch

John Lee lived not at the ferry site, but in the much more congenial surroundings of the **Lonely Dell Ranch**, nestled in a fertile curve of the Paria River about a half-mile up from the confluence. Back across the river from the modern boat ramp, make an immediate right on the unpaved road to reach the Park Service's replanted approximation of Lee's **orchards**, rich with apple, pear, plum, and peach trees.

His original **log cabin** stands not far beyond, constructed largely of driftwood and chinked with thick red river mud. The smaller adjacent **blacksmith shop** was also Lee's; it lies in the shade of a large mulberry tree that was planted to help raise silkworms. Various other structures were added by Lee's successors, some of whom now lie in the tranquil little **cemetery** at the end of the road. Uninhabited since the 1940s, its fields dotted with derelict green farm machinery, the ranch these days has the feel of a desert oasis and is a popular halt for migratory birds.

For serious backpackers, Lonely Dell Ranch marks the end of an epic four- to six-day hike that traces the full length of the Paria Canyon, starting at the White House trailhead off US-89 between Kanab and Page. The canyon forms part of the Paria Canyon–Vermilion Cliffs Wilderness, itself encompassed within Vermilion Cliffs National Monument.

Vermilion Cliffs

For the first thirty miles west of Marble Canyon, US-89A curves along the foot of the **Vermilion Cliffs**. In November 2000, in one of his final acts as president, Bill Clinton designated a vast 294,000-acre expanse that encompasses the cliffs, the Paria Plateau above them, and Paria Canyon as **Vermilion Cliffs National Monument**. Administered by the Bureau of Land Management from its office in St George, Utah (☎435/688-3200, ⓦwww.az.blm.gov), the monument is not expected to change significantly or to open up for tourism in the foreseeable future.

Although the road itself is all but featureless, and the desert almost entirely devoid of vegetation, the drive along the Vermilion Cliffs is superbly dramatic, as the soaring sandstone walls glow a magnificent red at sunrise and sunset. However, only a couple of small **motels** offer any incentive to get out of your car. You'd never know the Grand Canyon was out there to the east, slicing through the Marble Platform, unless you detour two miles down a dirt road that leaves the highway a couple of hundred yards south of *Lees Ferry Lodge*; at road's end lies the **Badger Canyon–Marble Canyon Overlook**.

Lees Ferry Lodge

Boasting great views from a pretty location three miles west of *Marble Canyon Lodge*, the smaller **Lees Ferry Lodge** complex dates from 1929 (☎928/355-2231 or 1-800/451-2231, ⓦwww.leesferrylodge.com; ❸). Besides offering appealingly rustic guest cabins of varying sizes, the lodge is centered on the friendly little *Vermilion Cliffs Bar & Grille*, which serves good food washed down with an extraordinary range of bottled beers and includes its own fly shop for anglers.

Cliff Dweller's Lodge

Originally built in 1890 as a mock ancient ruin and run these days as a standard-issue Western motel, the **Cliff Dweller's Lodge** (☎928/355-2261 or 1-800/962-9755, ⓦwww.leesferry.com; ❹) occupies another dramatic spot, amid the jumbled rocks a half-dozen miles beyond *Lees Ferry Lodge*. Like its neighbors, it's geared primarily toward river runners, who flock to its restaurant and adjoining attractive shady patio early in the morning (Mon–Thurs 5–10am & 4–10pm, Fri–Sun 5am–10pm).

House Rock Valley

US-89A rounds the southernmost promontory of the Vermilion Cliffs just under twenty miles out from Navajo Bridge. Not far beyond, as the highway begins its arrow-straight run across the desert toward the Kaibab Mountains, a dirt road sets off south between mile markers 559 and 560. It leads to the **House Rock Buffalo Ranch**, headquarters for a hundred-strong herd of buffalo that roams free across **House Rock Valley**. In recent years the buffalo have also wandered up onto the Kaibab Plateau and along the North Rim, so your chances of spotting them are pretty minimal; you'd have to be desperate indeed to think it worth driving the slow fifty-mile round-trip to road's end and back.

Another five miles up the highway, a northbound gravel road just past mile marker 565 – signed to Vermilion Cliffs National Monument, it closely parallels House Rock Wash – leads a few miles to the **Condor Release Site**. This

On July 29, 1776 – three weeks after Congress endorsed the Declaration of Independence – a party of twenty explorers set off from Santa Fe, the capital of the Spanish province of New Mexico. Led by two Franciscan friars, **Atanasio Domínguez** and **Silvestre Vélez de Escalante**, they hoped to establish a route to the Spanish mission at Monterey, California. Knowing that the Grand Canyon blocked their path, but not knowing how far it stretched, they headed north, planning to turn west once they felt confident the canyon had petered out. They eventually crossed the Colorado River somewhere east of modern Grand Junction, Colorado, then continued north and west as far as what's now Provo, Utah, which they named San Antonio de Padua. By October, they were in southern Utah, at what they calculated was the same latitude as Monterey. However, snowcapped mountains lined the distant western horizon, and winter blizzards were setting in.

By casting lots, the expedition made the difficult decision to head home and attempt to blaze a more direct trail back to Santa Fe. Their Indian guides steered them across the Kaibab Plateau and down through House Rock Valley to the Vermilion Cliffs. Eighteen miles southwest of Navajo Bridge on US-89A, a roadside plaque near mile marker 557 commemorates the **San Bartolome Campsite**, where they halted on October 25.

The following day, they approached the Colorado at Marble Canyon, a spot they described as "a corner all hemmed in by very lofty bluffs and big hogbacks of red earth which ... present a pleasingly jumbled scene." Crossing the mouth of the Paria River, they then made their camp amid the more difficult terrain of what's now Lees Ferry, roughly a hundred yards downstream from the present-day boat-launch site. Two members of the party managed to swim across the Colorado – at the cost of losing all their clothes – but returned, having been too exhausted to climb the cliffs on the far side. Next they built a raft, but three times failed to pole it all the way across. After eleven days, convinced of the impossibility of coaxing their horses (some of which by now they were forced to eat) through quicksand and onto makeshift rafts, they gave up.

They headed north instead, managing to climb out of Paria Canyon a few miles along, and eventually forded the Colorado on horseback on November 7 at what became known as the **Crossing of the Fathers** in Glen Canyon. Mormon settlers dynamited that uniquely shallow ford in the 1870s to thwart its use by Navajo cattle raiders, and it now lies drowned beneath the waters of Lake Powell.

The Franciscans eventually returned to Santa Fe on January 2, 1777, having promised to return to Utah to set up a mission among the Laguna. Following general cutbacks by the government in Spain, however, they never did so, and the vast new lands explored by the expedition remained virgin territory until the arrival of the Mormons seventy years later.

---

is mission control for the Peregrine Fund effort to repopulate Arizona with wild condors (see p.53). A roadside pavilion commands views of the precise spot, high on the Vermilion Cliffs, where the first six birds were released from a glorified coop on December 12, 1996. As the abundant guano stains prove, they and their siblings regularly return "home." With powerful binoculars, you may well see them perched atop the cliffs or flying far overhead, though you're more likely to get close-up views at Grand Canyon Village on the South Rim.

Not far beyond the release-site turnoff, US-89A reaches the **Kaibab Mountains** and begins the final eleven-mile climb to Jacob Lake. A panoramic viewpoint past the first few switchbacks, before the road plunges into the thick forests of the Kaibab Plateau, commands a superb prospect of the cliffs, the Marble Platform, and the slender crease of Marble Canyon.

Jacob Lake

Set deep in the forest forty miles up from Navajo Bridge, the crossroads community of **JACOB LAKE** looks more like a Canadian logging camp than anything you'd expect to find in Arizona. Named for Jacob Hamblin, a Mormon missionary to the Paiute and Navajo, it guards the sole access route to the North Rim of the Grand Canyon: **AZ-67**, whose 44-mile southbound run to *Grand Canyon Lodge* closes to all traffic between the first serious winter snowfall and the following spring thaw. Jacob Lake thus goes into a state of quasi-hibernation in the winter, emerging in summer to make its living from the constant stream of tourists.

The *Jacob Lake Inn*, a sprawling, welcoming complex of timber-frame buildings at the road junction, stays open year-round (☎928/643-7232, ⓦwww.jacoblake.com). In addition to offering simple **motel** rooms (ⓖ) and log cabins (ⓖ), it incorporates pricier family units capable of sleeping up to six (ⓖ), plus a gas station, a general store, an old-fashioned diner counter and a restaurant where chicken, trout, or steak entrees cost $10–15. The Forest Service's adjacent **Kaibab Plateau Visitor Center** presents displays and information on the surrounding area (daily 8am–5pm; ☎928/643-7298, ⓦwww.fs.fed.us/r3/kai).

The Forest Service also oversees the lovely *Jacob Lake Campground*, on US-89A just west of the intersection, which has facilities for **tent campers** only (mid-May to Oct; ☎928/643-7395). **RVs** are welcome at the equally attractive *Kaibab Camper Village*, well off AZ-67 a mile southwest of the inn, near the eponymous lake, which is actually a collapsed limestone sinkhole (mid-May to mid-Oct; ☎928/643-7804).

DeMotte Park

Mormon settlers made little use of the forests that lie south of Jacob Lake, aside from grazing their cattle in the large clearings that punctuate the road to the canyon. No one knows quite how these meadows came into being; the theory that some natural mechanism deters trees from encroaching is undermined by the fact that the trees are doing just that, year after year.

One such meadow, the especially idyllic **DEMOTTE PARK**, 27 miles down AZ-67 from Jacob Lake, harbors the *Kaibab Lodge* (mid-May to mid-Oct only; ☎928/638-2389 in summer, 928/526-0924 in winter, or 1-800/525-0924, ⓦwww.kaibablodge.com). The lodge offers two different cabin types – characterful older ones with bare wooden floors (ⓖ) and a few slightly more expensive ones with motel-style trimmings (ⓖ) – plus a basic restaurant open daily for breakfast and dinner. Immediately south is the Forest Service's tent-only *DeMotte Park Campground* (mid-May to Oct; ☎928/643-7298), which was revamped and upgraded for the 2006 season. The nearby **gas station** is the last one outside the park; the North Entrance Station is five miles down the road, while visitor facilities, including a gas station, lie nine miles beyond that.

With a good map – ideally the Forest Service's *North Kaibab Ranger District* and not AAA's otherwise reliable *Guide to Indian Country* – it's possible to navigate the dirt roads that branch off of AZ-67 near DeMotte Park to several dramatic viewpoints. These include overlooks of the Marble Platform to the east, as well as the canyon views from Parissawampitts, Crazy Jug, and Monument points (see p.84) to the west. For advice on conditions along these backcountry roads, call in at the Forest Service visitor center in Jacob Lake.

The Arizona Strip

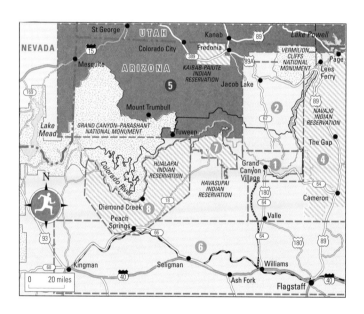

CHAPTER 5

Highlights

✳ **Kanab** Just across the state line in Utah, this former movie town provides plentiful food and lodging options in an otherwise underpopulated region. **See p.141**

✳ **Pipe Spring National Monument** Desert outpost that owes its tangled and fascinating history to its precious perennial water supply. **See p.144**

✳ **Toroweap Overlook** The remotest canyon overlook within the national park offers unique and extraordinary views of the inner gorge. **See p.148**

✳ **Lava Falls Overlook** Spectacular viewpoint, commanding the spot where a vast volcanic lava flow once blocked the entire Grand Canyon. **See p.148**

△ Picnicking at the Lava Falls Overlook

The Arizona Strip

Thanks to its sheer remoteness, the **Arizona Strip** – the anomalous area of northern Arizona sandwiched between the North Rim and the Utah state line – remains one of the least visited regions in the Southwest. Nonetheless, it makes a very rewarding destination for travelers eager to get the full Grand Canyon experience. Writer Wallace Stegner described it as "scenically the most spectacular and humanly the least usable of all our regions … as terrible and beautiful wasteland as the world can show," and much of it remains absolute wilderness. Almost no one ever sees the colossal canyon formed by **Kanab Creek**, which splits this region in two, while the million-acre **Grand Canyon–Parashant National Monument**, created in 2000, makes no provision for tourism whatsoever.

Virtually no roads cross the Strip, and those that do hold just a few tiny, secretive, and often semi-derelict hamlets. Although you have to pass this way in order to complete a full circuit of the Grand Canyon, most visitors here are simply racing between the canyon and southern Utah's national parks. Few are aware they're missing perhaps the most spectacular section of Grand Canyon National Park: the **Tuweep** district, home to two stunning overlooks at **Toroweap Point** that provide a rare opportunity to see the canyon's innermost core.

The Arizona Strip has never held more than five thousand inhabitants. Roughly that many **Kaibab Paiute** were living here – mostly as nomads, but also farming what little arable land it holds – when **Mormon** explorers arrived in the 1850s and set up ranches wherever they found water. By 1909, decimated by diseases and inevitable conflicts, the Paiute population had dwindled to just 89. The ranchers themselves largely gave up by the mid-twentieth century, and only a couple of their settlements, **Fredonia** and **Colorado City**, ever grew to any significant size.

By any logic, you'd expect the Strip to belong to Utah rather than Arizona. In 1864, Mormon leader Brigham Young called on Congress to grant the Mormons all territory that lay within two degrees of latitude of either side of the Colorado River; the boundary was drawn instead along the 37th parallel, and that remains the Utah-Arizona border. At least four attempts to incorporate the Strip into Utah failed, largely because many of the Mormons who chose to remain in this remote region were renegades who didn't accept their church's doctrinal reversal on multiple marriages. Continued effective isolation from both the Utah and Arizona state authorities suits these die-hard **polygamists** just fine.

Other than plenty of time and a reliable vehicle, the principal requirement needed to explore the Arizona Strip is a good **map** – ideally, the BLM Arizona Strip Field Office *Visitor Map* ($9).

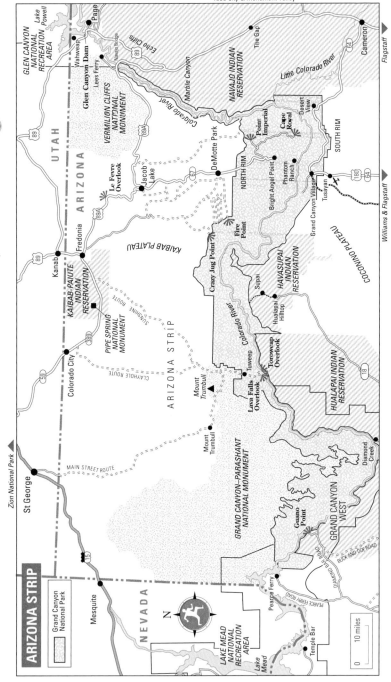

ARIZONA STRIP

☐ Grand Canyon National Park

Le Fevre Overlook

The Kaibab Plateau extends a full fifty miles north of the North Rim. Only after you've driven the length of AZ-67 and continued northwest on US-89A from the junction at **Jacob Lake** (see p.136) does the ground finally begin to slope downward.

Ten miles past the intersection, between mile markers 590 and 591, the roadside **Le Fevre Overlook** presents a jaw-dropping panorama across the Arizona Strip and into southern Utah. Tier upon tier of cliffs rise one behind the other into the distance, making it abundantly clear why geologists refer to this region as the **Grand Staircase**. First come the red sandstone of the Vermilion Cliffs, the formation pierced by **Zion Canyon**; next are the White Cliffs, which form the **Kolob Canyons** district of Zion National Park; then the grayish black mudstone, coal, shale, and sandstone of the Gray Cliffs; and finally, beyond them, forty miles away, stand the softer Pink Cliffs, sculpted into the hoodoos within **Bryce Canyon**. Apart from the occasional jewelry stand, the lookout holds no facilities of any kind.

Fredonia

US-89A eventually levels out at the foot of the Grand Staircase on **Muggins Flat**, reaching the very hot – in terms of temperature, not nightlife – little town of **FREDONIA**, just over thirty miles from, and 3000ft lower than, Jacob Lake. Mormon farmers founded Fredonia alongside Kanab Creek in 1885, under the more down-to-earth name of Hardscrabble. It remains a dusty, unadorned desert outpost.

While its population of around 1300 makes Fredonia the largest town on the Arizona Strip, the presence of the bigger and more interesting **Kanab**, a mere seven miles north across the Utah border, means that few visitors spend the night here. The very helpful modern **welcome center** (℡928/643-7241; Mon–Sat 9am–5pm), on the east side of US-89A near the state line at the north end of town, is the best place to seek advice on the Strip's backcountry routes and buy the necessary maps.

Practicalities

Fredonia holds a few small but adequate **motels**. Driving south to north on US-89A, you pass the very plain log-built *Crazy Jug*, 465 S Main St (℡928/643-7752; ❷); the ivy-covered *Grand Canyon*, 175 S Main St (℡928/643-7646; ❷), which boasts a red British telephone box in the garden; and the slightly run-down *Blue Sage*, 330 S Main St (℡928/643-7125; closed winter; ❷), which also accommodates RVs. The *Crazy Jug* has its own on-site diner, while *Nedra's Café*, 165 N Main St (℡928/643-7591), is a surprisingly good **Mexican restaurant**, where, if you're a newcomer to this neck of the woods, you might want to sample your first Navajo taco; for the uninitiated, it's a pizza-like cheese-topped slab of frybread.

Kanab

Until crews built new roads across the region in the 1950s, **KANAB**, Utah, just two miles north of the Arizona state line, was renowned as perhaps the most inaccessible town in the US. Now it's a significant tourist stop, thanks to its location midway between the Grand Canyon, 80 miles southeast, and Bryce Canyon, 83 miles northeast.

Kanab started life in 1864 as **Fort Kanab**, a frontier outpost so prone to Indian attacks that it was abandoned after just two years. Jacob Hamblin founded the town itself in 1870 as a God-fearing ranching community with a sideline in harboring Mormons who fell foul of the federal government, among them several perpetrators of the Mountain Meadows Massacre (see p.132). Pulp novelist Zane Grey later cultivated that lawless image, setting many of his Westerns nearby. Kanab's rugged surroundings also drew Western film greats, from Tom Mix, who filmed *Deadwood Coach* here in 1924, to Clint Eastwood, who swept into town with *The Outlaw Josey Wales* in 1976. The town soon earned the nickname "Utah's Little Hollywood."

While ranching has long been in decline in southern Utah, Kanab's citizens would still much prefer to wrest their living from the earth. Their biggest payday came in the late 1950s, when the town served as the construction base for the **Glen Canyon Dam**. During the eighteen months it took to upgrade the 72-mile dirt road to the damsite, not to mention build the new town of Page, Arizona, locals scurried to grab their share of the 200 million federal dollars pumped into the project. In November 1958, the workers decamped for Page, and the boom was over.

For many years thereafter, Kanab pinned its hopes on the prospect of large-scale coal mining operations on the **Kaiparowits Plateau** to the northeast. The politicians and environmentalists who thwarted such plans in the 1970s were burned in effigy on the streets of Kanab – "victims" included Robert Redford, which might explain why not so many movies get made around here any more – and the town closed down in protest for an hour in October 1996 when President Clinton's proclamation of Grand Staircase–Escalante National Monument precluded that possibility.

Kanab has thus been left to survive by catering to tourists, which it does with reasonably good grace. US-89 is lined with an above-par assortment of motels and restaurants, most of which are clustered along the stretch of highway that doglegs east-west along **Center Street**. A few blocks south, US-89 veers east toward Page, while US-89A ducks south into Arizona.

Apart from a few large Western-themed souvenir stores, such as Denny's Wigwam, opposite *Parry Lodge* at 78 E Center St (☎435/644-2452), there's almost nothing to do in Kanab, though hikers may enjoy the views from the **Squaw Trail**, which climbs the escarpment just north of town.

Information and tours

Operating under the slogan "The Greatest Earth on Show," Kanab's **visitor center** stands just south of Center Street at 78 S 100 East (March–Oct Mon–Fri 9am–7pm, Sat & Sun 9am–5pm; Nov–Feb Mon–Fri 9am–5pm; ☎435/644-5033 or 1-800/733-5263, ⓦwww.kaneutah.com). Interesting displays relate the story of the town's filmmaking past. The local **BLM** office, 318 N 100 East (Mon–Fri 7.45am–5pm; ☎435/644-4600, ⓦwww.ut.blm.gov), provides information on nearby public lands, including Grand Canyon–Parashant National Monument, as well as current driving conditions.

Several local companies offer one- or multi-day **tours** of the surrounding backcountry. Operators include Canyon Rim Adventures (☎435/644-8512 or 1-800/897-9633, ⓦwww.canyonrimadventures.com), whose camping, biking, and/or backpacking trips run $575 and up for three days, and Canyon Country Out-Back Tours (☎435/644-3807 or 1-888/783-3807, ⓦwww.ccobtours.com), which offers 4WD tours to nearby slot canyons ($25 per person per hour) and an excursion down to Toroweap (a six-hour round-trip that costs $300 for two people).

Accommodation

Kanab hosts a number of decent budget **motels**, so don't feel compelled to pay extra for a brand name. All are within easy walking distance of downtown – though since there's nowhere much to walk to, it makes little difference.

Aiken's Lodge – National 9 Inn 74 W Center St ☎435/644-2625 or 1-800/790-0380, ⓦwww .aikenslodge.com. This low-slung and not desperately aesthetic option is nonetheless the ideal budget motel: crisp and clean, right in the heart of town, and with its own pool. ❸

Holiday Inn Express 815 E AZ-99 ☎435/644-8888 or 1-800/574-4061, ⓦwww.hikanabutah.com. Large new motel, perched atop a bluff on the eastern edge of town. Somewhat isolated but offers the highest standard of rooms in Kanab, plus a free breakfast bar. Winter ❹, summer ❺

Parry Lodge 89 E Center St ☎435/644-2601 or 1-800/748-4104, ⒻＦ644-2605, ⓦwww.parrylodge .com. Opened in 1931, Kanab's oldest motel has an undeniable air of romance. Photos of celebrity guests festoon the lobby and restaurant, while nameplates identify the rooms in which they slept; you can even bathe in John Wayne's extra-large bathtub. *Parry*'s isn't *that* great, though, even if you can get room service from the restaurant; some of the newer rooms are dingy and noisy. Rates include

a full cooked breakfast. Winter ❸, summer ❹

Shilo Inn 296 W 100 North ☎435/644-2562 or 1-800/222-2244, ⓦwww.shiloinns.com/utah/kanab. Large, presentable motel at the north end of town. Some rooms have kitchens, and there's a breakfast buffet, pool, and spa. Winter ❸, summer ❹

Super 8 70 S 200 West ☎435/644-5500 or 1-800/800-8000, ⒻＦ644-5576. Dependable budget motel in a quiet zone a block south of Center Street, with a large pool and hot tub. Winter ❷, summer ❹

USA Hostels Grand Canyon 143 E 100 South ☎435/644-5554 or 1-877/205-7136, ⓦwww .usahostels.com. Although its name is misleading, considering the canyon lies 83 miles away in a different state, this is a friendly, straightforward hostel, housed in a small, primary-painted converted motel a block east of the highway near the visitor center. Dorm rooms for men, women, and couples, each with a shower and priced at $15 per bed, plus one private room at $32. There's also a kitchen, library, and laundry. ❶/❷

Eating

Twenty or so largely formulaic **restaurants** cling to the edge of the highway as it passes through Kanab. One or two make the effort to be distinctive, while the others rest safe in the knowledge that however bad they may be, there's precious little choice for a hundred miles in any direction.

Four Seasons Fifties-Style Restaurant 36 N 300 West ☎435/644-2415. Fun mock-'50s diner, with a 10¢ jukebox and a menu of burgers, sandwiches, and fried meats, with nothing stronger than copious malts and shakes to wash them down. Closes 7pm in winter.

Houston's Trails' End 32 E Center St ☎435/644-2488, ⓦwww.houstons.net. Western-themed family diner, serving chicken-fried steaks, ribs, fish, and fried breakfasts. Open daily for all meals, but closed mid-Nov to mid-March.

Nedra's Too 310 S 100 East ☎435/644-2030. Informal local hangout at the junction of US-89 and US-89A on the south side of town, with a sister restaurant in Fredonia (see p.141). The unifying factor of the Mexican/American menu is the fryer;

even the ice cream comes deep-fried. Open daily for all meals.

Parry Lodge 89 E Center St ☎435/644-2601. Attractive dining room where the menu occasionally hints at the healthy, in the form of dishes like poached salmon; unlike most places in Kanab, it has a license to sell alcohol. Open for all meals in summer, breakfast and dinner only in spring and fall, and closed Nov–March.

Rocking V Café 97 W Center St ☎435/644-8001. This valiant and largely successful bid to improve Kanab's culinary reputation is housed in a former bank, one of the town's oldest buildings. Classic French and Italian dishes for dinner at around $15 per entree; cheaper, lighter lunches. Open daily for lunch and dinner.

Pipe Spring National Monument

Thirteen miles west of Fredonia, just off AZ-389, **PIPE SPRING NATIONAL MONUMENT** (daily 8am–5pm; $5; free under age 16; ☎928/643-7105, ⓦwww.nps.gov/pisp) marks the site of one of the few water sources on the Arizona Strip. Not surprisingly, ownership of this precious spring has been much contested: It has spent time in both Utah and Arizona and belonged to three different counties. In 1863, Mormon rancher Dr James Whitmore appropriated it from the Paiutes, who knew it as *Mu-tum-wa-va*, or Dripping Rock. After Paiute and Navajo raiders killed Whitmore three years later, Brigham Young ordered the Mormons to withdraw. However, they returned in 1870 and enclosed the spring in a fort, named **Winsor Castle** for its first superintendent. Young personally dedicated the fort in a ceremony attended by John Wesley Powell.

In 1907, the federal government established the **Kaibab Paiute Indian Reservation**, which measured eighteen miles by twelve miles and included the spring. No provision was made concerning its water, however, and Mormon cattle ranchers continued to bring their herds here. The situation was further confused in 1923, when both spring and fort were designated as **Winsor Castle National Monument**, thanks to founding Park Service Director Stephen Mather, who had discovered its charms after his car broke down nearby. The idea was ostensibly to preserve the fort as a "memorial to Western pioneer life," though the declaration owed as much to the spring's position midway between the Grand Canyon and Zion National Park as to any intrinsic interest.

Bitter legal disputes between cattlemen, Paiutes, and the Park Service dragged on for another fifty years before water rights to Pipe Spring were largely granted to the Paiutes. By then, overgrazing had reduced the surrounding rich grassland to virtual desert. Local history debates endure. The Paiute argue that the fort was built to protect not so much valiant Mormon settlers from Indians as defiant polygamists from the government, and that the Mormon practice of recruiting Paiute into indentured servitude differed little from the earlier Navajo and Ute tradition of kidnapping them into slavery.

Considerable care has been taken to ensure the monument reflects both Paiute and Mormon history. The visitor center doubles as an interesting museum, whose staff can also advise you on local road conditions. The fort itself, a short walk away, remains in good condition and is open for half-hourly guided tours that illuminate early ranching life. An Ancestral Puebloan ruin said to lie beneath its outbuildings has yet to be excavated. With its small herd of longhorn cattle, scattered old wagons and farming implements, and long-range views across the desert, the monument is a pleasant enough spot, though you're unlikely to spend much time here.

A quarter-mile north of the monument, the Paiute run a small **campground** (☎928/643-7245), where sites run $5 per tent or $10 for RVs. At the peak of the 1990s Indian gaming boom, they also had a casino, but that's now defunct.

Colorado City

Continuing northwest from Pipe Spring, AZ-389 serves as the most direct route between the North Rim and I-15, which in turn connects Las Vegas and Salt Lake City. About a mile shy of the Utah border, a spur road to the right runs up to the renegade and notoriously polygamist Mormon community of **COLORADO CITY**. Set beneath the towering Vermilion Cliffs and devoid of either

Polygamy on the Arizona Strip

Although not officially founded until 1913, as **Short Creek**, Colorado City had long been an important Mormon settlement. After the Mormon Church disavowed **polygamy** in 1890, the Arizona Strip was a major refuge for recalcitrant polygamists. During the 1930s, Short Creek became the home of the Fundamentalist Church of Jesus Christ of Latter-Day Saints, who preached that by maintaining polygamy they were keeping true Mormonism alive. The community straddled the state line, making it easier to avoid outside investigation, as residents could simply cross between Arizona and Utah to avoid inquisitive police. Nonetheless, repeated state and federal inquiries culminated in the **Short Creek Raid** of 1953, when Arizona Governor Howard Pyle ordered a massive police sweep that saw 23 polygamist men hauled off for trial in Kingman.

Pyle's anti-polygamy campaign backfired, amid much negative publicity about separated families and children left without their fathers. Each of the accused menfolk of Short Creek received a year's probation, while Pyle lost his bid for reelection. To erase the name Short Creek from public memory, residents voted in 1958 to split the town in two, becoming **Colorado City** in Arizona, and **Hildale** in Utah.

The issue of polygamy in Colorado City has returned to the headlines in recent years, sparking furious political controversy in Arizona. Exposé after exposé has revealed the almost unbelievable truth that while Colorado City continues to benefit hugely from state and federal funding, it is run as the virtual fiefdom of a small group of Mormon polygamists. Until his death in 2002, the octogenarian self-styled "Prophet" Rulon Jeffs was its effective ruler. Not only did he assign the town's young women, often in their early teens, as brides to his middle-aged and already multiply married cronies – and conduct the wedding ceremonies himself – but he also presided over a system in which the young men, their own children, were run out of town as they came of age, so they could not become rival bridegrooms.

Rulon's son Warren, who succeeded him as Prophet and is said to have "inherited" around sixty of his wives, is thought to remain in control of the community, despite having fled town in 2004. The town's police and sheriff have shown marked reluctance to intervene and are widely believed to be close Warren associates. A federal warrant for Warren's arrest was issued in June 2005, on charges of sexual conduct with a minor and conspiracy to commit sexual conduct with a minor, and he has subsequently landed on the FBI's Ten Most Wanted list. As this book went to press, he was thought to be hiding out, along with many of the town's menfolk, in associated polygamist communities in either Texas or British Columbia.

accommodation or dining options, this is a surreal-looking place, laid out on a small grid of extremely broad, largely unpaved streets that see very few cars but plenty of gingham pinafores. On every corner stand massive homes built to shelter multiple wives and their predictably large families, and since much of the male population is either on the run or has been hounded out of town (see box above), you're likely to see only female faces. As young women are forbidden to cut their hair before marriage, most flaunt extraordinary swept-back coifs. Everyone will assume you're a magazine journalist hoping to write a sensational article about polygamy, and there's no encouragement to linger.

Toroweap

The Arizona Strip holds one tremendous prize for visitors prepared to venture off the paved highways: **Toroweap Point**, the only place where you can drive to the very lip of the canyon's Granite Gorge and peer down sheer 3000ft cliffs

△ The long dirt road to Toroweap nears its end

to the Colorado River. As the crow flies, the overlook lies less than sixty miles west of Bright Angel Point, the North Rim tourism hub. By road, however, it's nearly 150 miles, as you first must circumvent Kanab Canyon by heading all the way north to Fredonia.

Is it worth it? An unequivocal yes – Toroweap is not just another overlook. However, don't underestimate the amount of time and effort it takes to get there. Even a fleeting visit requires at least six hours of laborious driving on gravel roads.

There are two main routes: the eastern **Sunshine Route**, which starts on AZ-389 seven miles west of **Fredonia** and runs for 61 miles southwest, and the more scenic but longer western **Main Street Route**, which runs ninety miles from the heart of **St George**, Utah, but is closed by snow for much of the winter. What follows is the obvious east-west road trip itinerary, starting from Fredonia and returning via St George. A third possibility, the sixty-mile **Clayhole Route** from Colorado City, is not recommended, since it's less convenient for onward travel and liable to become impassable not only during wet weather, but also, thanks to drifting sand, during prolonged dry spells.

When open – typically year-round in the case of the Sunshine Route – these roads are generally passable in standard vehicles. Four-wheel-drive is only necessary in spots over the last few miles; if you don't have 4WD, you can always park and hike the final stretch to the overlooks. Be sure to ask locally about current driving conditions before you set off; the best sources are the visitor centers in Fredonia and Jacob Lake, at Pipe Spring, and on the North Rim. In addition, carry all the food, water, and gas you might need, plus a spare tire and emergency repair kit for your vehicle.

Sunshine Route

The **Sunshine Route** to Toroweap begins with a turn south off AZ-389 onto **BLM road 109**, seven miles west of Fredonia. This is a broad, well-surfaced gravel road, albeit subject to "washboarding" (becoming corrugated with

President Bill Clinton flew to the Toroweap Valley by helicopter on January 11, 2000, to designate the vast **Grand Canyon–Parashant National Monument**, which covers more than a million acres of northwestern Arizona. Such presidential proclamations skirt the usual legal requirements for public discussion and approval by state legislators; Theodore Roosevelt used the same strategy when he proclaimed the original Grand Canyon National Monument back in 1908. Both the governor of Arizona and the majority of its congressional delegation opposed the Clinton move.

The monument borders the Nevada state line to the west and the Virgin River drainage to the east and northeast. To the south, it either abuts **Grand Canyon National Park** at or near the canyon rim or meets and shares jurisdiction with the **Lake Mead National Recreation Area**. The **Bureau of Land Management** manages the 808,000 of its acres that lie outside the Lake Mead NRA, while the **National Park Service** oversees the rest. It's also dotted with parcels of Arizona state land, a few private landholdings, and several designated wilderness areas.

The point of creating Grand Canyon–Parashant was not to increase tourist visitation, but to preserve this little-known region's archeological, geologic, and natural resources. The new monument straddles the boundary between two major geologic provinces: the "basin and range" country to the west and the Colorado Plateau to the east. Its central feature, the **Shivwits Plateau**, is the westernmost segment of the Colorado Plateau, which descends the dramatic escarpment of the **Grand Wash Cliffs** on its western edge to meet the eastern **Mohave Desert**. While boasting a rich fossil record, it remains home to many rare animal and plant species; some sections have been set aside as sanctuaries for **desert tortoises**, and the **Californian condor** release program (see p.53) has been active here too. Although few visitors are aware the monument even exists, ecologists insist it has effectively doubled the reach of Grand Canyon National Park by protecting the broader canyon ecosystem.

While human presence here has ranged from early hunters to Ancestral Puebloans and Mormon ranchers, the region remains all but uninhabited and only minimally exploited. The new monument is obliged to respect existing grazing and hunting rights, but no new mining or geothermal activity will be permitted.

Very few roads penetrate the monument, and none of them is paved. With a high-clearance 4WD vehicle, it's possible to visit remote western Grand Canyon viewpoints such as Whitmore Point, Twin Point, and Kelly Point, though all entail demanding multi-day expeditions for which you'll need demonstrated survival skills. Before setting off, contact the visitor centers in Kanab or Fredonia or check **online** at ⓦ www.az.blm.gov/natmon2.htm.

bone-jarring undulations), that passes through a succession of open valleys first recorded by the Domínguez and Escalante party of 1776 (see p.135). Much of the country here is rangeland, grazed within an inch of its life. You don't see so much as a tree during the first hour and precious little vegetation thereafter.

Thirty miles in, the road leaves the plain and enters a range of smooth volcanic cinder cones. Ten miles farther, it meets **BLM road 5** – the aforementioned Clayhole Route – coming down from Colorado City. The final thirteen miles south to the national park lie just within the eastern boundary of **Grand Canyon–Parashant National Monument**. Halfway along, BLM road 5 veers west toward Mount Trumbull, while **BLM road 115** continues to Toroweap.

Tuweep

A sign about six miles short of Toroweap Point welcomes visitors to the **Tuweep Area** of Grand Canyon National Park. While the conspicuous roadside ranger station immediately beyond is unreachable by phone and not open set hours, a ranger is in residence year-round, though not always available on-site.

From this point to the overlook is by far the roughest stretch of the drive. Allow about two hours to reach the ranger station from the highway, then another half-hour to nurse your protesting vehicle to the canyon rim. A mile before road's end, you'll reach the Park Service's exposed **primitive campground**, which offers ten first-come, first-served sites. Reservations are accepted for the lone group site (☎928/638-7870). Fires are allowed, but you have to bring your own firewood, and you'll find composting toilets but no water. **No fee** is charged for day use or overnights at the campground, but you do need to buy a **backcountry camping** permit in advance (see p.92).

Incidentally, although the Paiute terms *Tuweep* and *Toroweap* are used more or less interchangeably in these parts, strictly speaking, Toroweap, which means "dry valley," is applied to a valley, the geologic fault that created that valley, a geologic strata within the larger canyon, and an overlook, while Tuweep, meaning "the earth," referred first to a Mormon settlement in the valley and now to this district of the park.

Toroweap Overlook

What doesn't quite sink in until you reach road's end at Toroweap is that this is an utterly unique segment of the Grand Canyon. Elsewhere you'll find effectively two canyons in one: mighty rim-side cliffs that tower over a broad plateau, and the deep, narrow chasm that holds the Colorado River. Here, thanks to volcanic action along the **Toroweap Fault**, that high outer rim is absent on the north side of the river, and the road follows the **Toroweap Valley** right to the brink of the inner Granite Gorge. From the overlook, it's therefore possible to gaze straight down on the river.

The **Toroweap Overlook** occupies a wide, rocky crest that holds a couple of picnic tables. If you're used to viewpoints farther east, you may find it hard to believe you've arrived at the Grand Canyon, as there's not a butte, pyramid, labyrinthine spur, or mesa in sight. You'll soon be convinced, however, when you inch to the southern edge of the parking lot, where the ground abruptly drops 3000ft from your toes. While the river is visible on its approach from the east and retreat to the west, it passes so directly below the point that in places you may have to lie full length and peep over the edge to see it.

At 4600ft, Toroweap is the lowest rim overlook in the national park. Soaring thousands of feet higher, the opposite cliffs belong to the Hualapai Indian Reservation (see p.183).

Lava Falls Overlook

A five-minute hike over the boulder-strewn hilltop west of the Toroweap Overlook – there's no fixed trail – leads to the stupendous west-facing **Lava Falls Overlook**. Here, the view of the river, interspersed with mighty white rapids and turning from green to blue as it recedes toward the horizon, is so spellbinding that you may initially overlook the most awesome feature of the landscape. Straight ahead, a few hundred feet below eye level, a colossal black **lava cascade** spills over the North Rim and down to within a few feet of the Colorado.

This flow bears witness to some of the most dramatic episodes in the canyon's history. On at least eight separate occasions, **volcanic eruptions** on the adjacent Esplanade Plateau have filled the Grand Canyon to a depth of as much as 2330ft, thus **blocking the Colorado**. The largest flow, about 1.2 million

△ A bird's eye view of the inner gorge from the Toroweap Overlook

years ago, created the long-vanished **Prospect Dam**, which backed up the river in a lake that stretched all the way east to Lees Ferry; geologists estimate it would have taken about 23 years to fill to the brim. Eventually, the Colorado spilled over the top and gradually wore away the dam. Vestiges of such events – the most recent was around 140,000 years ago – are visible at various heights on the canyon walls and make it possible to work out the speed at which the canyon deepens.

The same flow that dammed the canyon also filled a number of side canyons up to the brim, including **Prospect Canyon**, south of the river, and **Toroweap Valley** here. That explains why the valley cuts such a low profile and why the road runs flat all the way to the rim. Capping the ancient valley mouth is **Vulcan's Throne**, a 567ft cinder cone, which blocks any water that flows down the valley; in the wake of heavy rains, a small lake forms on its north side.

Below, a solitary black basalt column known as **Vulcan's Anvil** rises forty feet from the middle of the river. This formation cues rafters to the approach of **Lava Falls Rapid**, a fearsome torrent created by debris washed down from Prospect Canyon. From the overlook, you can both see the rapid and hear its roar. Until a flash flood radically restructured Crystal Rapid in 1966 (see p.201), Lava Falls was generally recognized as the most difficult white-water challenge in the canyon.

Main Street Route

Though described here as an alternative route from Toroweap back to civilization, the **Main Street Route** is also the most direct path to Toroweap if you're approaching from the west; its terminus, **St George**, Utah, lies on I-15 between Las Vegas and Salt Lake City. A spectacular ninety-mile, three-hour desert drive on gravel roads, Main Street is straightforward in summer, but liable to be closed altogether in winter.

From the Tuweep ranger station, drive 7.5 miles north, then turn left onto **BLM road 5**. You'll climb west into the **Uinkaret Mountains**, the volcanic field responsible for all those eruptions. *Uinkaret* is a Paiute word meaning "place of pines"; you'll see why ten miles along, when you reach the high, pine-forested saddle between **Mount Logan** to the south and 8026ft **Mount Trumbull** to the north. In the late nineteenth century, timber was shipped from here north to construct the Mormon Temple at St George. Five miles farther, you'll crest a final ridge before a hair-raising descent into the huge **Hurricane Valley**.

Within but not part of Grand Canyon–Parashant National Monument, Hurricane Valley was once home to a Mormon ranching and mining community. Founded by Abraham Bundy in 1916 as **Mount Trumbull**, it was universally known as "Bundyville," as most of its peak population of almost three hundred inhabitants seemed to be Bundys. Within fifty years, the settlement was driven out of existence, partly by drought and partly because improved roads and vehicles meant ranchers could live in St George and commute to their land.

The flat, desolate crossroads at the heart of the valley holds the last remaining vestige of Bundyville, the **Mount Trumbull Schoolhouse**, which is generally open during daylight hours. Built in 1922, the schoolhouse burned to the ground in 2000 but has since been rebuilt from scratch; displays include old schoolbooks and scores of photos of Bundys.

Turn right at the schoolhouse to remain on BLM road 5. Head due north, on what eventually becomes **BLM road 1069**, and after another 49 miles, past the dramatic **Wolf Hole Valley** and down into eerie gray badlands beside the **Mokaac Wash**, you'll reach the sanctuary of a paved road in suburban St George.

6

Flagstaff and Route 66

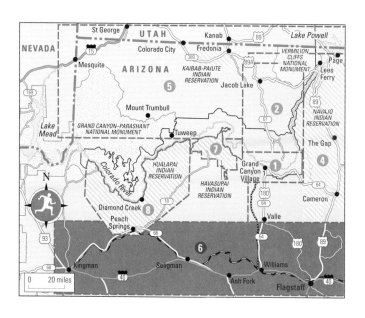

CHAPTER 6

Highlights

* **DuBeau and Grand Canyon International Hostels** These sister hostels in downtown Flagstaff offer budget travelers bargain lodging and cut-rate canyon tours. See p.157

* **Monte Vista** Characterful old Western hotel with attractive rooms and a lively downstairs bar. See p.157

* **Downtown Flagstaff** Bisected by Route 66 and the Santa Fe Railroad, Flagstaff's bustling downtown abounds with Western atmosphere. See p.157

* **Museum of Northern Arizona** Just outside Flagstaff, this superb museum explains the history and geography of the Colorado Plateau in fascinating detail. See p.157

* **Wupatki National Monument** From these remarkably complete thousand-year-old pueblos in the remote desert, ancient astronomers plotted solar calendars. See p.162

* **Walnut Canyon National Monument** Extraordinary site east of Flagstaff, where the Sinagua people carved hundreds of homes into the canyon walls. See p.164

* **Pine Country Restaurant** The pies at this central Williams diner will leave your jaw dropping ... and then munching furiously. See p.167

* **Seligman** Soak up genuine Route 66 ambience in this time-forgotten desert outpost. See p.167

△ *Museum Club*, on Route 66 in Flagstaff

6

Flagstaff and Route 66

Thanks to the region's forbidding terrain, of which the Grand Canyon is merely the most extreme example, Arizona's northernmost hundred miles remain largely impassable to east-west traffic. That makes **I-40**, which runs pretty much straight across the state roughly sixty miles south of the canyon, a crucial lifeline. Before the interstate was pushed through, the legendary **Route 66** followed much the same path; before either road, there was the Santa Fe Railroad; and before the railroad arrived, little more than a century ago, there were no significant Anglo settlements in the region.

The pick of the various communities along this corridor that compete to serve as "gateways" for Grand Canyon travelers is unquestionably the college town of **Flagstaff**. Set amid the world's largest forest of sweet-smelling **ponderosa pines** – lumber from which provided the basis for the region's nineteenth-century pioneer economy – it ranks among the Southwest's most appealing small towns, while the deserts just east of town hold the intriguing ancient sites of **Wupatki** and **Walnut Canyon**.

While **Williams**, just over 30 miles west, is closer to the canyon and serves as the starting point for excursion trains up to the South Rim, it's unlikely to hold your attention for any length of time. Farther west, both **Ash Fork** and **Seligman** are tiny desert outposts, while the larger **Kingman** lacks much sense of identity. That said, all of these places thrived on tourism during the heyday of **Route 66**, and driving through any one of them can always bring on a frisson of that era's romance.

Flagstaff

Northern Arizona's liveliest and most attractive town, **FLAGSTAFF** occupies a dramatic location beneath the San Francisco Peaks, halfway between New Mexico and California. Straddling I-40 and I-17, it's a major way station for tourists en route to the Grand Canyon, about eighty miles northwest, and a worthwhile destination in its own right.

Downtown, where few buildings rise more than three stories, oozes Wild West charm. Its main thoroughfare, Santa Fe Avenue, was once part of **Route**

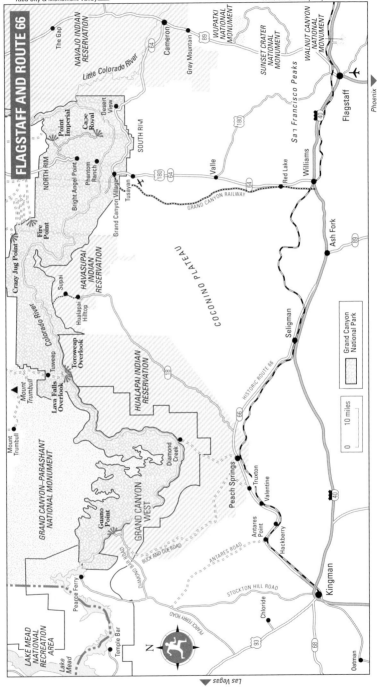

FLAGSTAFF AND ROUTE 66

66, while before that it was the pioneer trail west. Its few central blocks are gloriously evocative of the past, though these days the diners and saloons are interspersed with outdoor outfitters and coffee bars, and the local cowboys and Indians share the sidewalks with liberal-minded students from Northern Arizona University. Adding to the atmosphere, the tracks of the Santa Fe Railroad still run through downtown, so life here remains punctuated both day and night by the mournful wail of passing trains.

Flagstaff's first settlers arrived in 1876, lured from Boston by widely publicized accounts of mineral wealth and fertile land. Although they soon moved on, disappointed, toward Prescott, they stayed long enough to celebrate the centenary of American independence by flying the Stars and Stripes from a towering pine tree. This flagpole became a familiar landmark on the route west, and as the town grew, it inevitably became known as Flagstaff. Right from the start it was a cosmopolitan place, welcoming Navajo and Hopi traders from the nearby reservations and a strong black and Hispanic workforce in the (originally Mormon-owned) lumber mills and cattle industry.

Modern Flagstaff, with a population just over fifty thousand, makes an ideal base for travelers. You'll find abundant hotels, restaurants, bars, and shops within easy walking distance of downtown, food and lodging chain outlets along the interstates slightly farther afield, as well as hostels and diners that cater to budget travelers. The area also hosts a couple of good museums, ancient cultural sites, and wonderful scenery. Just one word of warning: The altitude here is almost 7000ft, which means the nights may well be colder than you'd expect. It can even snow in July.

Arrival, information, and getting around

While the Santa Fe Railroad still hauls freight, Amtrak's daily **Southwest Chief**, between Chicago and Los Angeles, is now the only passenger **train** that stops at Flagstaff's venerable wooden stationhouse, in the heart of town. In summer, the eastbound service leaves at 5.01am for Albuquerque and the westbound at 8.57pm for Los Angeles; winter times are one hour later.

Open Road Tours & Transportation (℡928/226-8060 or 1-877/226-8060, ⓦwww.openroadtours.com), based at the Amtrak station, runs twice-daily **bus service** via Williams to the Grand Canyon. The first bus leaves Flagstaff at 8.30am, the second at 3pm; the one-way fare is $27 for adults, and $19 for children 11 and under. Open Road also offers tours to Sedona and Monument Valley and around Flagstaff itself, as well as five daily **buses** between Flagstaff and **Phoenix** ($39). As detailed below, two local hostels, the *DuBeau* and the *Grand Canyon*, can arrange inexpensive excursions to the Grand Canyon and Sedona. Greyhound, a few blocks south of downtown at 399 S Malpais Lane (℡928/774-4573 or 1-800/231-2222), runs four daily buses to Phoenix and also heads east toward Albuquerque and west to Las Vegas, LA, San Diego, and San Francisco.

Flagstaff's helpful **visitor center** occupies half of the Amtrak stationhouse at 1 E Route 66 (Mon–Sat 8am–5pm, Sun 9am–4pm; ℡928/774-9541 or 1-800/842-7293, ⓦwww.flagstaffarizona.org). Even when it's not staffed, the building remains open for rail passengers, so visitors can still pick up brochures and **discount coupons** for local motels. You'll also find a courtesy phone in the Amtrak lobby for making hotel and hostel reservations (daily 8am–5pm).

The least expensive **car rental** agency is Budget, 175 W Aspen Ave (℡928/813-0156); Avis, Hertz, Enterprise, and National also have outlets.

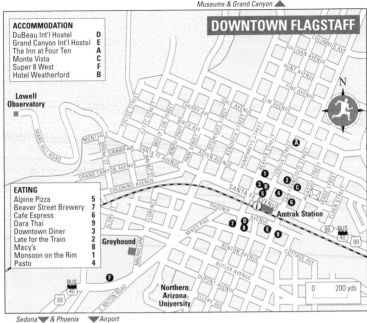

DOWNTOWN FLAGSTAFF

ACCOMMODATION

DuBeau Int'l Hostel	D
Grand Canyon Int'l Hostel	E
The Inn at Four Ten	A
Monte Vista	C
Super 8 West	F
Hotel Weatherford	B

Lowell Observatory

EATING

Alpine Pizza	5
Beaver Street Brewery	7
Cafe Espress	6
Dara Thai	9
Downtown Diner	3
Late for the Train	2
Macy's	8
Monsoon on the Rim	1
Pasto	4

Greyhound

Amtrak Station

Northern Arizona University

Sedona ▼ & Phoenix   ▼ Airport

0   200 yds

Absolute Bikes, 18 N San Francisco St (open daily; ☎928/779-5969, ⓦwww .absolutebikes.net), rents **mountain bikes** at $35 for the first day and $20 for subsequent days, while Arizona Mountain Bike Tours (☎928/779-4161 or 1-800/277-7985) runs local and regional **cycling tours**. Perhaps the best of several local **outfitters** offering equipment for outdoor activities and backpacking expeditions is Aspen Sports, 15 N San Francisco St (☎928/779-1935 or 1-800/771-1935).

Accommodation

As Flagstaff is considerably more than just another interstate pit stop, its dozens of **motels** and **B&Bs** get away with charging higher rates than its I-40 neighbors. They're still not bad value, however, and **budget** travelers can choose between two hostels, as well as a historic hotel that offers hostel-style dorm beds as well as private rooms. Most of the major chain motels are clustered well to the east, along Butler Avenue and Lucky Lane, but staying close to downtown is much more fun. It's worth knowing that if you do manage to find a room where the lonesome whistle of freight trains doesn't wake you up in the night, it's unlikely to be anywhere near Flagstaff.

If you arrive without a reservation, use the free **courtesy phones** in the visitor center (see p.155) to compare options. Above all, plan ahead on summer weekends, when the town is likely to be booked solid.

The best local **campground** lies three miles south on US-89A, at *Fort Tuthill County Park* (May–Sept; ☎928/774-3464), though Flagstaff also holds the year-round Flagstaff/Grand Canyon KOA at 5803 N AZ-89A (☎928/526-9926 or 1-800/562-3524, ⓦwww.koa.com/az/flagstaff).

DuBeau International Hostel 19 W Phoenix Ave ☎928/774-6731 or 1-800/398-7112, ⓦwww .dubeauhostel.com. Welcoming independent hostel just south of the tracks, whose appealingly converted en suite motel rooms serve as four-person dorms at $18 per bed or private doubles at $38 Sun–Thurs or $41 Fri & Sat. Internet access is available, and breakfast is free, but the common areas can get noisy at times. The *DuBeau* offers the same program of tours as its sister property, the *Grand Canyon International Hostel* (see below). Closed Nov–Feb. ❶/❷

Grand Canyon International Hostel 19 S San Francisco St ☎928/779-9421 or 1-888/442-2696, ⓦwww.grandcanyonhostel.com. Independent hostel, under the same friendly management as the similar nearby *DuBeau*, that offers dorm beds at $18 in summer or $16 in winter and six private rooms priced at $32–39, depending on the season and day of the week. Provides tours to the Grand Canyon (Mon, Wed, Fri & Sat, plus Tues in summer only; $55) and Sedona (Thurs & Sun; $25), as well as car rental discounts. ❶/❷

Holiday Inn 2320 E Lucky Lane ☎928/714-1000, ⓦwww.holidayinnflagstaff.com. Large motel in a rather characterless area just off the interstate, with a handful of nearby diners. Winter ❹, summer ❺

The Inn at Four Ten 410 N Leroux St ☎928/774-0088 or 1-800/774-2008, ⓦwww .inn410.com. Bright ranch home operating as a luxurious antique-furnished B&B; all nine rooms are en suite, most with fireplaces and three with whirlpool tubs. On summer evenings, the porch and patio make welcoming, convivial retreats. ❼

Little America 2515 E Butler Ave ☎928/779-7900 or 1-800/865-1399, ⓦwww.flagstaff .littleamerica.com. Large motel-cum-resort near the interstate, where the 1950s-style ambience conceals a higher standard of accommodation than you might expect. Good pool. ❺

Monte Vista 100 N San Francisco St ☎928/779-6971 or 1-800/545-3068, ⓦwww.hotelmontevista .com. Attractive landmark 1920s hotel in the heart of downtown. The assorted restored rooms, with and without attached bathrooms, are named for celebrity guests, from Bob Hope to Michael Stipe. Many of the guests are young international travelers, drawn by the local nightlife, including the hotel's own bar (see p.160). Weekend rates rise by as much as $20. ❸–❺

Super 8 Motel 3725 N Kasper Ave ☎928/526-0818 or 1-888/324-9131, ⓦwww.dknhotels.com. Decent budget motel four miles east of downtown, right where Route 66 joins US-89. Winter ❸, summer ❹

Super 8 West 602 W Route 66; ☎928/774-4581 or 1-800/654-4667, ⓦwww.dknhotels.com. Attractive chain motel centered on an enclosed swimming pool, adjacent to a Barnes & Noble bookstore less than a mile southwest of downtown, just past the US-89 turnoff toward Sedona. Winter ❸, summer ❹

Hotel Weatherford 23 N Leroux St ☎928/779-1919, ⓦwww.weatherfordhotel.com. Attractive old downtown hotel, with elegant wooden fittings, which bit by bit is restoring its fading rooms to offer tasteful though basic accommodation, without telephones or TVs. The upstairs lounge offers Wild West ambience, but can make for a noisy night. ❹

The Town

Flagstaff's longstanding **downtown** stretches for a few redbrick blocks north of the railroad. Filled with cafés, bars, and stores that hawk Route 66 souvenirs and Native American crafts, as well as outfitters that specialize in tents, clothing, and all sorts of contraptions for outdoor adventures, it's a fun place to wander around, even if it holds no significant tourist attractions. Although the visitor center suggests several walking tours, few specific buildings are especially historic; by the time you've browsed a few bookstores, downed a few coffees, and peeped into the old *Weatherford* and *Monte Vista* hotels, you may well be ready to move on. Your most lasting impression is likely to be of the magnificent volcanic **San Francisco Peaks**, which rise to a jagged crest from the plains on the northern horizon.

Museum of Northern Arizona

The exceptional **Museum of Northern Arizona**, three miles northwest of downtown on US-180, rivals Phoenix's Heard Museum as the state's best and is an essential stop for any first-time visitor to the Colorado Plateau (daily 9am–5pm; $5

△ *Monte Vista*, downtown Flagstaff

adults, $2 under age 18; ☎928/774-5213, ⓦwww.musnaz.org).Although it covers local geology, geography, flora, and fauna and explores various theories regarding the Grand Canyon's origins, the museum's main focus is **Native American** life. It provides an excellent run-through of the region's Ancestral Puebloan past, as well as contemporary Navajo, Havasupai, Zuni, and Hopi culture, from an overview in the initial gallery followed by rooms devoted to pots, rugs, Hopi kachina dolls, and silver and turquoise jewelry. It also offers temporary shows of local (not always Native American) arts and crafts, a well-stocked bookstore, and a **nature trail** that skirts the adjacent small piñon-fringed canyon.

Since its founding in 1928, the museum has actively encouraged development of traditional and new skills among Native American craftspeople. The exquisite inlaid silver jewelry now made by the Hopi, for example, stems from a museum-backed program to find work for Hopi servicemen returning from World War II. During its annual Native American Marketplaces, every item is for sale; the **Hopi** show is held on the weekend closest to July 4, the **Navajo** one at the start of August.

For details on **Museum of Northern Arizona Ventures**, an extensive program of tours and expeditions, including multi-day Grand Canyon trips, check on the museum's website.

Pioneer Museum

Off US-180, closer to town than the Museum of Northern Arizona, an impressive steam train marks the **Pioneer Museum** (Mon–Sat 9am–5pm; donation; ☎928/774-6272, ⓦwww.arizonahistoricalsociety.org). Run by the Arizona Historical Society and housed in the onetime county hospital, the museum holds a random but reasonably entertaining assortment of objects and images from old Flagstaff.

Sharing the same grounds, the **Coconino Center for the Arts** is a gallery and concert hall specializing in works by local artists, while the adjacent **Art Barn** cooperative (daily 9am–5pm) sells a wide selection of crafts.

Lowell Observatory

Flagstaff's **Lowell Observatory**, in the pine forest atop Mars Hill, a mile west of downtown, is renowned as the place where the existence of the planet Pluto was first confirmed. Many of the necessary calculations were performed by Dr Percival Lowell, who founded the observatory in 1894 and deluded himself that he'd discovered canals on Mars. Lowell died in 1916 and is buried in a small domed mausoleum of blue glass on the hilltop. It wasn't until 1930 that Clyde Tombaugh actually spotted the ninth planet.

From the **visitor center** (daily: May–Oct 9am–5pm, Feb–March noon–5pm; $5 adults, $2 under age 18; ☎928/774-3358, ⓦwww.lowell.edu), where only the most technically minded visitors are likely to get much joy from playing with computers or watching explanatory videos, the **Pluto Walk** footpath climbs to the tiny original observatory. Signs tick off the relative positions of the planets; to show the position of the nearest star, Alpha Centauri, the display would have to extend more than six hundred miles, beyond Boise, Idaho.

Astronomy remains a passion in Flagstaff, and the town has won awards for minimizing nighttime light pollution. The observatory reopens most evenings for **stargazing sessions** (June–Aug Mon–Sat 8pm; Sept–May Wed, Fri & Sat 7.30pm; no additional charge).

Eating

Though surprisingly short of high-end **restaurants**, central Flagstaff more than compensates with its lively assortment of both old-style Western **diners** and eclectic **budget** options. Thanks to all those students, the area around San Francisco Street, both north and south of the tracks, is filled with vegetarian cafés and espresso bars.

Alpine Pizza 7 N Leroux St ☎928/779-4109. Raucous downtown student hangout, with decent pizzas and lots of different beers. Mon–Sat 11.30am–2pm & 5–11pm, Sun 5–11pm.

Black Bart's 2760 E Butler Ave ☎928/779-3142. Enjoyable Western-themed steakhouse, across from *Little America* on the east edge of town, with a waitstaff that sings and dances onstage between servings of barbecued steak, ribs, and chicken ($18–26). Daily 5–10pm.

Café Espress 16 N San Francisco St ☎928/774-0541. Great vegetarian breakfasts, then salads, sandwiches, and veggie specials for the rest of the day, plus espresso. Mon, Tues & Sun 7am–3pm, Wed–Sat 7am–9pm.

Charly's Pub & Grill *Hotel Weatherford*, 23 N Leroux St ☎928/779-1919. Café-restaurant in a classy Western setting, serving good, inexpensive meals accompanied by live music (cocktail piano at lunch, bands at night). Sun–Thurs 7am–10pm, Fri & Sat 7am–1am.

Dara Thai 14 S San Francisco St ☎928/774-0047. Large Thai place just south of the tracks, where the service is great and a plate of delicious pad Thai noodles costs just $7 at lunch, $9 at dinner. Mon–Sat 11am–10pm, Sun noon–9pm.

Downtown Diner 7 E Aspen Ave ☎928/774-3492. Classic Route 66 diner a block north of the main drag, featuring leatherette booths and hefty burgers and sandwiches. Mon–Sat 7am–9pm, Sun noon–8pm.

Late for the Train 107 N San Francisco St ☎928/779-5975. Little coffee bar opposite the *Monte Vista* hotel that serves excellent house-roasted coffee and pastries to a slightly older, literary crowd. Mon–Thurs 6am–6pm, Fri 6am–10pm, Sat 7am–10pm, Sun 7am–5pm.

Macy's European Coffee House & Bakery 14 S Beaver St ☎928/774-2243. Not merely superb coffee, but heavenly pastries to go with it, in a chaotic but friendly student-oriented atmosphere. Substantial vegetarian dishes include black bean pizza and even couscous for breakfast. You'll also find free wireless Internet and an adjacent coin laundry. Daily 6am–10pm.

Monsoon on the Rim 6 E Aspen Ave ☎928/226-8844. This pan-Asian, sushi-centered restaurant, with huge plate-glass windows in a modern mall-like development in the heart of town, clearly has more to do with the new West than the Old West. While pretty good rather than wonderful, the food is surprisingly cheap, with most of the Thai and Chinese options priced under $10, and the people-watching is fun. Daily 11.30am–9pm.

Pasto 19 E Aspen Ave ☎928/779-1937. Downtown Italian joint, with pasta specials and chicken, shrimp, and vegetarian entrees for

$14–19. Mon–Thurs & Sun 11.30am–2.30pm & 5–9pm, Fri & Sat 11.30am–2.30pm & 5–9.30pm.

Nightlife

Milling with international travelers in summer and students the rest of the year, Flagstaff is the liveliest **nightspot** between Las Vegas and Santa Fe. Wander a block or two to either side of San Francisco Street downtown, and you can't go wrong. Besides the *Monte Vista Lounge*, hotel bars that feature live music include both the *Exchange Pub* and the upstairs *Zane Grey Ballroom* at the *Weatherford*.

Beaver Street Brewery & Whistle Stop Café 11 S Beaver St ☎928/779-0079. Popular microbrewery that also serves inventive and inexpensive food, with an outdoor summer barbecue in the beer garden. Daily 11.30am–midnight.

Flagstaff Brewing Company 16 E I-40 ☎928/773-1442. Bustling downtown pub, with outdoor seating, big windows, and live music Wed–Sat.

The Mad Italian 101 S San Francisco St ☎928/779-1820. Highly sociable downtown bar with several pool tables.

Monte Vista Lounge *Monte Vista*, 100 N San

Francisco St ☎928/779-6971. Hip little bar and dance club in the basement of a venerable old hotel, with DJs on weekdays and live music of all kinds on weekends.

The Museum Club 3404 E Route 66 ☎928/526-9434, ⓦwww.museumclub.com. A real oddity, this log-cabin taxidermy museum, popularly known as "The Zoo," somehow transmogrified into a classic Route 66 roadhouse, saloon, and country music venue that's a second home to hordes of dancing cowboys. Open daily noon–1am. Call ☎928/774-4444 for free shuttle service to and from your motel.

Around Flagstaff

Dominated by the striking **San Francisco Peaks**, the Flagstaff region is extraordinarily rich in natural and archeological wonders. Three national monuments – **Sunset Crater Volcano**, **Wupatki**, and **Walnut Canyon** – lie within 25 miles, all generally regarded as day trips from town; only Sunset Crater offers a campground.

San Francisco Peaks

North of Flagstaff, the **San Francisco Volcanic Field** comprises more than six hundred distinct cinder cones that have formed over the past two million years. During that time, glacial ice also sheathed the region on three separate occasions, shaving around 3000ft off the top of the volcanoes.

Capped by 12,643ft **Humphreys Peak** and visible from downtown Flagstaff, the serrated **SAN FRANCISCO PEAKS** are the remnants of a single ancient mountain. Spanish missionaries named the peaks in honor of St Francis of Assisi, although the Hopi already knew the range as *Nuvatukya'ovi*, home of the kachina spirits, and the Navajo referred to it as *Dook'o'ooslííd*, one of four sacred mountains. Seen from afar, wreathed in a semipermanent layer of clouds, it's obvious why the Hopi and Navajo regarded these mountains as the source of life-giving rain. The Hopi still make annual pilgrimages on foot from their mesas, 65 miles east, to hidden shrines in the upper reaches. Ironically, it is precisely because they were sacred to both tribes that the peaks now belong to neither; federal law dictates that Native American reservations can only include lands of which a tribe can prove it has "exclusive use."

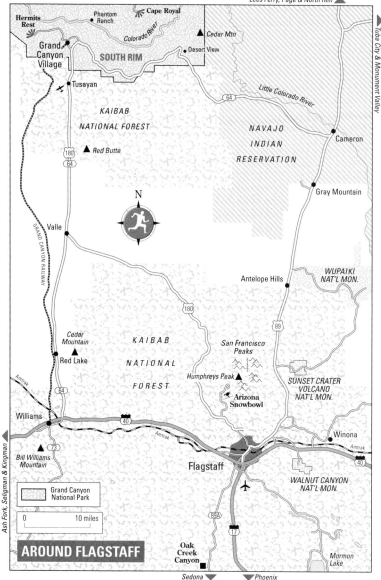

Lees Ferry, Page & North Rim ▲

Tuba City & Monument Valley ▶

Hermits Rest

Phantom Ranch

Cape Royal

Colorado River

Grand Canyon Village

SOUTH RIM

Cedar Mtn ▲

Desert View ●

Tusayan ●

Little Colorado River

64

KAIBAB

NATIONAL FOREST

NAVAJO

INDIAN

RESERVATION

Cameron ●

Red Butte ▲

180
64

N

Gray Mountain ●

Valle ●

GRAND CANYON RAILWAY

Antelope Hills ●

WUPATKI NAT'L MON.

180

89

Cedar Mountain

Red Lake ●

K A I B A B

N A T I O N A L

F O R E S T

San Francisco Peaks

Humphreys Peak ▲

Arizona Snowbowl

SUNSET CRATER VOLCANO NAT'L MON.

Amtrak

64

Williams ●

40

Amtrak

Winona ●

Amtrak

40

Bill Williams Mountain ▲ 73

Ash Fork, Seligman & Kingman ◀

Flagstaff

WALNUT CANYON NAT'L MON.

Grand Canyon National Park

0   10 miles

89A

17

AROUND FLAGSTAFF

Oak Creek Canyon ■

Mormon Lake

Sedona ▼   ▼ Phoenix

Arizona Snowbowl

While the San Francisco Peaks have lain dormant more than 220,000 years, the time may come when the gods decide that the **Arizona Snowbowl**, Flagstaff's own **ski resort**, is a desecration no longer to be tolerated. For the moment it survives, nestled between Humphreys and Agassiz peaks at the end of a seven-mile spur road north of US-180 and featuring such ski runs as Boo-

Boo and Bambi. There's not enough water up here to make artificial snow – an early name for the peaks was the **Sierra Sinagua**, or "waterless range" – so the season typically runs from mid-December through early April. That may change if the Forest Service is permitted to make snow here using treated wastewater from Flagstaff's municipal sewage system; Hopi and Navajo tribal leaders consider the plan a violation of sacred lands.

The *Ski Lift Lodge* provides both food and cabin lodgings (☎928/774-0729, or 1-800/472-3599 from Arizona and California only; Mon–Thurs & Sun ❹, Fri & Sat ❺), while lift tickets cost $44 for a full day (9am–4pm) or $36 for the afternoon. For more information, call ☎928/779-1951 or visit ⓦwww.arizonasnowbowl.com.

In summer, the longest of the Snowbowl's five chairlifts, which climbs to within a few hundred feet of the 12,350ft summit of Mount Agassiz, remains open as the **Scenic Skyride** (mid-May to mid-Sept daily 10am–4pm, mid-Sept to mid-Oct Fri–Sun 10am–4pm; $10 adults, $6 under age 13). To protect the fragile vegetation, onward hiking is prohibited, but you'll find plenty of other day-use **trails** in these mountains. One switchbacks to the summit of Mount Humphreys for seventy-mile views to the Grand Canyon and beyond.

Sunset Crater Volcano National Monument

Three miles east of US-89 along a loop road twelve miles north of Flagstaff, **SUNSET CRATER VOLCANO NATIONAL MONUMENT** centers on the youngest of the San Francisco volcanoes. Its most recent eruption, in AD 1065, had a profound impact on the local population and economy. Thick deposits of ash for miles around opened up previously infertile land to cultivation, accelerating – if not triggering – a land rush that threw differing Native American peoples into contact and competition for the first time.

John Wesley Powell named Sunset Crater for its multicolored cone, which swells from a black base through reds and oranges to a yellow-tinged crest. Unfortunately, its shifting cinders are too unstable to allow hikers to climb to the rim. Instead, the one-mile **Lava Flow Trail** at its base offers an up-close look at the jagged black lava that streamed out across the desert, while the steeper one-mile **Lenox Crater Trail** ascends a lesser cone nearby.

All is explained at the **visitor center** just off the highway (daily 8am–5pm; ☎928/526-0502, ⓦwww.nps.gov/sucr), opposite the Forest Service's *Bonito* **campground** (late May to mid-Oct; $10; ☎928/527-0866). The monument admission fee ($3 per person) also covers entry to Wupatki.

Wupatki National Monument

A dozen miles north of Sunset Crater along the same loop road (see above), **WUPATKI NATIONAL MONUMENT** comprises a cluster of several distinct and exceptionally well-preserved ancient ruins, dramatically poised between the volcanoes and the desert. The ruins evince a period in which different tribal groups lived side by side in seeming harmony. Some time after the Sunset Crater eruption – though not necessarily because of it, as archeologists formerly believed – the existing Sinagua people, who surely witnessed the explosion, were joined by many others, including Ancestral Puebloans and the Hohokam. Once the rich new soil had been exhausted, around 150 years later, they all moved on.

To get the most out of your visit, it's best to start at the monument's excellent **visitor center** (daily: summer 8am–7pm, winter 8am–5pm; $3 per person, includes admission to Sunset Crater; ☎928/679-2365, ⓦwww.nps.gov/wupa). If you're arriving from Sunset Crater, it's just past the turnoff for the Wukoki pueblo. Here you'll find informative displays on the history and culture of the Sinagua and their neighbors, placing them firmly with the context of the traditional migration story of their modern descendants, the Hopi.

A paved loop trail descends from the visitor center to the main three-story, hundred-room pueblo of **Wupatki** ("long cut house"), which blends into a sandstone hillock that conceals a number of natural caves. The site's most intriguing features, however, lie a bit farther along. First comes what looks like an amphitheater, a walled circular plaza whose purpose remains unknown. Beyond it is an oval **ball court**, the northernmost such court ever found. Similar arenas throughout Central America were used for a game – part ritual, part sport – in which players tried to propel a rubber ball through a stone hoop high on a wall, using their knees and elbows alone, much like modern basketball (although losers of this contest may have been sacrificed). Alongside the ball court, cracks in the ground form a natural **blowhole**, through which air is either sucked or blown, depending on pressure and temperature. The audible "breathing" of the earth made this a sacred shrine for Wupatki's ancient inhabitants.

At the end of its own 2.5-mile spur road, the **Wukoki** pueblo takes its name from a modern Hopi word meaning "big house." Reminiscent of the castlelike structures at Hovenweep in southern Utah, it's within sight of a procession of rounded cinder cones, but was probably positioned for its commanding prospect of the Painted Desert to the north and east. Windows in its central tower, which traces the contours of a red-rock outcrop and is built with bricks of the same material, point in all directions; archeologists believe some are precisely aligned to the position of sunrise at significant moments in the annual calendar. As the Little Colorado River lies a full five miles distant, pueblo inhabitants must have been desperately short of water.

The loop road through Sunset Crater Volcano and Wupatki rejoins US-89 twenty miles south of Cameron (see p.121). Outcrops along its final few miles hold more pueblos, including **The Citadel**, which occupies a hilltop. While its interior,

△ Wukoki pueblo at Wupatki National Monument

which appears to hold a large circular kiva, remains unexcavated, much of its outer wall is intact, incorporating striped bands of black lava boulders. It too is dotted with tiny windows that may have served defensive or astronomical purposes.

Walnut Canyon National Monument

WALNUT CANYON NATIONAL MONUMENT is another Sinagua site, as spectacular in its own way as Wupatki. It lies just south of I-40, ten miles east of Flagstaff, or eight miles from downtown via Route 66. Between AD 1125 and 1250, this shallow canyon was home to a thriving community of Sinagua, who lived in small family groups rather than communal pueblos. Literally hundreds of their **cliff dwellings** remain nestled beneath overhangs along the canyon walls. They simply walled off alcoves where softer rock had eroded and put up partitions to make separate rooms. No single dwelling is on the same scale as at Wupatki, and only a handful are accessible to visitors, but collectively they make an impressive spectacle.

A large scenic window in the **visitor center** (daily: June–Aug 8am–6pm, March–May & Sept–Nov 8am–5pm, Dec–Feb 9am–5pm; $5; ☏928/526-3367, ⓦwww.nps.gov/waca) offers an excellent overview. **Walnut Creek** was long ago diverted to provide Flagstaff with drinking water, but you can imagine how fertile this valley must have been when the Sinagua first arrived. Trees cling to the porous rock, shading the ancient dwellings, and the vegetation thickens down to a valley floor dense with black walnut and oak trees.

Only visitors who arrive more than an hour before closing time are permitted to set off down the mile-long **Island Loop Trail**; as the dwellings are at their most photogenic in late afternoon, that calls for careful timing. Following a steep descent from the visitor center, the trail crosses a narrow causeway to a few accessible structures on a rocky isthmus high above a gooseneck in the creek. Note the T-shaped doorways, which could only be entered headfirst, and ceilings blackened by smoke from generations of fires. While petroglyphs adorn other visible ruins, none remain along the trail.

Offering a less strenuous walk, the separate **Rim Trail** skirts the edge of the canyon to a picnic area and surface ruins in the dissimilar pueblo style, consisting of large clusters of rooms.

Between June and August each year, rangers lead two- to three-hour **guided hikes** to lesser-known and otherwise inaccessible sites within the monument (Tues, Sat & Sun at 10am; call to confirm). The park offers no accommodation and only minimal snack food.

Williams

Although Flagstaff is widely regarded as the main gateway for visits to the South Rim, **WILLIAMS**, 32 miles west, is in fact the closest interstate town to the national park. While it lacks its neighbor's pizzazz, Williams is a nice enough little place, filled with Route 66–era motels and diners but retaining a certain individuality despite the constant stream of tourists. Part of its charm lies in its setting, cupped in a high grassy valley amid pine-covered hills. The highest visible peak is 9264ft **Bill Williams Mountain**, to the south, named for pioneer trapper and mountain man Bill Williams (1787–1849). The town was founded thirty years after Williams' death.

Like Flagstaff, Williams originally based both its architecture and economy on the surrounding ponderosa forests. Since 1901, however, when the Santa Fe

△ An historical relic at Williams' Grand Canyon Railway depot

Railroad first linked it with the canyon rim, sixty miles due north, Williams has lived off tourism. Though the rail line shut down in 1968, it reopened in 1989 as the **Grand Canyon Railway**, promoted as a fun ride rather than a serious means of transportation. Most people who spend the night in Williams are here to take the morning train up to the canyon.

Arrival and information

Amtrak's *Southwest Chief* **trains** call in twice daily at **Williams Junction**, three miles east of town, heading east at 4.20am and west at 9.33pm. The *Grand Canyon Railway Hotel* (see below) runs free connecting shuttle buses into town.

See p.40 for schedule and fare information for the **Grand Canyon Railway** (☎928/773-1976 or 1-800/843-8724, ⓦwww.thetrain.com), which sets off daily at 10am from the downtown **Williams Depot**.

Williams' **visitor center**, near the depot at 200 W Railroad Ave (daily: summer 8am–6.30pm, winter 8am–5pm; ☎928/635-4061 or 1-800/863-0546), serves as an entertaining local history **museum** and offers a range of brochures, including details of a town walking tour and driving tours in the Kaibab National Forest.

Marvelous Marv's Tours (☎928/635-4061 or 1-800/655-4948; ⓦwww.marvelousmarv.com) runs daily **guided van tours** up to the South Rim; the $85 adult rate includes park admission.

Accommodation

The large *Grand Canyon Railway Hotel* ranks as Williams' leading **accommodation**, though you'll find plenty of alternatives. Vintage motels and the odd B&B line downtown's main thoroughfares, while the national chains congregate near the interstate exits at either end of town. North of town, the *Red Lake Hostel* caters to budget travelers.

Those interested in **camping** can choose between two *KOA* camp-grounds – *Circle Pines* (☎928/635-2626), three miles east, and *Grand Canyon* (☎928/635-2307 or 1-800/562-5771; closed Nov–Feb), five miles north – or ask at the Chalender Ranger Station, 501 W Route 66 (☎928/635-2676), for details about secluded summer-only mountain sites in the Kaibab National Forest.

Best Value Inn 1001 W Route 66 ☎928/635-2202. Small Japanese-owned motel, just west of the junction where the separate spurs of Route 66 rejoin; a cut above most budget options, with its own pool and spa. Winter ❸, summer ❹

Best Western Inn of Williams 2600 W Route 66 ☎928/635-4400 or 1-800/635-4445. Spacious, well-equipped motel-resort, with a pool and hot tub, perched near I-40 exit 161 at the west end of town. Winter ❹, summer ❻

Grand Canyon Railway Hotel 1 Fray Marcos Blvd ☎928/635-4010 or 1-800/843-8724, ☜www.thetrain.com. The Grand Canyon Railway's flag-ship hotel originally opened in 1908 as the *Fray Marcos*; since rebuilt and renamed, it lacks much character, though the large open lobby is a pleas-ant enough place to sit, and there's also an indoor pool, spa, and saloon. All rooms provide two queen beds. Mid-Oct to mid-March ❺, mid-March to mid-Oct ❼

Mountain Side Inn 642 E Route 66 ☎928/635-4431 or 1-800/462-9381. Large, comfortable motel, set back from the road at the east end of

town, with an outdoor pool and surprising giraffes in the lobby. Winter ❸, summer ❺

Red Garter Bed & Bakery 137 W Railroad Ave ☎928/635-1484 or 1 800/328-1484, ☜www.redgarter.com. Plush four-room B&B in a former downtown bordello, serving fresh-baked breakfasts from its own downstairs bakery. Closed mid-Dec to mid-Feb. ❺

Red Lake Hostel AZ-64 ☎928/635-4753 or 1-800/581-4753, ✉redlake@azaccess.com. Adjoining a Mustang gas station at a lonely curve on AZ-64 nine miles north of town, this bright red converted motel offers rudimentary accommoda-tion; $12 for a dorm bed, or $22 for a private room. Also offers tent and RV camping. ❶/❷

Super 8 911 W Route 66 ☎928/635-4045 or 1-800/800-8000. Standard chain motel – the more central of Williams' two *Super 8*s – not far west of downtown. The interior hallways are rather faded, but the rooms are fine, and there's an indoor pool. Winter ❷, summer ❹

Travelodge 430 E Route 66 ☎928/635-2651 or 1-800/578-7878. Reliable, clean, downtown motel, with a pool and hot tub. Winter ❸, summer ❹

The Town

Williams holds definite romantic appeal as the very last town along **Route 66** to have been bypassed by I-40. Until October 13, 1984, when Bobby Troup of *(Get Your Kicks On) Route 66* fame fronted a closing ceremony, the only stoplight on the interstate between Chicago and Los Angeles stood outside the Williams visitor center.

Much of the former Route 66 frontage remains unchanged, and several quirky antique stores sell both vintage memorabilia and Native American crafts and jewelry. But while it's fun to explore downtown along the two parallel one-way streets – eastbound Route 66 and westbound **Railroad Avenue** – an hour-long morning or evening stroll is probably enough; Williams is not really a place to spend the day.

For rail enthusiasts, the Williams Depot holds the slowly expanding **Grand Canyon Railway Museum** (daily 7.30am–5.30pm; free). In addition to myriad old photos, including several great hand-tinted ones, the museum is bursting with vintage tools and implements, as well as cases of antique armrests and window catches. In due course, it hopes to unveil a 650ft model of the route up to the canyon.

Highlights on Williams' annual events calendar include the Labor Day **rodeo** and **Rendezvous Days**, on Memorial Day weekend, when locals dress up as buckskinned pioneers.

Eating

Williams' **restaurant** selection is generally disappointing. A few places conjure up the feel of its Route 66 heyday, but no place serves anything out of the ordinary.

Grand Canyon Coffee & Café 125 W Route 66 ☎928/635-1255. Tiny downtown café that serves espressos, juices, and pastries throughout the day, then switches to simple Asian dishes such as Korean barbecue in the evenings. Mon–Fri 8am–8pm, Sat 8am–2pm.

Max & Thelma's Williams Depot ☎928/635-8970. Named for the owners of the Grand Canyon Railway, *Max & Thelma's* is an adequate but dull family restaurant aimed at speedily satisfying hungry tour groups. All-you-can-eat buffets are available at every meal – breakfast is $9, lunch $11, and dinner $14 – and you can also order predictable à la carte options. Daily 6.30am–9pm.

Pancho McGillicuddy's 141 W Railroad Ave ☎928/635-4150. Popular but very average Mexican cantina, housed in an attractive tin-ceilinged building downtown, with its own authentic-looking saloon. The usual south-of-the border standards, like flautas, tostadas, tamales, or carnitas, cost under $10, while three mixed platters go for $14; also serves steaks and grills. Daily 7am–10pm.

Pine Country Restaurant 107 N Grand Canyon Blvd ☎928/635-9718. Traditional central diner with friendly waitstaff, where the predictable fare is actually pretty good, and the homemade pies are irresistible. Daily 5.30am–9pm.

Ash Fork

Stretched along a brief arc of Route 66 that juts north of I-40 twenty miles west of Williams, the ranching community of **ASH FORK** is smaller, less picturesque, and far less involved in catering to travelers. On the western fringes of the Kaibab National Forest, its downtown features buildings constructed with the yellowish local sandstone rather than timber.

While major **motel** chains haven't bothered to set up shop in Ash Fork, there are a few homespun alternatives, including the large, pink *Ash Fork Inn*, at the west end of town near I-40 exit 144 (☎928/637-2514; ❷). You'll also find a *KOA* **campground**, 783 Old Route 66 (☎928/637-2521), and a couple of basic diners in the thick of what few things Ash Fork can claim.

Seligman

A few miles west of Ash Fork, Route 66 parallels its modern replacement for the twenty or so miles to **SELIGMAN**. This flyblown desert outpost a mile or two north of the interstate feels more than a little stranded, but if you're in the mood to be seduced by its kitsch diners and drive-ins, it makes a mildly diverting stop after a long day's drive. Every business in town strives to outdo the others with eye-catching displays – mannequins of Elvis and Marilyn waving from oddball parked vehicles and the like – and the passing traffic is worth watching too, as all kinds of vintage roadsters make pilgrimages along the "Mother Road."

You might even choose to continue along Route 66, which curves north-west from I-40 through a dozen fading villages and a corner of the **Hualapai Indian Reservation** (see p.183), then dips south to Kingman – a diverting drive of 88 miles, versus the dreary 65-mile run west on I-40.

Seligman offers the only **lodgings** along the interstate between Ash Fork and Kingman, though motels like the *Historic Route 66*, 500 W Route 66 (☎928/422-3204; ❸), and the *Canyon Lodge*, 114 E Route 66 (☎928/422-

3255; ❷), all reflect an indifferent sameness. The wackiest of the local **diners** has to be *Delgadillo's Snow Cap*, 301 E Route 66 (☎928/422-3291), where every malt or burger comes with a side order of outrageous puns and put-ons. If you're just looking for a square meal, the *Copper Cart*, in the former railroad station (☎928/422-3241), serves a standard all-American menu.

Kingman

With a population exceeding thirty thousand, **KINGMAN**, sixty-five miles west of Seligman and thirty miles short of the California border, ranks second to Flagstaff among Arizona's I-40 towns. **Las Vegas** lies a mere hundred miles northwest on US-93, and as all traffic bound there from Phoenix or the Grand Canyon is obliged to pass this way, Kingman welcomes enough tourists to keep more than thirty motels busy year-round. The best that can be said for it, however, is that it's not lifeless, nor is it particularly ugly – with the exception of a commercial sprawl beside the railroad tracks north of the interstate. It's just a humdrum pit stop with a tinge of Route 66 ambience.

Curving alongside the tracks, Kingman's main street is named in honor of native son **Andy Devine**, the actor who drove the eponymous *Stagecoach* in John Ford's 1939 movie. As the town's promotional brochure puts it, "There must be somebody who hasn't heard of Andy Devine, but that person sure doesn't live in Kingman." To learn about his career, Hualapai culture and basketwork, and sundry other aspects of Mohave County heritage, stop by the **Mohave Museum of History & Arts**, 400 W Beale St (Mon–Fri 10am–5pm, Sat & Sun 1–5pm; $3 adults, free under age 13; ☎928/753-3195). The year 1939, incidentally, was a big one for Kingman: Carole Lombard and Clark Gable were married here on March 29.

Arrival and information

On the western edge of downtown stands Kingman's large **Powerhouse visitor center**, 120 W Andy Devine Ave (daily 9am–6pm; ☎928/753-6106); in addition to offering tourist brochures, the center displays and sells lots of Route 66 memorabilia.

The old station in the midst of town welcomes Amtrak **trains** on the run between Flagstaff and LA, though at unearthly hours of the night, while Greyhound **buses** traveling between Phoenix and Las Vegas, as well as east-west routes, use a terminal up near the interstate at 3264 E Andy Devine Ave (☎928/757-8400).

Accommodation

As you're unlikely to spend more than one night in Kingman or to linger here in the morning, its range of ordinary, inexpensive **motels** should meet your needs. Others prefer **camping** in the beautiful hills five miles southeast of town at county-run **Hualapai Mountain Park** (☎928/757-3859), which also holds the *Hualapai Mountain Lodge Resort* (☎928/757-3545; closed Mon; ❹).

Brunswick 315 E Andy Devine Ave ☎928/718-1800 or 1-888/559-1800, ⓦ www.hotel-brunswick.com. This century-old "historical boutique hotel" is downtown Kingman's most characterful lodging, with antique-styled rooms that range from a basic, single-bedded cowboy or cowgirl option, with shared bathroom, to lavish suites. Triple-paned windows keep noise from the nearby railroad to a minimum. All rates include breakfast. ❷–❻

Quality Inn Kingman 1400 E Andy Devine Ave ☎928/753-4747 or 1-800/228-5151. Standard motel a half-mile from downtown, with small but adequate rooms, that offers a bit of character via a strong Route 66 theme, including a retro breakfast room and outdoor vintage gas pumps. ❸
Ramblin' Rose 1001 E Andy Devine Ave

☎928/753-5541. Appealing, spruced-up independent motel just east of downtown that provides some of Kingman's best budget rooms. ❷
Super 8 3401 E Andy Devine Ave ☎928/757-4808 or 1-800/800-8000. Reliable, inexpensive chain motel well east of town, just north of I-40 exit 53. Winter ❷, summer ❹

Eating

Most of Kingman's **restaurants** play up the Route 66 angle in some form or another. The options are too scattered for you to stroll around comparing menus, but hop in your car and you'll find something.

Dambar & Steakhouse 1960 E Andy Devine Ave ☎928/753-3523. Atop the hill, this is a classic Western steakhouse, all sawdust and bare timber and serving grilled and barbecued ribs and chicken, as well as massive steaks. All entrees come in under $20 at dinner and more like $10 at lunch. Mon–Thurs & Sun 11am–10pm, Fri & Sat 11am–11pm.
Hubb's Café *Brunswick*, 315 E Andy Devine Ave ☎928/718-1800. The *Brunswick's* attractively restored dinner-only dining room prepares an eclectic menu of international cuisine, from rich Continental sauces to spicy Asian curries, as well as American standards. Few entrees cost over $20. Mon–Sat 5–9pm.

Mr D'z Route 66 Diner 105 E Andy Devine Ave ☎928/718-0066. Across from the visitor center, this loving recreation of a classic Route 66 roadhouse is bursting with neon, lurid molded trimmings, and memorabilia and serves up good burgers and shakes, malts and floats, and fries with everything. Tues–Sun 10am–5pm.
Old Town Coffeehouse 616 E Beale St ☎928/753-2244. Slightly chintzy café on the eastern fringes of downtown, where you can enjoy espressos, soups, and sandwiches on a small outdoor patio. Mon–Fri 7am–4pm, Sat 8am–5pm.

Havasupai Indian Reservation

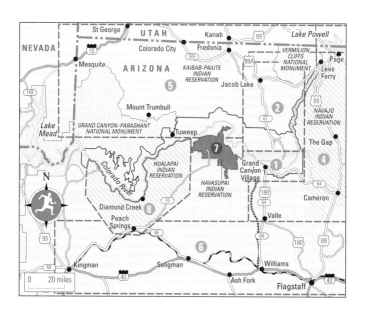

CHAPTER 7

Highlights

✳ **Hualapai Trail** Busy with hikers and Havasupai alike, not to mention mules and horses, the sandy Hualapai Trail is the only way to reach the heart of the reservation. **See p.178**

✳ **Helicopter from the South Rim** If you don't have time to hike, Papillon's day trip via chopper from the South Rim is an extravagant treat. **See p.178**

✳ **Guided hiking** Join one of the Grand Canyon Field Institute's expert-led backpacking trips to Havasupai. **See p.178**

✳ **Havasu Falls** These astonishing, lush, turquoise waterfalls, buried deep within Havasu Canyon, are the main reason visitors flock to the reservation. **See p.180**

✳ **Havasu Campground** Gorgeous riverside campground, shaded by beautiful cottonwood trees. **See p.181**

✳ **Mooney Falls** The hair-raising hike to the foot of these falls, named for a prospector who died in the attempt, is rewarded with magnificent views. **See p.182**

△ Havasupai tribal members hike down to the falls

7

Havasupai Indian Reservation

Nestled deep within the Grand Canyon, at the heart of the **Havasupai Indian Reservation**, is **Havasu Canyon**, one of the most spellbindingly beautiful places in the southwestern US. Though it lies a mere 35 miles west of the national park headquarters on the South Rim, the only approach is from the southwest – a road trip of nearly two hundred miles. Once you leave the interstate, the last ninety miles cross the endless Coconino Plateau.

From road's end, the eight-mile **Hualapai Trail** provides the only route down into the canyon itself. Those who brave this desert hike are rewarded by a stunning oasis of **turquoise waterfalls** and lush vegetation, a Shangri-la that has been home for centuries beyond record to the same small group of Native Americans. The **Havasupai** owe their existence here to a geologic fluke: Although the canyon receives only nine inches of rain each year, almost all the water that falls in the surrounding three thousand square miles funnels down this one narrow gorge, creating the year-round torrent of **Havasu Creek**.

One 1930s anthropologist described Havasu Canyon as "the only spot in the United States where native culture has remained in anything like its pristine condition." Since then, tourism has become the mainstay of the tribal economy, but visitor numbers are kept deliberately low, at around 35,000 per year. The Havasupai have rejected all suggestions of building a road – or even a tramway – down into the canyon, to minimize the impact on the traditional way of life. Instead, the five hundred or so tribal members earn their keep by ferrying non-hikers up and down the trail on pack mules and horses and operating a creekside **campground** and a comfortable lodge in the village of **Supai**. While visitors should not expect sweeping views of the Grand Canyon – or to have much interaction with residents – for spectacular desert scenery and sheer romance, the Havasupai reservation is beyond compare.

The one crucial factor to bear in mind if you're planning a trip is that you *must* have an advance reservation for either the lodge or campground. That's easier said than done; between May and October, the lodge is almost invariably booked months in advance, and the campground is usually full

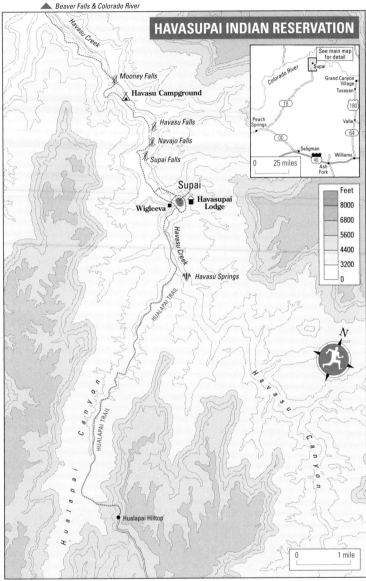

Beaver Falls & Colorado River

HAVASUPAI INDIAN RESERVATION

Havasu Creek

Mooney Falls

Havasu Campground

Havasu Falls

Navajo Falls

Supai Falls

Supai

Wigleeva   Havasupai Lodge

Havasu Creek

Havasu Springs

HUALAPAI TRAIL

HUALAPAI TRAIL

Canyon

Hualapai Canyon

Havasu Canyon

Hualapai Hilltop

See main map for detail
Supai
Colorado River
Grand Canyon Village
Tusayan
Peach Springs
18
180
00
Valle
64
Seligman
Williams
40
Ash Fork

0   25 miles

Feet
8000
6800
5600
4400
3200
0

N

0   1 mile

on weekends. On top of that, the telephone line down to Supai can fail for weeks at a time.

Unless you travel by **helicopter** (see p.178), it's impossible to visit Havasu Canyon as a **day trip**; aside from the long drive to the trailhead, the twenty-mile round-trip hike to the falls would take well over ten hours.

A history of the Havasupai

Archeologists have identified the earliest inhabitants of Havasu Canyon as the **Cohonina**. Like the Ancestral Puebloans, their neighbors to the east, they are thought to have occupied the region roughly between AD 700 and 1100. During that period, a Yuman-speaking group who call themselves the **Pai** – a word that simply means "people" – made their first appearance in the Southwest. So little is known about the Cohonina that no one knows whether the Pai were their cousins, their descendants, or an entirely new group.

What is certain, however, is that by 1300, a couple of hundred years after the Cohonina abandoned the canyon, a band of Pai had taken their place. The Pai as a whole had by this time quarreled and split to form the **Hualapai** ("People of the Tall Pines") of northwest Arizona and the **Yavapai** ("Almost People," who no longer quite deserved to be regarded as people), who settled along the Colorado farther south. It was a group of Hualapai families who moved into the canyon and became the **Havasupai** – the "People of the Blue-green Water." Although not related to any of the various Pueblo peoples, the Hualapai established close links with the Hopi and the Zuni, from whom they eventually acquired the art of raising sheep, horses, and crops such as peaches.

Despite naming themselves for the turquoise river that watered the fields, the Havasupai only lived along the canyon floor in summer, in houses of hide-covered branches. In winter, the canyon made a cold, miserable home, lacking big game and firewood and receiving as little as five hours of sunlight per day. The Havasupai would instead move up onto the plateau to hunt deer, elk, and antelope, creating artificial watering holes to lure them closer. Their territory covered perhaps 2.3 million acres, extending far beyond the region now occupied by Grand Canyon Village, south to the San Francisco Peaks near modern Flagstaff, and as far north as what's now Tuba City, Arizona.

In June 1776, shortly before the Declaration of Independence was signed in Philadelphia, the Havasupai welcomed their first white visitor. **Father Francisco Tomás Garcés**, a missionary from San Xavier del Bac near Tucson who made several pioneering expeditions into the frontier West, was greeted with five days of feasting. Describing the Grand Canyon as a "calaboose of cliffs and canyons," he dubbed it the Puerto de Bucareli in honor of the viceroy who had dispatched him; more enduringly, he was the first to name the **Río Colorado**. Garcés himself traveled eastward along the South Rim to meet the Hopi, while the rest of his expedition blazed a trail to California, where they founded San Francisco.

The Havasupai remained undisturbed for another eighty years, until Anglo prospectors and surveyors began to enter the region. Conflict arose in 1866, when, to encourage the spread of the railroads, Congress granted the Atlantic and Pacific Railroad company ownership of swathes of land adjoining its tracks across northern Arizona. Native resistance soon escalated into a disastrous **war**, after which the defeated Hualapai spent several years confined to a reservation near Ehrenberg, 150 miles downstream along the Colorado. Because the Havasupai did not participate in the fighting, they were allowed to remain in their traditional territory, then known to US authorities as **Cataract Canyon**. Only then did they begin to regard themselves as a separate tribe rather than just another band of Hualapai.

In negotiations over the extents of a permanent Havasupai reservation, the government was as usual only prepared to acknowledge Native American ownership of land that held permanent settlements and cultivated fields. Areas used for hunting, gathering, or even grazing weren't recognized, especially if use was shared by more than one band. Fearful of being removed, the Havasupai settled in 1882 for a tiny plot at the bottom of Havasu Canyon – at a mere 518 acres, it amounted to less than one square mile. Restricted to a fraction of their former range, they were obliged to farm what little land they were granted as intensively as possible.

A century of hardship was to follow, during which the Havasupai repeatedly petitioned to have their reservation enlarged. Suffering great spiritual uncertainty, both the Havasupai and Hualapai took part in the **Ghost Dance** movement in the 1890s, when Native Americans throughout the West joined in trancelike rituals designed to ensure that white men would vanish from the land and the old ways would return. The Havasupai also briefly adopted the rainmaking kachina dances of the Hopi, until a catastrophic **flood** on January 1, 1910, destroyed their village, which then stood half a mile from its current site.

The creation of **Grand Canyon National Park** in 1919 placed further restrictions on Havasupai use of traditional lands. One early supervisor avowed that the Grand Canyon "should be preserved for the everlasting pleasure and instruction of our intelligent citizens, as well as those from foreign countries; I therefore deem it just and necessary to keep the wild and inappreciable Indians from off the Reserve." Park proposals during the 1920s to build a direct road along the South Rim and down into Havasu Canyon were probably only thwarted by the Crash of 1929; such suggestions would resurface repeatedly in subsequent decades.

Although Coconino National Forest, south of the reservation, takes its name from the Hopi word for the Havasupai (which also, anachronistically, explains how the Cohonina got their name), tribal members could only graze animals there by annual permit. The Havasupai survived by simply disobeying whatever unenforceable regulations outsiders sought to impose and continuing to spend winters up on the plateau. In due course, many Havasupai found jobs in Grand Canyon Village, while tourism to Havasu Canyon itself became an important element in the tribal economy.

Nonetheless, the Park Service and the Havasupai remained at loggerheads. During the 1950s, the park surreptitiously bought up defunct mining claims in the canyon and then opened its own campground – the same one that remains in use today under Havasupai control – on a former Havasupai burial ground. Meanwhile, the Havasupai petitioned tirelessly for the return of their lands. It may sound strange now, but their greatest ally was Republican Senator **Barry Goldwater**, while ranged against them were such environmental groups as the **Sierra Club** and **Friends of the Earth**, who had yet to be convinced that Native Americans could look after wilderness lands as well as the Park Service.

Despite having agreed in 1968 to accept $1.24 million as final compensation for their lost lands, the Havasupai finally won their battle in 1975. The reservation was expanded by 185,000 acres, and the Havasupai were also awarded rights over 95,300 acres of traditional-use land that lay within the park. This was the largest tract of land ever returned to Native Americans, but it came with the proviso that it must remain forever wild; no mining, logging, or manufacturing was to be permitted on the traditional-use lands, and no dams or railroads could be built.

The settlement came just in time, as the Grand Canyon region soon experienced a boom in **uranium** mining, with more than 3500 claims filed in the Arizona Strip over the ensuing decade. In 1988, Energy Fuels Nuclear was granted rights to develop a uranium mine in the Kaibab National Forest near **Red Butte**, which, though it lies outside the reservation, is sacred to the Havasupai.

Despite fears that the mine might contaminate Havasu Creek, Havasu Canyon, and ultimately the Colorado itself, federal courts blocked Havasupai attempts to stop it. **Canyon Mine** was built, but never went into operation, thanks to a drop in prices caused by a worldwide glut of uranium. It now belongs to the International Uranium Corporation, which despite denying rumors that the mine might soon be reactivated, insists that the low price of uranium is the only factor holding it back.

The other major threat facing the Havasupai is that any future tourist development on the South Rim – along the lines of the abortive Canyon Forest Village scheme (see p.214) – could deplete the water table for hundreds of miles around and render Havasu Creek dry.

Getting to the reservation

Since the enlargement of their reservation in 1975, the Havasupai have closed all but one of the possible access routes into their land. Now the only way to get here by car is from **I-40**, turning off at **Seligman** if you're driving from Flagstaff or Grand Canyon Village or at **Kingman** from Las Vegas or California; allow three to four hours for the drive from Flagstaff and more like five or six from Las Vegas. From I-40, you'll follow **AZ-66** – the longest remaining segment of Route 66, which roughly parallels the main east-west railroad – to the poorly marked intersection with **Arrowhead Hwy 18**, six miles east of **Peach Springs**. From Seligman, it's a straight run of around 29 miles; from Kingman it's more like sixty miles, but you'll have the option of an overnight stop at the *Hualapai Lodge* in Peach Springs (see p.188). Stock up with food, water, and gas when you leave the interstate.

Hwy 18 runs 56 miles across bare sagebrush desert interrupted by patches of thick ponderosa forest, with hardly a building in sight. Despite maps to the contrary, it's fully paved, and there's no possibility of losing your way. Eventually it winds down through burgeoning canyons to road's end atop the large plateau known as **Hualapai Hilltop**. At an elevation of 5200ft, the hilltop commands a long view of white-walled **Hualapai Canyon**, which cuts into the tablelands as it stretches north toward its junction with Havasu Canyon. As this remote hilltop holds no more than a small cluster of dilapidated shacks, with no lodgings, food, or gas, you'll likely be surprised at the number of parked vehicles.

Hikers are free to set off from Hualapai Hilltop whenever they choose. From the end of the parking lot, the Hualapai Trail to Supai village zigzags steeply down the hillside to the right, then threads its way across the valley floor. Again, do not hike down without advance lodging reservations.

Horse rides

If you prefer to **ride** down on either horse or mule, make a reservation at the same time as you book your accommodation. The mule train leaves the hilltop sometime between 10am and noon; if you arrive any later than noon, you won't be able to ride down and will lose both your reservation and your deposit. The ride down to the **village** costs $70 per person one-way or $120 round-trip and is arranged through the lodge (☎928/448-2111); continuing to the campground costs $75 one-way or $150 round-trip and is arranged

through the Havasupai Tourist Enterprise (☎928/448-2121 or 2141, ⓦwww
.havasupaitribe.com). Riders are limited to ten pounds of baggage each and
must pay for another horse or mule to carry any additional gear; hikers can
also arrange to have their bags carried. One animal can carry up to four packs,
for the same charge as a rider. On the return trip, the mules are scheduled
to leave the campground at 7am between April and October and at 8am
in winter; they set off from the lodge at 8am year-round. Visitors can also
arrange a round-trip horseback ride from the village down to Havasu Falls
(see p.180).

Helicopters

A **helicopter shuttle** service operates between Hualapai Hilltop and Supai. In
recent years, flights have been available between 10am and 1pm on Thurs, Fri,
Sat, and Sun from mid-March to October and on Fri & Sun only from November to mid-March. The service operates on a first-come, first-served basis, with
a one-way fare of around $85. Call the Havasupai Tourist Enterprise to check
whether the service is available.

Hualapai Trail

Apart from steep initial switchbacks down the Coconino Sandstone hillside, the
Hualapai Trail is not especially difficult. It is, however, a long eight-mile walk,
with no shade for the first three miles and no reliable water source until very
near the end. Allow around three hours to reach the village (and four or more
to come back up again) and be sure to carry all the food and water you'll need
for a day in the desert.

Guided tours and excursions

If you're short on time, an expensive but undeniably wonderful way to see Havasu
Canyon is to take a **one-day helicopter trip** from **Tusayan**, just outside Grand
Canyon Village on the South Rim, with **Papillon Grand Canyon Helicopters** ($455
adults, $435 under age 12; ☎928/638-2419 or 1-800/528-2418, ⓦwww.papillon
.com). While the flight from Tusayan won't venture over the Grand Canyon proper,
the descent into Havasupai through assorted side canyons is an exhilarating adventure. From the landing pad, you'll have time to either hike or ride a horse down to
Havasu Falls and back and linger at the various cascades along the way; meals are
not included. When lodge accommodation is available, visitors can stay overnight
and fly back the next day.

Various organizations offer guided expeditions to the Havasupai Reservation.
Highly recommended is the **Grand Canyon Field Institute** (see p.94), which runs
several four-day hiking and camping tours in summer, one for women only and each
costing around $525 (☎928/638-2485 or 1-866/471-4435, ⓦwww.grandcanyon
.org/fieldinstitute).

Commercial operators offer a few more amenities on their tours. **Arizona Outback
Adventures** (☎480/945-2881 or 1-866/455-1601, ⓦwww.azoutbackadventures
.com) offers three-, four-, and five-day trips, with stays at its private base camp and
options regarding whether to hike and/or take a helicopter in or out, from $1375 up
to $1635. **Discovery Treks** (☎520/404-1151 or 1-888/256-8731, ⓦwww.discovery
treks.com) arranges three-day trips via foot, horseback, or helicopter that include
either camping or lodge stays; prices range from $900 up.

The well-trodden route is busy throughout the day with small supply trains of mules and horses. Once on the valley floor, it follows the bed of a dry wash between red-rock cliffs that slowly but inexorably rise to form the flanking walls of deep, narrow Hualapai Canyon. While the sand underfoot is so thick that it splashes at every step, the potential for flash floods is clear from the much-scoured rocks to either side. In places, mighty boulders all but block the path, while solitary cottonwoods reach up toward the thin strip of sky overhead. Atop the Esplanade Plateau straight ahead, the pale, stark butte of **Mount Sinyala** repeatedly looms into view.

After almost seven miles, the trail reaches its intersection with Havasu Canyon; until the disastrous flood of 1910 (see p.176), this was the site of Supai village. All of Havasu Canyon was formerly known as **Cataract Canyon**, but now that old name only applies to its dry segment, to the right of the junction. Whatever you do, don't turn right – it took three weeks to rescue a dehydrated camper who did so in 1975. That said, however, what little tourist traffic the Havasupai received a century ago arrived along the latter route, on the **Topocoba Trail**, which reaches Cataract Canyon via Lee Canyon, at the end of a thirty-mile dirt road from Grand Canyon Village. Although the Havasupai still make occasional use of that trail, recreational hikers are no longer permitted to do so.

Bear left at the trail junction instead, at a dense cluster of small trees. The sound of rushing water soon signals the emergence of **Havasu Creek** from hidden springs in the rock. Before long it's flowing through the parched landscape in all its blue-green splendor, at an amazing average of 38 million gallons per day.

Not far beyond, you'll cross a low rise and follow irrigation ditches across the meadow that holds the modern village of Supai, watched over by two red-rock pillars atop the high canyon wall on the far side. Known as the **Wigleeva**, these twin sentinels – one of which is considered to be male, the other female – are regarded as guardian spirits of the Havasupai.

Supai

Though in a superb natural setting – a wide, flat clearing surrounded on all sides by forbidding walls of red sandstone – the village of **SUPAI** is not in itself attractive. The Havasupai were only obliged to build a year-round settlement in the canyon by the loss of their lands on the plateau above (see p.176), and this site was their second choice after the first proved prone to flooding. This location has also suffered repeated flood damage, including four major inundations since 1990. It therefore comprises just a scattering of basic timber-frame houses and prefabricated cabins. Even the name itself is a flimsy fabrication: *Supai* is a meaningless abbreviation of Havasupai, invented by the US Postal Service.

Once the Hualapai Trail widens into what is jokingly called "Main Street" and shepherds you into the village, the first building you'll reach holds the tribal **registration office**. Only campers are obliged to pay the $20 reservation **entrance fee** here; for lodge guests, it's added to their bill. A back room holds a small **museum** (daily 7am–7pm; $1), with a random but reasonably interesting assortment of century-old photographs and newspaper clippings. You'll also find a case of assorted baskets, a craft for which the Havasupai are famous; one basket is coated with pine pitch to make it waterproof. On the whole, however, ancient artifacts have become too expensive for the museum to afford.

Fifty yards farther, beyond the only post office in the US that still receives its mail by pack mule, lies Supai's dusty, flyblown **plaza**. To the right, benches outside the lone **grocery store** form Supai's main social center, where the older Havasupai gather each evening. The younger set, together with a vast population of dogs, are more likely to be found on the terrace of the **café**, opposite. Onward, the trail skirts the edge of the village school, then branches left and descends toward the campground. Visitors are forbidden to wander off the main trail into the surrounding farmland.

Havasupai Lodge

Havasupai Lodge (☎928/448-2111 or 448-2201, ℮lodge@havasupaitribe .com; ⊙) sits slightly apart from things, near the canyon wall behind the school. It's a simple two-story structure, built in the style of a functional motel rather than a grand park lodge, where the plain but comfortable air-conditioned rooms lack phones or TVs; each sleeps up to four people. As mentioned earlier, advance bookings are essential and are hard to secure between May and October.

Note that the $20 reservation entrance fee is added to guests' lodge bills, which, like all prices on the Havasupai reservation, are subject to an additional five percent **tribal sales tax**.

Eating

Although the lodge has a pleasant little garden, the only place to get a **meal** in Supai is the *Tribal Café* (daily: hours vary from 6am–7pm in summer to 8am–5pm in winter; ☎928/448-2981). The food is far from exciting, with fried breakfasts and a lunch or dinner of beef stew, fry bread, or burritos; most items cost around $7 (cash only), more if you want grated cheese on top. **Alcohol** is not available here or anywhere on the reservation.

The **grocery store** across the plaza sells a limited selection of processed items, all carried in by mule and priced accordingly.

Below Supai: the falls

The reservation's renowned **waterfalls** lie farther down the canyon beyond Supai. To get there, follow the footpath near the lodge out of the village; it will take you several minutes to clear the straggle of farms and homes. Flash floods and erosion are forever reshaping the riverbed immediately below the village, and **Navajo Falls**, which thunders audibly off to the left about a mile and a half down, often looks different one day to the next. Clearings in the undergrowth at regular intervals should offer glimpses of its foamy white course, though it's seldom possible to approach any closer.

Incidentally, the waterfall was named for **Chief Navajo**, who led the Havas-upai when the reservation was first established and who died in 1900. His own confusing moniker is owed to the fact that he was kidnapped by the Navajo as a child and only returned to his people in adult life.

Havasu Falls

Scoured by floods in 1993, the trail beyond Navajo Falls was reconstructed higher up the canyon wall. It now crosses the river on two successive foot-bridges before reaching the stupendous twin cascade of **Havasu Falls**. You'll first catch sight of the falls from an overlook at rim level – an absolutely breathtaking view. The creek foams white as it hurtles over a 150ft cliff into shallow terraces filled with limpid turquoise water. The surrounding rock formations are composed of water-deposited limestone known as **travertine** – the same stuff that clogs the inside of domestic kettles. It's a light travertine coating on the river-bed that lends the water its astonishing blue-green glow. Be sure not to walk onto it in bare feet, however; travertine is horrendously sharp stuff.

In the days when it was known to the Park Service as **Bridal Veil Falls**, Havasu was a broad cascade, which explains the solidified sheets and curtains of travertine that span its wide brim. Then a flash flood punched a notch dead center, through which the cascade now gushes to either side of a small outcrop knitted together by a frail cottonwood sapling. Side trails off the main path lead down to an idyllic shaded beach beside the largest, deepest pool, where the ceaseless roar makes conversation difficult, but swimming is all but irresistible. Dividing the various terraces are natural travertine dams, partially reconstructed after the 1993 flood using artificial support groins now buried beneath new deposits. Cross to the far side of the creek along these dams to reach a group of picnic tables in a cottonwood grove at the mouth of a side canyon.

△ The travertine pools below Havasu Falls

A short **horseback excursion** from Supai to Havasu Falls costs $60; for reservations, contact Havasupai Tourist Enterprises (see p.178).

Havasu Campground

Just beyond Havasu Falls, two miles down from the village, **Havasu Campground** occupies an especially narrow, high-walled segment of the canyon. Once the tribal cremation and burial ground, this site was excluded from the original reservation on account of its rich deposits of lead, silver, and zinc. After mining activities ceased, but before the Havasupai wrested back control in 1975, it fell into the hands of the Park Service, which turned it into a campground in 1957. As one Havasupai bitterly complained during hearings before the US Senate in 1973, "Dead people's things have long since walked off with hikers."

Today, the campground stretches some three-quarters of a mile and can accommodate about three hundred campers. Tent sites lie in clearings amid the woods on either side of the shallow creek, which is spanned by a small footbridge. Facilities are primitive in the extreme, but it's a wonderful spot, with lush cottonwood shade trees and fresh drinking water from springs along the canyon wall. There are no showers or phones, and fires are not permitted. Reservations are required (☎928/448-2121, 448-2141, or 448-2237, ✉touristoffice@havasupaitribe.com), and the fee is $10 per person, per night. Although villagers are barred from entering the campground in summer by tribal edict, groups of horses stand tethered at the entrance, waiting to carry campers back up the hill.

Mooney Falls and the Colorado River

Havasu Campground abruptly ends atop the precipitous, and once again luridly turquoise, 196ft **Mooney Falls**. This natural barrier was long regarded as impassable, even by the Havasupai. It takes its modern name from an unfortunate prospector who fell to his death here in 1880, after a rope snagged as he was being lowered to the bottom. Colorful stories that he dangled for three days before the rope broke are untrue, but it did take several months before his companions managed to dig out his body, which by then lay beneath a thick coating of travertine.

The trail to the bottom is little better today. After scrambling down the travertine ledges and through two successive tunnels bored through the cliff face by Mooney's cohorts, you arrive at a sheer section that was blasted away by the 1993 flood and now comprises a vertical series of footholds aided by an iron chain affixed to the rock. The prospect of having to climb back up intimidates many hikers into turning back at this point; those who do continue also have to contend with two steep ladders. The gorgeous pools and swimming holes at the foot of the falls are worth the effort.

A long day hike from the campground continues for three miles to the quick-fire set of rapids at **Beaver Falls**, as far as the Havasupai recommend visitors should go. The onward route involves a climb up to and along a high ledge, followed by a four-mile descent to the Colorado. You may just encounter river runners, who got here the easy way – shooting the 157 miles of white-water from Lees Ferry (see p.130).

△ Spectacular limestone deposits at Mooney Falls

Hualapai Indian Reservation

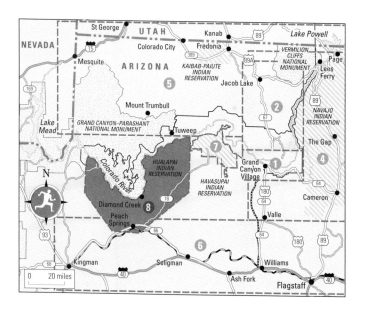

CHAPTER 8

Highlights

✳ **Rafting day trip** The only one-day rafting trip available anywhere in the Grand Canyon starts daily from Peach Springs. See p.189

✳ **Flying to the river** Only at Grand Canyon West is it possible to ride a helicopter on a fearsome plummet to the Colorado River. See p.190

✳ **Eagle Point** Earmarked as the site of the amazing Skywalk, Eagle Point is a stunning canyon viewpoint. See p.191

✳ **Indian Village** Featuring authentic Native American dwellings, cultural performances, and crafts, Indian Village strives to lend Grand Canyon West a genuine Hualapai identity. See p.191

✳ **Guano Point** The focal point of Grand Canyon West, Guano Point features fascinating historical relics and commands a superb prospect of the canyon as it nears its end. See p.192

△ Las Vegas visitors pledge their vows beside the Colorado

8

Hualapai Indian Reservation

The **Hualapai Indian Reservation** spreads across almost a million acres of northwest Arizona. Its northern border comprises a 108-mile stretch of the Colorado at the extreme western end of the Grand Canyon, from which the reservation extends south on average between twenty and thirty miles – just far enough to include thirteen-mile sections of both the original **Route 66** and parallel transcontinental **railroad**. Straddling the highway is the reservation's only town, **Peach Springs**, home to just under a thousand of the total Hualapai population of around 1500.

The tribe's main business these days is **tourism** – specifically, promoting a cluster of rim-side overlooks as **Grand Canyon West**, or the **West Rim** of the Grand Canyon. This canny piece of marketing is aimed squarely at the 35 million tourists who flock to **Las Vegas** each year. The Hualapai reservation is the closest spot to Vegas that offers canyon views, and most of its visitors are first-time day-trippers who are unaware they're not seeing the canyon at its best. As it starts to peter out, the canyon here lacks the colossal depth and width of its central section, and it holds none of the towering mesas, buttes, and temples so conspicuous from the South or North rim viewpoints. Neither, unfortunately for the Hualapai, is there anything to match the sumptuous waterfalls of the neighboring Havasupai reservation.

Even so, for anyone new to the Southwest canyonlands, the so-called West Rim presents a tremendous spectacle. The Hualapai are also engaged in a remarkable bid to maximize the commercial potential of their rim-side holdings. Their plans are so ambitious, it's hard to say what will truly materialize, but they've clearly attracted a great deal of investment, and the infrastructure (for example, road conditions) is rapidly being transformed.

The Hualapai take full advantage of their independent status, outside the national park and free from federal regulations. For several years already they've been offering two unique enticements for visitors: **helicopter flights** that drop below the rim and land by the river and **one-day white-water rafting** trips on the Colorado. As this book went to press, they were also constructing a glass-bottomed, U-shaped **Skywalk** that loops out from the rim atop a 4000ft cliff. As of late 2005, there were just a few holes drilled in the ground, but the tribe confidently predicted the Skywalk would open in 2006. If all goes according to plan, it could well become one of the world's most famous tourist attractions.

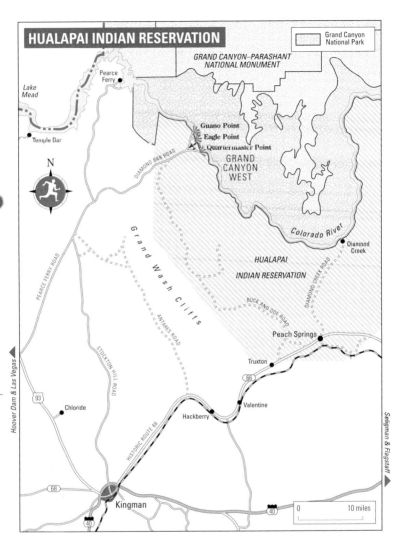

Ultimately, the Hualapai and their business partners hope to develop a high-end resort close to the Skywalk and make Grand Canyon West more than just a day-trip destination. For the moment, however, virtually all of its roughly 300,000 annual visitors fly in from Las Vegas for just a few hours. If you're among the very few who drive here, the long, empty route evokes a sense of unexplored wilderness you certainly *don't* get from driving to the South Rim.

A history of the Hualapai

Though the Hualapai – whose name is pronounced *Wa-la-pie* – are not as well known as the Havasupai, the latter were originally a minor offshoot of the Hualapai tribe. As detailed on p.175, both were descended from a group known as the **Pai** – "The People" – who make their first appearance in the archeological record shortly after AD 700. Also called the **Cerbat**, the Pai trace their tribal origin to Spirit Mountain, farther down the Colorado near modern-day Bullhead City, Arizona. The Hualapai lived in the South Rim forests from around 1100 – hence their name, "People of the Tall Pines." While their original base was **Meriwhitica Canyon**, a side canyon on the western end of the current reservation, the Hualapai seem to have supplanted Ancestral Puebloans throughout most of the Grand Canyon proper, in many cases inheriting their craft skills, survival techniques, and even their homes.

The Hualapai were a nomadic people, who planted crops and collected wild plants on the canyon floor in summer and spent the winter hunting on the plateaus and amid the mountains farther south. Significant contact with outsiders only came in the 1860s, when prospectors established a wagon route deep into Hualapai territory to pursue the copper, lead, silver, and gold deposits in the Cerbat Mountains to the west. Conflict soon escalated into the **Hualapai War**, a guerrilla struggle that lasted from 1865 to 1869. With a quarter of all Hualapai men killed in the fighting, and the tribe further decimated by disease, the survivors were rounded up and force-marched into internment at La Paz, near modern-day Parker, Arizona. They soon escaped and returned to their ancestral lands, a situation formalized in 1883 – two years after the railroad reached Peach Springs – by the establishment of their own reservation.

From the 1950s through the 1970s, Hualapai leaders vociferously supported plans to construct the **Bridge Canyon Dam** on their reservation, to block the Grand Canyon at its narrowest point. The Hualapai stood to gain not only in terms of construction jobs, but also in long-term royalties and increased visitation. When environmentalists, appalled at the notion of damming the canyon, campaigned against the project, the Hualapai accused them of "condemning our families to lifelong poverty by forcing us to keep our

△ The Hualapai flag flies at Grand Canyon West

homeland a wilderness." The proposals were nevertheless defeated, and the Hualapai turned their attention exclusively to promoting tourism. Development of Grand Canyon West started in 1988, and the current generation of leaders now speaks of preserving the canyon.

Peach Springs

The lone sizable Hualapai community, **PEACH SPRINGS** stands at the northern extremity of Route 66's sweeping curve away from I-40, 53 miles northeast of Kingman and 35 miles northwest of Seligman. Entirely distinct from, and not conveniently connected with, Grand Canyon West, it lies just six miles west of the turnoff for Arrowhead Hwy 18, the one road into the Havasupai Indian Reservation. Aside from Seligman itself, there's a disappointing lack of kitsch Americana along Route 66, but driving the much-mythologized **Mother Road**, crossing vast desert expanses with only the railroad for company, remains an evocative experience.

Peach Springs is no more than a straggle of buildings along the highway, of which the most prominent by far is the shiny, modern **Hualapai Lodge**, which opened in 1997. Its sixty good-sized bedrooms are broadly equivalent to what you'd expect to find in one of the slightly more upmarket hotel chains, as is the **dining room**, open daily for all meals (☎1-888/255-9550 or 928/769-2230, ⓦwww.grandcanyonresort.com; April–Oct ❺, Nov–March ❹).

A desk in the lobby serves as the headquarters of the **Hualapai Office of Tourism** (Mon–Fri 9am–5pm; same phone and website). As well as organizing the rafting trips described below, this office sells **permits** for visits to Grand Canyon West (though very few of the drivers heading there come via Peach Springs; see p.190), backcountry sightseeing ($5 per day), and camping on Diamond Creek Road ($10, including sightseeing fee; see opposite). The tribe's separate **Wildlife Office** (Mon–Fri 8am–4.30pm; ☎928/769-2227), a short

Who owns the river?

When the Hualapai began offering one-day river trips, in 1973, it was with a permit from the National Park Service, which is officially responsible for the entire course of the Colorado through the canyon. However, an ongoing dispute has festered ever since. The Park Service argues that the Hualapai reservation extends only as far as the high-water mark of the Colorado, thus not to the river itself; the Hualapai claim that it extends not merely to the banks of the Colorado, but to a notional line in mid-river, thus obviating the need for permission to operate the rafting trips. For many years, the Park Service tacitly tolerated the situation, its sensitivity to charges that tours are improperly regulated outweighed by an even greater sensitivity to accusations of provoking conflict with the canyon's rightful "owners."

However, the rapid expansion of tourism on the Hualapai reservation has thrown the tribe increasingly into conflict with the Park Service, which has long been drafting the Colorado River Management Plan to regulate river trips. Around twelve thousand annual visitors take the Hualapai river trips, but the Hualapai want to be able to carry up to 960 passengers per day; the Park Service wants to cap the figure at a maximum of 150 per day. As this book went to press, it seemed inevitable the issue would end up in court, and the Hualapai were threatening that if they lose, they'll start charging substantial fees to the many rafters on multi-day trips who exit the canyon at Diamond Creek, on Hualapai land.

distance west across the highway, issues similar sightseeing permits for exploration elsewhere on the reservation, as well as permits to fish (an extra $8 per day) and hunt (up to $20,000 for a trophy bighorn sheep).

One-day rafting trip

Operating under the name **Hualapai River Runners** (☎1-888/255-9550 or 928/769-2219, ⓦwww.grandcanyonresort.com), the Hualapai run the only **one-day rafting trip** offered within the Grand Canyon – a 35-mile ride from **Diamond Creek** to **Quartermaster Canyon** that includes significant stretches of white water. No rowing or paddling is involved; instead they use motorized pontoons, capable of carrying up to ten passengers aged 8 or over. The price is a hefty $280. At a potential cost of more than $1000 for a family of four, it makes a very expensive day out, and simply getting here in the first place takes quite a commitment, but the trips are nonetheless popular with those who lack the time for a longer river trip.

While the future of the Hualapai trips is uncertain (see box opposite), for now they depart the *Hualapai Lodge* by van at 8am daily between mid-March and mid-October. After a ninety-minute drive down to the river at Diamond Creek, you'll board the rafts and immediately confront white water. The first ten miles shoot the canyon's final ten rapids, with a maximum difficulty rating of 7 (see p.201). Following a riverside picnic lunch and optional short hike, the trip winds down with a tranquil 25-mile float to Quartermaster Canyon, where a **helicopter** awaits to fly you up to the canyon rim. It's a two-hour drive back to Peach Springs, with a typical return time of around 7pm. Many passengers overnight at the lodge before or after the trip.

Diamond Creek

The unpaved twenty-mile road that leads due north of Peach Springs to the river at **Diamond Creek** is used almost exclusively by rafters, either leaving the Colorado after a multi-day expedition or taking one of the Hualapai's day trips. However, with the appropriate permit from the lodge (see opposite), you can simply drive down for a look.

Thanks to deep **Peach Springs Canyon**, Diamond Creek is the only place within the Grand Canyon where a road runs all the way to the river, dropping 3000ft en route. Not much of a road, though: The views of soaring canyon walls on either side are great, but the surface is terrible and liable to be rendered impassable to standard cars by the slightest rain. The final two miles are often washed out altogether by summer flash floods.

Despite the difficult terrain, there was a hotel down here between 1884 and 1889, before access improved to what's now called the South Rim. These days, there's just a rather rudimentary tribal **campground**, set back from the river amid the sand dunes ($10 per night).

Grand Canyon West

Grand Canyon West, also known as the **West Rim**, is a remote group of inner canyon viewpoints roughly fifty miles northwest of Peach Springs and 120 miles east of Las Vegas. If you're touring the canyon region, the West Rim is perhaps the least essential stop to include on your itinerary; its sole *raison d'être* is to generate income for the Hualapai by granting tourists from Vegas a glimpse of the canyon on an easy day trip. That said, it's only easy if you come by air; by car, it's a long detour down barren desert roads.

While **Guano Point** offers an undeniably great prospect of the inner gorge, the canyon as a whole here is simply not as majestic as in its better-known segments. Come expecting natural wonders and you may well end up feeling shortchanged. Instead, the success of your visit will probably depend on whether the **Skywalk** is in place when you arrive (and lives up to expectations) or whether you're prepared to spend the necessary money on a hair-raising **helicopter** ride to the canyon floor.

Driving to Grand Canyon West

In terms of road conditions, the best routes to Grand Canyon West approach not from the east via Peach Springs, but from the west and south. In recent years the Hualapai have finally paved two roads to the West Rim. The busiest of the pair, **Pearce Ferry Road**, heads northeast from **US-93** (the main highway between Arizona and Las Vegas), thirty miles north of Kingman and forty miles south of the Hoover Dam. Twenty-eight miles along, you'll turn east on **Diamond Bar Road**. After a rocky fourteen-mile climb through foothills scattered with Joshua trees and up the Grand Wash Cliffs, you'll enter the Hualapai reservation; the airstrip and Grand Canyon West headquarters lie five miles farther up the road. Alternatively, from central Kingman you can take the forty-mile **Stockton Hill Road**, which runs due north and T-junctions with Pearce Ferry Road some 26 miles short of Grand Canyon West.

Two more routes may have been paved by the time you read this; ask locally before taking either of them. The more likely of the two is **Antares Road**, which runs north from Route 66, eighteen miles northeast of Kingman, and meets Pearce Ferry Road at much the same juncture as Stockton Hill Road. The fifty-mile **Buck and Doe Road**, which heads north from Route 66, four miles west of Peach Springs, and meets Diamond Bar Road three miles short of the end, will probably remain unpaved and impassable to standard vehicles indefinitely.

In 2005, plans were announced for a **visitor center** at the intersection of Pearce Ferry Road and US-93; visitors would then have the option of taking a shuttle to Grand Canyon West for a projected round-trip fare of $7–10. Missing Link Tours already offers day trips by bus from Las Vegas, starting at $139 (T1-800/209-8586, Wwww.tmltours.com).

Flying to Grand Canyon West

Several companies offer day-trip **flights from Las Vegas** to the rudimentary airstrip beside West Rim headquarters. Papillon Grand Canyon Helicopters (T928/699-3993 or 1-800/528-2418, Wwww.papillon.com), Maverick Helicopter Tours (T702/261-0007 or 1-888/261-4414, Wwww .maverickhelicopter.com), and Sundance Helicopters (T702/736-0606 or 1-800/653-1881, Wwww.helicoptour.com) offer **helicopter** tours, starting at around $230, while **fixed-wing** operators include Scenic Airlines (T702/638-3200 or 1-800/634-6801, Wwww.scenic.com), which charges $249 with the bus tour described opposite or $379 with a helicopter flight into the canyon.

Both Papillon and Sundance operate **helicopter flights** down to the Colorado from the Grand Canyon West terminal; prices are detailed in the box opposite.

Below we've detailed the packages available for **touring Grand Canyon West**; all prices are subject to an additional seven percent **tribal tax**.

Basic tour packages
Earth ($29). Bus tour to Eagle Point to visit the Indian Village and Hualapai Market and watch a cultural performance, then to Guano Point for a stroll; no meal included.

Spirit ($50). Everything on the Earth tour, plus a hike at Guano Point, a photo op with Hualapai tribal members, a visit to the Hualapai Ranch for a wagon wheel ride and Wild West show, and either a buffet at Guano Point or a cookout at the ranch.

Explorer ($109). Everything on the Spirit tour, plus either a Hummer tour or a horseback ride.

Optional add-ons to tour packages
Skywalk	$25
Horseback ride	
Traditional	$59
Extended	$79
Hummer tour	
Original	$59
Extended	$89
Helicopter packages	
Helicopter/Hummer tour	$169
Helicopter/jet boat	$169
Helicopter/float trip	$149

Exploring Grand Canyon West

Your first impression of Grand Canyon West will likely be of the featureless gray desert plateau that leads to the edge of the abyss. All visitors report to a small, single-story building to the right of the highway, a few hundred yards short of the rim, which serves as the **tribal headquarters** for tours and permits and as the **terminal** for both the adjacent helicopter pad and airstrip across the road.

To reach the two main viewpoints, farther down the road, you'll have to join a Hualapai-run **bus tour** from the terminal. If you've flown in, a package tour will be included in your overall price; otherwise, the various permutations and possibilities are outlined in the box above.

Eagle Point
Eagle Point does not perch on the rim, but faces across a narrow, unnamed side canyon. In the right light – especially morning – shadows play along the knife-edged sandstone spur that forms the canyon's opposite wall, calling to mind a massive eagle with outstretched wings. The point is the setting for the **Skywalk**, the glass-floored, horseshoe-shaped walkway that will become the centerpiece of Grand Canyon West. Visitors will be asked to pay something like $25 for the thrill of walking out over the sheer 4000ft drop. If it is in operation when you arrive, you should also find an adjacent high-end restaurant, though the ground had yet to be broken at press time.

A short trail from Eagle Point leads to the **Indian Village**, which consists of various authentic dwellings built by the Hualapai and other local Native

American tribes, including the Navajo, Hopi, and Apache. Tribal representatives are on hand to explain their history and symbolism, there are regular dance performances, and crafts are sold in the **Hualapai Market**.

Guano Point

At road's end, two miles beyond the terminal, the buses reach appetizingly named **Guano Point**. This windswept rounded headland, poised atop sheer 3000ft cliffs, surveys long stretches of the Colorado in both directions. Though the Grand Canyon looks as if it could go on forever, it actually peters out just beyond the next bend in the river to the west, where it bisects the Grand Wash Cliffs.

Follow the short loop trail just below the point and you'll find large pylons and chunks of abandoned machinery littering the landscape. Dating from the 1940s and 1950s, these are relics of the days when guano – bat dung, an excellent fertilizer – was commercially mined from the so-called **Bat Cave**, still visible on the far side of the river. A cable car carried the congealed dung across the canyon. The mine was eventually shut down after a rabies scare, and it's said that low-flying Air Force fighters cut the suspended cables during a training mission; unlike the National Park Service, the Hualapai allow the Air Force to conduct flight training within the canyon.

An ugly, rather futuristic shelter on the point serves all-you-can-eat **buffet lunches** – chicken, ribs, and the like – included in certain tour packages.

Hualapai Ranch

Roughly two miles from the terminal in the opposite direction from Eagle and Guano points, **Hualapai Ranch** is perhaps the strangest of the attractions the Hualapai have built at Grand Canyon West. Bearing little relevance to either the tribe or the canyon, it's basically a themed Wild West stockade set well back from the rim. In addition to serving as the headquarters for horseback rides, it stages such Western-style events as country music and professional bison riding and also offers cookout lunches – a fancy way of saying an outdoor café ladles out plates of beans and barbecued chickens.

Quartermaster Point

A third viewpoint, **Quartermaster Point**, lies beyond Hualapai Ranch. Perched just west of deep Quartermaster Canyon, the overlook commands views straight up Burnt Canyon, across the Colorado, toward the long promontory of Kelly Point on the North Rim.

The Colorado River

While no hiking trails connect Grand Canyon West with the river below, a high proportion of visitors take the four-minute helicopter ride down from the terminal. The flight in itself is a major adventure, though it's also a thrill to stroll along the **Colorado** in the depths of the inner gorge. You'll land close to the south bank, which is much broader than its northern counterpart and, more important, belongs to the Hualapai. Though you won't find much in the way of amenities, apart from a basic arbor for shade, this is an attractive and fascinating spot, lush with tamarisk thickets and flowering cacti.

A short footpath leads from the landing pad to the river's edge, where wooden jetties serve as a base for pontoons and jet boats that sweep visitors out for a quick swirl on the river. The adjoining beach is the terminus for the Hualapai's one-day rafting trips (see p.189); participants fly out from here.

△ Pontoon excursion on the Colorado below Grand Canyon West

Note that if you take a one-day helicopter tour from Las Vegas to Grand Canyon West, and that tour lands within the canyon but does *not* include a river trip, your landing will likely be at a different vantage point, roughly a mile or so upriver, which offers arguably better views but not access to the river itself.

Rafting the Colorado River

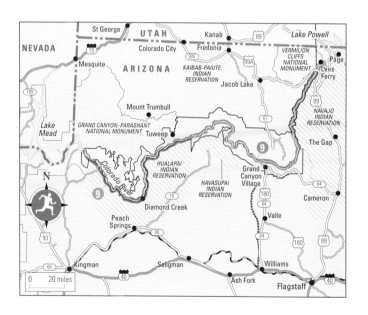

CHAPTER 9

Highlights

* **Dory trips** Follow in the wake of John Wesley Powell by tackling the Colorado in a genuine wooden dory. See p.200

* **The sound of strings** Remarkably, Canyon Explorations offers two rafting trips each year during which participants are serenaded by a string quartet. See p.201

* **Specialist trips** Arizona Raft Adventures' many rafting expeditions include trips designed for hikers, natural historians, and even geologists. See p.202

* **Marble Canyon float trip** Floating the Colorado from Glen Canyon Dam to Lees Ferry gives you a spectacular taste of river rafting in just half a day. See p.204

* **Hualapai River Runners** At the far western end of the Grand Canyon, the Hualapai tribe offers a one-day rafting trip that culminates in an exhilarating helicopter ride. See p.204

△ Rafters set off from the beach near Phantom Ranch

Rafting the Colorado River

I conclude the Colorado is not a very easy stream to navigate.
— Diary entry of George Bradley, member of the first Powell expedition,
at the end of the first-ever day's boating on the Colorado

Part white-knuckle ride, part leisurely scenic cruise, **rafting** the **Colorado River** through the Grand Canyon has been repeatedly rated among the greatest outdoor adventures our planet has to offer. Yes, you can admire the canyon from the safety of the rim, but only when you've raced its every rapid, drenched to the skin and deafened by its thundering roar, can you truly claim to know it inside out. And a river trip offers much more than pure adrenaline: You can also picnic on sandy riverside beaches; camp beneath the stars; hike up little-known side canyons to hidden waterfalls, mysterious caves, and narrow sandstone slots; swim in streams and water holes; and generally escape from the modern world into a remote, timeless wilderness.

When **John Wesley Powell**'s crew set out in 1869 to become the first party to travel down the Colorado by boat (see p.212), they had no way of knowing whether such a voyage was possible. Along the way, they were haunted by fear, perhaps that a mighty waterfall might lie around the next bend or that some fearsome rapid might fill the canyon wall to wall at a point that offered no way to climb out. As it turned out, there were no waterfalls, and it *is* possible to float the full length of the Colorado. Of course, it remains far from easy and is not something you should even dream of attempting without the most expert guidance and advice. Nevertheless, river craft and techniques have become so refined that professional rafting companies can carry thousands of inexperienced passengers through the canyon each year in safety. Yet as weather and water levels fluctuate and flash floods reshape the canyon contours, the thrill of uncertainty remains, and every trip presents a new challenge.

The prime reason why rafting the Grand Canyon is so exciting is the estimated 161 sets of **rapids** along the way. The Colorado here is what's known as a "**pool and drop**" river, consisting of tranquil sections, where it meanders along at an average six miles per hour, that alternate with hectic rapids, where the water is constricted into narrow, debris-strewn channels. The latter often occur where rocks washed down a side canyon by a tributary stream have tumbled

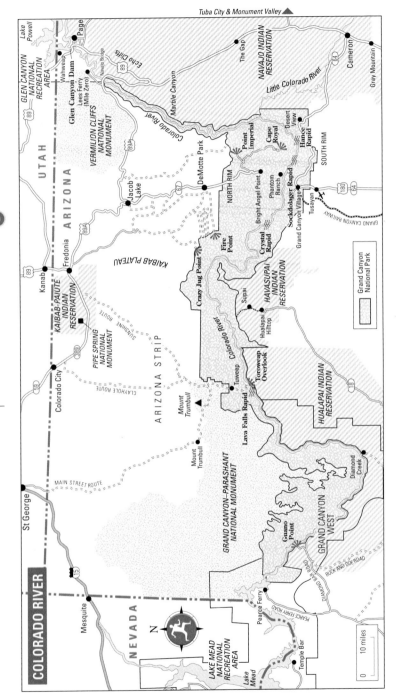

into the riverbed. The resultant **white water** charges along at perhaps twenty or thirty miles per hour, creating an obstacle course of concealed boulders and treacherous whirlpools that canyon boatmen learn to navigate by both instinct and experience.

The **rafting season** begins in mid-April and runs until mid-September for motorized trips or as late as early November for oar-powered expeditions. The busiest period is **summer**, between June and August, despite the fact that daytime temperatures often exceed 100°F and thunderstorms are common from late July into September. In **spring** and **fall**, when temperatures are cooler and the canyon quieter, many operators offer longer trips to allow for extra hiking. Spring also ushers in canyon flora at its most colorful. Typical daytime highs are in the 60–80°F range in April and November, more like 70–100°F in May, September, and October. Nightly lows vary from as low as 40°F in April up to a muggy 90°F in July. Whenever you come, however, you must be prepared for extremes of both heat and cold, as well as potential rain. Although the Colorado itself remains consistently cool year-round, barely straying from 48°F – cold enough to cause hypothermia – streams and pools in the side canyons present great swimming opportunities in summer.

There are two basic types of rafting trip, both strictly regulated by the Park Service – you certainly can't just turn up at the Colorado with your own raft and set off. You can either join a **commercial** trip with one of the accredited concessionaires listed on pp.202–204 or, if you have a great deal of white-water experience and an even greater amount of patience, put together your own **noncommercial** party and join the waiting list for a time slot. As it currently takes around nine years to reach the head of the line, the commercial option is much more realistic.

Commercial rafting trips

Anyone considering a commercial rafting trip through the Grand Canyon must choose between joining a **motorized** or an **oar-powered** expedition. Typical costs range between **$200 and $300 per person per day**, though oar-powered trips often cost a bit more and take longer overall. On a motorized trip, a professional guide is wholly responsible for the actual work of running the river, while on an oar-powered boat, you don't necessarily have to do any rowing, but guides often allow passengers to paddle some or even all of the way. As a rule, the **minimum age** for participants on motorized trips is 8, while on oar-powered trips it's 12.

Although purists insist that the comparative silence and sense of physical involvement of an oar-powered trip provides a far more "authentic" river-running experience than a motorized trip, the actual day-to-day routine is actually quite similar whichever type you choose. Even the fastest trips of either type spend little more than five hours actually on the river each day; it's taken for granted that everyone wants to stop for picnics and hikes.

The boats

For the most part, commercial operators use different kinds of **inflatable rubberized rafts**. Powell's wooden boats were built for speed, very hard to maneuver, and rowed by two men, seated in traditional rowboat style with their backs to what lay ahead. Modern rafts are flat-bottomed, extremely maneuverable, and capable of bouncing undamaged off obstacles; the single boatman faces

△ Mile Zero of the Grand Canyon, beneath the Vermilion Cliffs at Lees Ferry

forward and often slows down by paddling against the current, jockeying for position until a route opens up.

Naturally, **motorized** trips travel significantly faster. Each raft can be up to thirty feet long, equipped with outriggers for extra stability, and carry up to ten passengers. The Park Service has long considered banning motorized craft altogether, arguing that they increase both noise and environmental pollution. Industry lobbyists have so far managed to stymie a complete ban, but motorized expeditions remain restricted in terms of both the total passengers permitted each year and the season they can operate (mid-April to mid-September).

Nonmotorized, or **oar-powered**, rafts average around eighteen feet long and are usually rowed and steered by a guide with a single oar while the four or five passengers simply enjoy the ride. Some outfitters also offer **paddle rafts**, of a similar size and passenger capacity, on which everyone has their own paddle, and the guide is only responsible for steering. Adventure sports enthusiasts often opt for **paddle-only** trips, during which paying customers are expected to paddle all the way; it's also possible to take a **hybrid** trip, which incorporates both vessel types and allows passengers to choose each day whether to ride in a paddle boat or be rowed by a guide.

For those determined to echo the conditions experienced by river pioneers, two operators, **Grand Canyon Expeditions** and **O.A.R.S.** (under the name Grand Canyon Dories), offer significantly more expensive rowing trips in hard-bodied **dories**. These are the closest modern approximation to Powell's boats, albeit extensively adapted for Grand Canyon use. Because dories require such skilled handling, only the crew may row.

Choosing a trip

The Grand Canyon is officially 277 miles long, with each river mile extending downstream from Mile 0 at **Lees Ferry** (see p.131). Just under sixteen miles downstream from Glen Canyon Dam, Lees Ferry is the only spot from which it's possible to **launch** a rafting expedition. Boats and/or passengers can, however, **leave** at differing junctures.

The canyon ends at Mile 277, where the Colorado emerges on the open waters of **Lake Mead**; three miles farther, at Mile 280, a paved road accesses the lake at **Pearce Ferry**. However, over the final 43 miles of the canyon, the true channel lies submerged beneath calmer lake waters. Many river trips, therefore, end at **Diamond Creek**, on Hualapai land at Mile 226, where boats and passengers can be driven out of the canyon along a gravel road. Some operators end their trips even sooner, at **Whitmore Wash** (Mile 187), scooping up customers from river level by helicopter and whisking them to the **Bar 10 Ranch** on the North Rim, where an airstrip enables onward flights to Las Vegas or elsewhere. **Phantom Ranch**, at Mile 87, offers another potential stopping place en route, from which passengers can hike out to either the South or North rims. Passengers may also join an existing trip at Phantom Ranch, though there's no way to get a boat down to the Colorado at that point.

The permutations for possible trips are endless. What are advertised as full-length Grand Canyon expeditions may be 187, 226, or 280 miles long and take anything from six motorized days to 22 oar-powered days. (The record, incidentally, for the full 277 miles is just under 37 hours, by an unauthorized expedition undertaken in 1983 during dangerous flooding, when the canyon was closed to all craft.) Most operators also offer an **upper canyon** option, starting at Lees Ferry and ending with a hike out from Phantom Ranch, which typically takes four days/three nights, as well as a **lower canyon** trip, starting with a hike down to Phantom Ranch and taking out somewhere downstream after four or five nights.

You can also take a **two-day/one-night** river trip if you fly down into the canyon at Whitmore Wash with Arizona River Runners (see p.202) or a **day trip** from Diamond Creek with Hualapai River Runners (see p.204).

Neither an upper nor a lower canyon trip is "better" than the other. On an upper canyon trip, you and your fellow passengers will set out together, versus joining an established group, and you'll get a gentler, more progressive introduction to the canyon and its rapids. On the other hand, there's less placid water overall, and you'll have to hike out at the end. A lower canyon trip offers a slightly longer ride, but also plunges you straight away into some really major rapids.

Although white-water experts traditionally grade rapids on a difficulty scale of 1 to 6, on the Colorado they're ranked from 1 to 10, so a "4" here won't be the same as one elsewhere. Both of the Grand Canyon's two unquestioned 10s lie downstream from Phantom Ranch – **Crystal Rapid** at Mile 98, created by a flash flood in 1966, and **Lava Falls Rapid** farther west at Mile 179, which is visible from Toroweap Point (see p.148). There are, however, a couple of almost-as-intense rapids in the upper canyon: **Hance Rapid** at Mile 76, and **Sockdolager Rapid** – named by Powell for a contemporary word meaning "knockout punch" – just past the start of the Granite Gorge at Mile 78.

Other highlights in the upper canyon include **Vasey's Paradise**, a flower-filled natural garden at Mile 31; the **Redwall Cavern** at Mile 33, a vast sand-floored alcove which Powell overeagerly estimated could hold fifty thousand people; and the confluence with the **Little Colorado** at Mile 61, which, thanks to a rich concentration of salts from springs not far upstream, flows in from the east as a resplendent turquoise stream.

The biggest treats for **hikers** come in the lower canyon, with the successive **Olo**, **Matkatamiba**, and **Havasu** canyons between miles 145 and 156. The first two are narrow slot canyons, interspersed with hidden pools and waterfalls and boasting rock walls sculpted by flash floods into beautiful swirling patterns; the splendors of Havasu Canyon are described in full in **Chapter Seven**, though rafters seldom hike any farther up the canyon than Beaver Falls, four miles up but two miles shy of Mooney Falls.

Commercial rafting operators

Following is a complete list of operators authorized to conduct commercial river trips within the Grand Canyon; you can also find the current list online, with active links, at Ⓦ www.nps.gov/grca/river/river_concessioners.htm. For an overview of available excursions, contact **Rivers & Oceans**, 12620 N Copeland Lane, Flagstaff, AZ 86004 (☎ 1-800/473-4576 or 928/526-4575, Ⓦ www.rivers-oceans.com), a travel broker that specializes in making bookings with all of the outfitters.

When considering a company, ask whether its published rates include any **transportation** and/or overnight **accommodation** that may be required before or after your trip. While you might be tempted to cut costs by driving yourself to Lees Ferry, that can leave you with a serious logistical problem. Also, if you're a long way from home, choosing a trip that includes round-trip transportation to and from Flagstaff or Las Vegas can spare you from having to pay for a **rental car** you won't be using for several days.

Listed rates include unlimited **food** and **beverages** for the duration, though you'll have to supply any alcoholic drinks yourself. You should, however, confirm exactly what **equipment** is included in the price. Some operators charge rental fees to passengers who don't bring their own sleeping bags and mats, while others provide everything.

Companies also provide checklists of what you should and shouldn't bring. Recommended **clothing** includes a full set of raingear, insulating base layers, a fleece jacket and hat, a swimsuit, and sandals with soft rubber soles. Among items not to carry are mobile or satellite phones, radios, and other electrical devices.

Finally, bear in mind that it's customary to **tip** your river guides between five and ten percent of the total cost at the end of your trip.

Arizona Raft Adventures 4050-F E Huntington Rd, Flagstaff, AZ 86004 ☎ 1-800/786-7238 or 928/526-8200, Ⓦ www.azraft.com. ARA's motorized rafts operate between May and mid-August, costing around $2000 for the eight-day standard trip, $2360 for the ten-day Hiker's Discovery in Sept, $2460 for the ten-day Natural History Discovery in May, and $2810 for the twelve-day Geology Discovery in September. Paddle-only trips leave once monthly between May and mid-September, at around $1625 for six days, $2375 for nine days, and $3110 for fourteen days. For slightly cheaper rates, you can also join one of a dozen hybrid trips between May and September. **Arizona River Runners** PO Box 47788, Phoenix, AZ 85068-7788 ☎ 1-800/477-7238 or 602/867-4866, Ⓦ www.raftarizona.com. Motorized trips down the full length of the canyon, available between May and September, cost $1755 for six days, $1925 for seven days, or $1945 for eight days. Oar-powered expeditions run four times

between June and October, though not in midsummer, and cost $1310 for the six-day upper canyon voyage, $1770 for the eight-day trip from Phantom Ranch to Diamond Creek, and $2700 for the full thirteen-day voyage from Lees Ferry to Diamond Creek. Every few days between May and September, the company also offers a three-day Grand Canyon Escape from Las Vegas, in which you fly to the Bar 10 Ranch and spend a night there, take a helicopter down to the Colorado for a 1.5-day river trip, then return to Vegas from Lake Mead, all for $865.

Canyon Explorations/Canyon Expeditions PO Box 310, Flagstaff, AZ 86002 ☎ 1-800/654-0723 or 928/774-4559, Ⓦ www.canyonexplorations .com. An extensive program of river trips of differing lengths is available between April and October. All begin and end with transportation to and from Flagstaff, and several are extended to allow for extra hiking. Rates for hybrid trips, which also include inflatable kayaks, and paddle-only expeditions are the same, ranging from $1580 for six days or $2380 for nine days up to $3350 for fifteen days; a couple of the latter trips, bizarrely enough, take a string quartet along with them. Kayakers can join any trip for a $200 additional fee.

Canyoneers PO Box 2997, Flagstaff, AZ 86003 ☎1-800/525-0924 or 928/526-0924, ⊛www .canyoneers.com. Canyoneers, which also runs *Kaibab Camper Village* (see p.136) near the North Rim, specializes in sending massive powered pontoons down the Grand Canyon. Weekly between mid-April and early September, it runs the entire length in seven days/six nights for $1825 ($1495 in April only). In June and July, it also offers a handful of shorter trips, with a $705 two-day/two-night sprint through the upper canyon and a $1425 five-day/four-night trip through the lower canyon, which costs $1550 if you choose to overnight at Phantom Ranch first. In September only, it also offers oar-powered trips, costing $1450 for the five-day upper canyon segment, $1895 for the eight-day lower canyon stretch, or $2700 for the full twelve-day trip. All trips start and end in Flagstaff.

Colorado River & Trail Expeditions PO Box 57575, Salt Lake City, UT 84157-0575 ☎1-800/253-7328 or 801/261-1789, ⊛www.crateinc .com. Weekly motorized expeditions between mid-May and the end of August, at $925 for the four-day upper canyon run, $1450 for the six-day lower canyon run, and $1975 for the whole thing, in either eight or nine days. Rates for its first trip of the season, at the end of April, are a little lower, even though rafts linger five days over the upper canyon and seven in the lower, to allow more time for hiking. In late July and August, it also offers one hybrid trip and one paddle-only trip, both of which cost $1225 for the five days from Lees Ferry to Phantom Ranch, $2195 for the seven days from Phantom Ranch to Whitmore Wash, and $2895 for the eleven days from Lees Ferry to Whitmore Wash.

Diamond River Adventures PO Box 1300, Page, AZ 86040 ☎1-800/343-3121 or 928/645-8866, ⊛www.diamondriver.com. Female-owned and -managed rafting company, which offers Grand Canyon expeditions of between four and thirteen days by either oar or motorboat. The season runs from May to early September, with motorized trips setting off more or less weekly, and oar-powered ones somewhat less frequently. Four-day upper canyon motorized trips start at around $830, while to run the full length with a motor takes seven days and costs $1675. By oar, it's twelve days and $2600.

Grand Canyon Expeditions Company PO Box 0, Kanab, UT 84741 ☎1-800/544-2691 or 435/644-2691, ⊛www.gcex.com. Offers a huge number of motorized expeditions, with 65 departures between April and mid-September each year. Some are devoted to special interests like ecology, archeology, and photography and thus offer longer pauses at, and extra hikes to, sites of particular significance, with guidance from experts in the respective fields. The eight-day run from Lees Ferry to Lake Mead costs $2145. It also offers four rowing trips each summer, in May, June, July, and September, using modern dories, which take either fourteen days, for $3225, or sixteen days, for $3500.

Hatch River Expeditions PO Box 1200, Vernal, UT 84078 ☎1-800/433-8966 or 435/789-3813, ⊛www.hatchriverexpeditions.com. Hatch River Expeditions runs regular seven-day, 188-mile motorized trips between Lees Ferry and Whitmore Wash; passengers leave the canyon well before the end, via helicopter, for connecting flights to Las Vegas or Marble Canyon. Taking the whole cruise costs $1925, or you can take a four-day version, which costs $1000 for the upper canyon, exiting at Phantom Ranch, or $1050 for the lower canyon, entering at Phantom Ranch.

Moki Mac River Expeditions PO Box 71242, Salt Lake City, UT 84171-0242 ☎1-800/284-7280 or 801/268-6667, ⊛www.mokimac.com. Each summer, Moki Mac runs eleven fourteen-day oar-powered trips between Lees Ferry and Lake Mead – priced at $1650 for the upper canyon, $2205 for the lower canyon, and $3205 for the whole thing – and nine eight-day motorized trips on the same route, only sold as the entire trip and costing $2135. All rates cover round-trip transportation to and from Las Vegas.

O.A.R.S. PO Box 67, Angles Camp, CA 95222 ☎1-800/346-6277 or 209/736-2924, ⊛www .oars.com. Active throughout the West, this adventure-tour operator offers two separate kinds of Grand Canyon trips on a flexible program that runs from mid-April to early November. Among its conventional paddled raft trips, the full canyon voyage from Lees Ferry to Lake Mead takes either fifteen or seventeen days and costs around $4250 or $4500, respectively, while the many shorter stretches on offer include the usual Lees Ferry to Phantom Ranch stretch in six or seven days ($2050/2200) and Phantom Ranch to Diamond Creek in nine to eleven days ($2910–3285). Under the name Grand Canyon Dories, it also offers trips in flat-bottomed wooden dories (rowboats); the upper canyon takes seven to eight days for $2539, the lower canyon takes ten to twelve days for $3431, and the full canyon takes 21 days and costs $5068.

Outdoors Unlimited 6900 Townsend Winona Rd, Flagstaff, AZ 86004 ☎1-800/637-7238 or

928/526-4546, ⓦ www.outdoorsunlimited.com. Offers oar-powered trips, all of which take at least one paddle boat, and some of which are paddle-only. The full-length trip from Lees Ferry to Lake Mead costs $2900 for the full thirteen days, or you can take a five- or six-day upper canyon run for $1395 and $1595, respectively, or the eight- or nine-day lower Canyon segment for $2045/$2315. A paddle-only trip is slightly more expensive, while at the start or end of the season you can pay a little more again to join an extended trip that offers more hiking opportunities.

Tour West PO Box 333, Orem, UT 84059 ⓣ 1-800/453-9107 or 801/225-0755, ⓦ www.twriver.com. Between April and mid-September, Tour West sends 33 motorized expeditions down the canyon. A six-night trip from Lees Ferry to the Bar 10 Ranch costs $1975, an eight-night trip from Lees Ferry to Lake Mead costs $2165, and a three-night jaunt from the Bar 10 Ranch to Lake Mead costs $1130. In June and July each year, it also offers three twelve-night rowing trips for $2805.

Western River Expeditions 7258 Racquet Club Drive, Salt Lake City, UT 84121 ⓣ 1-800/453-7450 or 801/942-6669, ⓦ www.westernriver.com. Western River runs a slick program of brisk, motorized Grand Canyon expeditions, offering two basic choices on almost fifty separate expeditions between mid-April and September each year. You can either take the six-day run from Lees Ferry to the Bar 10 Ranch, which involves being heli-coptered out of the canyon 187 miles along, just after Lava Falls, or be choppered in at that point for a three-day float down to Lake Mead (with an optional extra first night at the ranch). The former costs around $2065, the latter more like $1025; both are ten percent cheaper in April.

Wilderness River Adventures PO Box 717, Page, AZ 86040 ⓣ 1-800/992-8022 or 928/645-3296, ⓦ www.riveradventures.com. Offers both oar-powered and motorized trips. The oar-powered ones use six boats, each capable of carrying four to six passengers, and set off every two to three weeks between mid-May and mid-September. They cost around $1630 for the five-day upper canyon ride; $2560 for the lower canyon, from Phantom Ranch to the Bar 10 Ranch, with a flight out to Las Vegas or Page; and $3100–3350 for the twelve- to fourteen-day full-length Grand Tradition trip. Motorized expeditions, using two fifteen-passenger boats, run regularly between mid-April and mid-September, taking 3.5 days for the upper canyon ($1000), 4.5 days for the lower canyon ($1950), and six to eight days for the whole thing ($2200–2500).

One-day trips

No one-day rafting trips are available within Grand Canyon National Park. If you only have a day to spare, however, there are two alternatives – one at either end of the canyon.

As described on p.128, Wilderness River Adventures (ⓣ928/645-3296 or 1-800/992-8022; ⓦwww.riveradventures.com) offers one-day **float trips** that start immediately below **Glen Canyon Dam** and take out at **Lees Ferry** (daily: 11.15am mid-March to mid-May and mid-September through May, 7.30am or 1pm June to mid-September; $62 adults, $52 age 12 and under). Participants rendezvous at Aramark's headquarters at 57 S Lake Powell Blvd in Page, Arizona, not far from the dam. Water and sodas are provided, but you're expected to bring your own picnic lunch.

Farther west, Hualapai River Runners offers daily 35-mile motorized trips through the western end of the canyon, including several rapids. You'll find full details in the **Hualapai Indian Reservation** chapter (see p.189).

Noncommercial trips

Between 250 and 300 **private rafting expeditions** are allowed onto the Colorado each year, with a maximum of sixteen participants each. The Park Service maintains a **waiting list** of more than 8000 applicants eager to organize their own trips, sufficient to fill all vacancies nine years in advance. Since December 2003, however, the Park Service has stopped adding names to the list, as an ongoing review of the Colorado River Management Plan is expected to change the whole way river rafting is regulated and organized. For details, contact the Grand Canyon River Permits Office, Grand Canyon National Park, PO Box 129, Grand Canyon, AZ 86023 (☎1-800/959-9164 or 928/638-7843, ⓕ928/638-7844). All those whose names are already on the list have to submit a **Continuing Interest** form every year by the end of January; miss this deadline more than once in any four-year period, and you'll be dropped from the list.

Should your name finally rise to the top, you'll be invited to pick a date within the next two years. A further fee of $100 per person is payable ninety days in advance. No participant on any trip can have been on another noncommercial trip within the last four years, and places are transferable only in very tightly controlled circumstances.

Around seventy **cancellations** come through each year. The freed-up dates are assigned to those on the waiting list, who must call on Friday evenings or all day Saturday or Sunday. Names higher up the list are favored, but if you're flexible, you may even get a cancellation the year you apply.

Contexts

Contexts

History

T he Grand Canyon might seem a supremely inhospitable, pristine environment, but it has been home to humans for around twelve thousand years. Native Americans once farmed along the canyon floor, across its plateaus, and up on the rims, while Spanish adventurers arrived here eighty years before the *Mayflower* set sail. Only within the last hundred years, however, has it occurred to anyone to come here for fun.

Native peoples

The oldest traces of a human presence at the Grand Canyon are a handful of flaked-stone spearheads that date back to around 10,000 BC. They were produced by the **Clovis** culture, which spread throughout North and South America until around 8000 BC. Living in small groups, constantly on the move, Clovis hunters pursued prey over long distances. They seem to have been such successful killers that they drove the indigenous fauna – which included giant sloths, camels, and even horses – to extinction.

As the large animals died out, the inhabitants of the Grand Canyon adapted to become **hunter–gatherers**, who migrated seasonally between the canyons and plateaus in search of food. Judging by small figurines found in caves in Marble Canyon and elsewhere – made from split willow twigs to represent deer and bighorn sheep and often run through by little "spears" – these nomads developed shamanistic rituals to encourage hunting success.

The so-called **Archaic Era** drew to a close following infiltration of influences from Mexico, especially **agriculture**. The skill of growing **corn**, passed northward from group to group and accompanied by prayers and rituals to ensure a good harvest, reached the canyon around 1000 BC. At first, low-level farming merely supplemented the traditional diet; large-scale cultivation of corn and also **squash** probably began around 100 BC. The people responsible, known as the **Basketmakers**, lived in extended family groups in shallow **pit houses** – rectangular pits, two to six feet deep, with earthen roofs that rose above ground level. They hunted using the atlatl – a spear-throwing device – and cooked by dropping hot rocks into yucca-leaf baskets lined with waterproof pitch. They also domesticated **dogs**, for hunting, and **turkeys**, used for feathers rather than food.

Pottery arrived a few centuries later, and with it the ability to boil **beans**, the third great staple Southwestern food. By around AD 500, the Basketmakers were also growing **cotton** and using **bows and arrows**. Sizable **villages** (what the Spanish later called **pueblos**) started to appear. Each centered on one pit house, larger than the rest, that was set aside for public or ritual use. These were the first **kivas** – the ceremonial underground chambers still at the heart of Pueblo religion. By AD 700, the Grand Canyon was populated by the ancestors of modern Pueblo Indians, a people now known as **Ancestral Puebloans**, in preference to the previously common term **Anasazi**, which comes from a Navajo word meaning "enemy ancestors."

The heyday of agriculture in the Grand Canyon came roughly one thousand years ago, when increased levels of precipitation meant that corn, beans, and squash could be planted throughout the canyon. Deltas at the mouths of major side canyons, such as **Unkar Creek** and **Chuar Creek**, made prized living spots. Modern visitors can see typical Puebloan dwellings both down in the canyon, close to Phantom Ranch (see p.106), and up on the plateaus, most notably at the **Tusayan Ruin** on the South Rim (see p.64) and **Walhalla Glades** on the North Rim (see p.81). Ancestral Puebloans seem to have roamed readily between rim and river; their ladders and even footbridges still survive in certain well-hidden places, while their trails form the basis of almost all the park's hiking routes.

By around 1150, rainfall had again diminished, the soil was becoming depleted, and an exodus from the region began. There are also indications of conflict for scant resources between competing groups. The Ancestral Puebloans of the canyon can be subdivided into the **Kayenta** peoples of its eastern and central reaches and the **Cohonina** farther west, who with less fertile farmland depended to a greater extent on roasting wild agave plants. Fortified watchtower-like structures along the rim suggest that these previously amicable neighbors may have fallen out, or that perhaps the Cohonina left the canyon earlier than the Kayenta and were supplanted by the less friendly **Cerbat** people. The **Paiute** also made their appearance around this time, along the western end of the North Rim.

Although only a minimal population remained in the canyon proper by 1250, Puebloan groups have maintained close spiritual links ever since. The many distinct Pueblo peoples that survive today came into being when groups of migrants coalesced in various locations well east of the canyon between around 1100 and 1300. Geographically the closest are the **Hopi**, whose mesas lie sixty miles east. They regard a dome-shaped hot spring known as the *sipapu*, not far up the Little Colorado from its confluence with the Colorado, as the hole through which they entered the world, and they still make pilgrimages to it along the **Salt Trail**. Some **Zuni**, who now live in New Mexico, also trace their origins back to the canyon, particularly to Rainbow Falls below the North Rim.

Farther west, the Cerbat never left the canyon vicinity. Their descendants became the **Hualapai**, as well as the **Havasupai**, whose continued existence deep in Havasu Canyon represents the closest modern approximation to the ancient way of life.

The coming of the Spanish

In 1540 – less than twenty years after Cortés conquered the Aztecs of Mexico and before any European settlements had been established anywhere in what's now the United States – the first **Spaniards** reached the Southwest. An expedition led by **Francisco Vásquez de Coronado**, hoping to find cities of gold and consisting of more than three hundred Spanish soldiers and hundreds more Native American "allies" and servants, marched up through Arizona and reached the Zuni pueblos on July 7. After a bloody battle – the first ever fought between Europeans and Native Americans – secured the area as a temporary base, exploring parties were sent out in all directions.

Reaching the Hopi mesas, one such group was told of a great river not far to the west, inhabited by people with very large bodies (presumably the Havasupai, who tend to be significantly bigger than the Hopi). Four men, under **García López de Cárdenas**, were dispatched to investigate. They reached the Grand Canyon after twenty days, a puzzlingly long march that suggests their Hopi guides were deliberately leading them astray. The Spaniards were assured that no trails extended down to the river and were taken to a spot where none was visible; no one knows exactly where, but it's generally reckoned to have been somewhere near Grandview Point.

Cárdenas' men spent three days on the South Rim, searching for a route to the bottom. Three eventually made an abortive attempt, only to discover that "some huge rocks on the sides of the cliffs [that] seemed to be about as tall as a man … were bigger than the great tower of Seville." They turned back a third of the way down, concluding that "it was impossible to descend."

The Spanish hoped to find a river route to the so-called "South Sea," the Gulf of California, and identified the Colorado as being the *Río Tíson*, or Firebrand River, up which a simultaneous naval expedition was attempting to sail. It managed 225 miles, reaching the modern site of the Hoover Dam. Cárdenas himself, who seems to have been an unsavory character, rejoined Coronado and was later responsible for burning two hundred Indian hostages alive at the Tiguex pueblo.

Although Coronado's expedition ultimately failed, the Spaniards returned in force in 1598 to establish the colony of **New Mexico**, the boundaries of which nominally included the Grand Canyon. However, no further Spanish visits to the canyon are recorded before **1776**, when a group of explorers from Santa Fe, led by the Franciscan friars **Domínguez** and **Escalante** (see p.135), set out to map what later became the Old Spanish Trail to California. On their return they wandered extensively across the Arizona Strip and failed to cross the river at the site of Lees Ferry. That same year, **Father Garcés** from Tucson penetrated what he called a "calaboose of cliffs and canyons" to visit the Havasupai in the western canyon.

John Wesley Powell

One or two mountain men and trappers may have seen the Grand Canyon during the first half of the nineteenth century, but by the time jurisdiction over the region passed from Mexico to the United States, in 1848, it had yet to be surveyed and did not even have a fixed **name**. To the Havasupai it was *Wikatata* ("Rough Rim"); Spanish maps showed it as the *Río Muy Grande* ("Very Big River"); and Yankee prospectors knew it as the Big Cañon.

The first serious attempt to explore it came in 1857, when the US War Department instructed **Lieutenant Joseph Christmas Ives** to find out if the Colorado River was navigable by **steamboat**. Like his Spanish predecessors, Ives got little farther than the future Hoover Dam site, but he then continued on foot all the way to the Little Colorado River. Though an accompanying geologist made the first accurate scientific observations of the canyon, the expedition is best remembered for Ives' own very negative assessment: "The region is, of course, altogether valueless. … Ours has been the first, and will doubtless be the last, party of whites to visit this profitless locality."

The name **Grand Canyon**, first used on a map in 1868, was popularized by the one-armed Civil War veteran **John Wesley Powell**, whose dramatic 1869 boat trip along the fearsome and uncharted Colorado captured public imagination. Such a trip had long been mulled, but in the words of John Frémont, the legendary "Pathfinder" of the West, "no trappers have been found bold enough to undertake a voyage which has so certain a prospect of a fatal termination."

Powell's ten-man **Colorado River Exploring Expedition** set off from Green River, Wyoming, on May 24, 1869. This was just two weeks after the completion of the transcontinental railroad, which carried his four heavy Whitehall oak rowing boats here from Chicago. Another expedition, led by Thomas Hook, set off a few days later, but was abandoned almost immediately, after Hook drowned in a rapid. Powell himself soon lost one of his boats, but he reached what would become Green River, Utah, on July 13; then the previously unseen confluence of the Green and (larger) Grand rivers, which marks the start of the Colorado, on July 16; and the mouth of the San Juan on July 31. From what's now Lees Ferry, he launched himself into the Grand Canyon on August 5.

It was a grueling, even nightmarish trip, for which Powell's boats were wholly unsuitable. His crew counted a total of 476 rapids, 62 of which they had to portage – that is, physically carry their boats over the riverside rocks. Eventually, however, the bedraggled, ravenous crew emerged from the canyon on August 29. In a dreadful irony, three members of the party, terrified by the interminable prospect of yet more rapids, had abandoned the river the day before, only to be murdered as they hiked out of Separation Canyon. Their deaths have traditionally been blamed on Native Americans, but compelling recent evidence suggests Mormon settlers may have killed them.

Powell was both a genuine hero and a consummate self-publicist, who, thanks in part to the acclaim he received for his journals – an unacknowledged amalgam of both this voyage and a second trek in 1871 – later became director of both the Bureau of American Ethnology and the US Geological Survey. He returned repeatedly to the canyon with scientific teams, one of which, in 1875, included the artist **Thomas Moran**. Moran's paintings and engravings, and the detailed geologic report prepared by **Clarence Dutton** in 1880–81 – the first to give quasi-religious names to the various "temples" and monuments below the rim – did much to place the canyon firmly in the American consciousness.

The growth of tourism

As the Grand Canyon was being recognized as the most extraordinary natural wonder in the US, settlers moved to the vicinity in ever-greater numbers. Isolated Mormon communities sprang up across the Arizona Strip, on the North Rim plateaus, while westbound pioneers began to stake claims close to the South Rim. There has been tension ever since between this new permanent population, determined to survive in such an unforgiving environment, and visitors hoping to find unspoiled wilderness. Broadly speaking, **logging** and **grazing** interests long retained control of the plateau forests, while in the canyon itself most attempts at **mining** were defeated by the difficult terrain; **tourism** soon proved a far more lucrative proposition.

When the **railroad** first crossed northern Arizona in 1882, visitors were taken by stagecoach from **Peach Springs**, the nearest station to the Grand Canyon, to stay at the *Diamond Creek Hotel* by the river. With the growth of the timber towns to the east, that locality soon declined; by the 1890s, **Flagstaff** was the main terminus, connected to the canyon by three weekly stages. The railroad reached the canyon itself, via a branch line from **Williams,** in September 1901. That triggered the growth of **Grand Canyon Village**, built under the auspices of the Fred Harvey Company, a subsidiary of the Santa Fe Railroad, and dependent on water carried by rail from Del Rio, 120 miles away. The company's grand *El Tovar* hotel – still the showpiece canyon-edge lodging – opened in January 1905, and its early marketing strategies influence the experience of canyon visitors to this day. Following an internal memo to "get some Indians to the Canyon at once," the company built the Hopi House souvenir store, modeled on the Hopi village of Old Oraibi, and staffed it with Hopi craftspeople. Similarly, the company exhorted Navajo weavers to produce rugs to suit tourist tastes, using nontraditional "earth" colors such as brown. Pseudo-Pueblo architecture became the dominant theme, in line with the vision of architect Mary Jane Colter (see p.55).

Late nineteenth-century proposals to create a **Grand Canyon National Park** aroused vigorous local opposition. In due course, however, naturalist **John Muir** – who had earlier championed Yosemite Valley in California and declared the Grand Canyon to be "unearthly … as if you had found it after death, on some other star" – found a powerful ally in **Theodore Roosevelt**. Presidential authority only entitled Roosevelt to protect sites of historical, rather than geologic, interest, so Roosevelt used the pretext of preserving Ancestral Puebloan ruins to proclaim **Grand Canyon National Monument** in 1908. Having failed to persuade the Supreme Court to overrule the president, Arizonan politicians finally came around to the idea of a national park after Arizona achieved statehood in 1912. Even so, by the time the boundaries of the new **Grand Canyon National Park** were fixed in 1919, they had trimmed away large tracts of grazing land. The park encompassed only about 1000 square miles and included just 56 miles of the actual canyon.

Meanwhile, tourism to the South Rim increased. **Ralph Cameron** had been accumulating bogus mining claims along the South Rim since 1890, which enabled him to charge a toll of $1 to riders using the Bright Angel Trail. In 1905, he built his own hotel beside the railroad terminal, forcing the Fred Harvey Company to relocate the station beyond sight of its upstart rival. When

△ Mary Jane Colter's arch and bell at Hermits Rest

the national park came into being, Cameron continued to be a thorn in its side. Elected to the US Senate in 1920, he spent a few years hacking at the park's budget before his mining claims were eventually invalidated. His control of the Bright Angel Trail had by then spurred development of the competing **Kaibab Trail**, which stretches from rim to rim by way of the Kaibab Suspension Bridge. Plans to pave that route never materialized, but a slight enlargement of the park in 1927 permitted construction of a road east to Desert View, which, with completion in 1928 of **Navajo Bridge** across Marble Canyon, reduced what had been a 600-mile drive between the rims to a more feasible 215 miles.

The first **automobile** showed up at the canyon in 1902, despite running out of gas twenty miles short. By 1926, more visitors were coming by car than by train, and Flagstaff was once again the major gateway. By 1938, the throngs of visitors necessitated advance reservations for both mule rides and lodging. Annual visitor numbers first exceeded a million in 1956 and ran over five million through most of the 1990s. Anticipating that visitation would continue to increase at an exponential rate, the Park Service drew up plans around the turn of the millennium to build a **light rail** network and a huge new tourism complex close to the South Rim, to be known as **Canyon Forest Village**. However, visitor numbers have now dropped back below five million – no one's sure why, though the downward trend has continued since the terrorist attacks of September 11, 2001 – and the political will to make major changes seems to have disappeared.

Environmental issues

The biggest issues to face the Grand Canyon during the twentieth century centered on the **environment**. The 1935 damming of Black Canyon, just west of the Grand Canyon, by the **Hoover Dam**, inspired a spree of dam-building in the Western US. Bureau of Reclamation proposals included damming the Green River in northwest Colorado, the San Juan in New Mexico, and the Colorado itself at both Arizona's Bridge Canyon and Utah's Glen Canyon. The ax eventually fell on **Glen Canyon**, which despite praise from John Wesley Powell was almost completely unknown.

The story of the construction of Glen Canyon Dam and creation of Lake Powell is told in full on p.126. Most environmentalists regard it as a disaster, and it's easy to forget that although the Grand Canyon itself has not been dammed, the dam at Glen Canyon has utterly changed the character of the Colorado River and thus the ecology of the inner Grand Canyon. At least no further dams have been built; green activists, for example, halted plans to construct the **Bridge Canyon Dam** on the Hualapai reservation in the 1970s, despite the eagerness of the Hualapai themselves (see p.187).

Commercial **logging** and **mining** were finally banned from the Grand Canyon when the park boundaries were redrawn and enlarged in 1975. President Clinton followed Roosevelt's example in 2000 by using his presidential prerogative to protect two vast enclaves within the overall Grand Canyon ecosystem, proclaiming the 294,000-acre **Vermilion Cliffs National Monument** (see p.134) and the million-acre **Grand Canyon–Parashant National Monument** (see p.147). Fears persist, however, that **uranium mining** may return to areas just outside the park along the South Rim, as evidenced by Havasupai concern over the prospective **Canyon Mine** (see p.177).

Geology

The merest glance at the Grand Canyon reveals that this vast landscape is composed of layer upon layer of different kinds of rock, each with its own distinct color and texture. Some layers form thin stripes, some sheer cliffs hundreds of feet tall; others vary in width and in places may disappear altogether. Taken as a whole, however, the consistency of these horizontal bands, identifiable throughout the canyon, acts as a reassuring counterpoint to the bewildering complexity of the terrain, with its tangle of buttes, mesas, and side canyons.

Geologists often talk of "reading" the various strata like a book, which tells the story not only of the canyon but also of the earth itself. What makes the Grand Canyon such a good read is that it's very rare for such an even, undisturbed set of rock layers to exist so high above sea level, and unique for them to be exposed to view to such an amazing depth. Common sense tells us that the deepest layers are the oldest, and the saga does indeed start at the bottom, almost **two billion** years ago. What's less obvious, however, is that in geologic terms the canyon is not old but very **new**. The processes that put all those buried strata into place were entirely separate from those that created the canyon itself.

At various times, the region that now holds the Grand Canyon has lain underwater, or at the edge of a very different continent, or even embedded in the planet's one massive supercontinent. As it swirled around the globe, it also spent long periods at the equator. Until less than six million years ago, there was no canyon here. Then the **Colorado Plateau** started to rise, somehow climbing several thousand feet without greatly deforming its thick layers of sedimentary rock, and its many rivers began to cut deeper and deeper.

While scientists still can't decide quite how it happened, the canyon took shape quickly. It had acquired essentially its present form a million years ago and since then has only burrowed a further fifty feet. A new phase began in 1963, when completion of the **Glen Canyon Dam** rendered the Colorado River barely capable of maintaining the canyon, let alone enlarging it.

The story in the stone

Almost every rock layer visible from the rim of the Grand Canyon is **sedimentary** and was originally deposited on the bed or along the shoreline of a shallow primeval sea. Such rocks can be further subdivided into **sandstone**, which consists mostly of sand, perhaps mixed with a little silt or clay, and cemented with silica or calcite; **limestone**, which is largely biological, comprising dead sea creatures and their shells; and **mudstone** such as shale and siltstone, carried down to the sea by rivers as mountain ranges rise and fall.

There are two other types of rock in the canyon. **Igneous** (fire-formed) rocks well up from the depths of the Earth, both in the ocean along the edges of the lithospheric plates that hold the separate continents and via volcanic action on the surface. **Metamorphic** rocks are those that have been altered by heat and pressure over time, which happens especially when continents collide.

The oldest rocks of all, in the **Vishnu schist** layer, are both igneous and metamorphic. This gnarled, dense bed of dark granite – which is not only exposed at river level, but forms the entire thousand-foot-deep **Granite Gorge** – was

△ The uppermost strata of the Grand Canyon, at Bright Angel Point

originally deposited by lava flows 1.84 billion years ago. (While that makes it old by any standard, the oldest visible rocks on the planet, dating back almost four billion years, lie along the shore of the Great Slave Lake in Canada's Northwest Territories.) The Vishnu schist subsequently metamorphosed when the seabed on which it rested collided with what became the North American continent around 1.7 billion years ago, and the schist became threaded with veins of pink Zoroaster granite. Life had already established its first tentative foothold on Earth during this **Precambrian Era**, but no fossils could hope to survive such an inferno of molten rock.

In parts but not all of the canyon, a further medley of both igneous and sedimentary Precambrian rocks lies immediately above the Vishnu schist. Where it exists (for example, in the Desert View vicinity), this **Grand Canyon Supergroup** is immediately recognizable, because, unusually for the canyon, the normally horizontal strata are tilted at a twenty-degree angle.

If we think of each layer as being a page of the canyon's great geologic textbook, then we have to bear in mind that many pages are missing altogether. Just as there are eras when new strata are being added, there are also periods, like our own, when not only is nothing new being deposited, but preexisting layers lie exposed to the elements and erode away. Such gaps in the record are known as **unconformities**. The most obvious, dubbed the **Great Unconformity** by John Wesley Powell, is the line that separates the Precambrian rocks of the inner gorge from the sedimentary strata of the **Paleozoic Era** above. It's especially striking when the Grand Canyon Supergroup is absent, representing an interlude of a billion years.

During the **Paleozoic Epoch**, which lasted from 550 million until 250 million years ago, much of what's now North America was covered by water. The oldest Paleozoic groups consist of three consecutive strata – **Tapeats sandstone**, **Bright Angel shale**, and **Muav limestone** – which collectively form the **Tonto Group**, as seen in the broad Tonto Platform, at 4000ft. Each in turn was created farther offshore, which is thought to reflect increasingly high water levels, possibly due to melting polar ice caps.

Next comes another unconformity, followed by the **Temple Butte Formation** from the **Devonian Era** and the distinctive **Redwall limestone** layer, responsible for the 500ft cliffs that pose such a problem on many inner canyon trails. Despite its namesake color, the Redwall is not naturally red, but dyed by leaching from the iron-rich rocks of the thick **Supai Group** above. These mingle limestone, sandstone, shale, and siltstone, testifying to an era when the coastline repeatedly rose and fell.

The Paleozoic ends with a final four-part sequence: **Hermit shale**, left by rivers on a coastal plain; pale **Coconino sandstone**, the solidified dunes from a windswept ancient desert; the **Toroweap Formation**, a mixture of limestone and shale that once more lay beneath the waves; and the **Kaibab Formation**, a similar but harder blend that tops the canyon rim all the way from Lees Ferry to the heart of the national park.

And there the story stops, roughly 250 million years ago, at which point all the world's landmasses were jammed together in a giant supercontinent known as **Pangaea**. Although only the tiniest traces of anything newer survive at the Grand Canyon, it's thought that another four or five thousand feet of rock was deposited on top during the **Mesozoic Era**. Those are the rocks that form the **Navajo sandstone** of Arizona's spectacular Canyon de Chelly, and the multi-colored shales of the nearby **Painted Desert**. The canyon is rich in marine fossils, but it holds nothing from the age of the dinosaurs, which ended a mere 65 million years ago.

Those final blank pages do hold one last footnote, however. A series of **lava cascades** inundated the western canyon during the last three million years, culminating around 1.2 million years ago when the largest flow created the **Prospect Dam**. That backed up the Colorado into a lake that stretched even farther upstream than modern-day Lake Powell and took around twenty thousand years to erode away. Volcanoes remain active in the vicinity; **Sunset Crater**, near Flagstaff (see p.162), last erupted in 1065.

The power of erosion

The physical mechanisms that have sculpted the Grand Canyon are well understood, not least because they remain active today. All fall under the broad heading of **erosion**, with **water** as the dominant force. Whatever intuition might suggest, however, the Colorado River alone did not carve the canyon. The river only operates at river level, so while it's responsible for the **depth** of the canyon – and continues to scour its way deeper – it did little to create its **width**. The fantastic pyramids and mesas that tower above the central gorge are the result of the interplay of water, wind, gravity, and extreme cycles of heat and cold.

Erosion is often pictured as a gradual process, under which grains of sand tumble one by one from the rim. In fact, the canyon has been shaped to a much greater extent by cataclysmic events, none more so than **flash floods**. The very fact that the Grand Canyon sits amid a desert means that what rain does fall can have a disproportionate impact. There's little soil cover to absorb the monsoon-like thunderstorms that hit the region each year, especially in late July and August. Instead they pour onto bare stone and quickly gather into storm channels that feed in turn into side canyons and the main canyon. Vast quantities of mud and rock are picked up and swept along in these violent upheavals, widening the old routes down to the river and battering out new ones.

An even more fearsome phenomenon is **debris flow**, in which a morass of gravel, stone, and sand becomes sufficiently sodden after rains that it begins to flow like concrete. Such flows occur somewhere in the canyon roughly twice every year. One created Crystal Rapid in 1966; another, in Monument Creek in 1984, threw boulders weighing as much 37 tons each into the Colorado.

Subtler activity can produce equally spectacular results. Some of the water that falls as rain or snow finds its way into cracks in the earth. As it subsequently freezes and expands, the water chisels vast slabs of stone away from their moorings, unseen and unsuspected until one day a mighty rockfall shatters the peace of the canyon.

Many of the **side canyons** in which so much of this activity takes place follow courses originally created by **earthquakes** and only later widened by water; seismic action, including the occasional earthquake, still continues. Major cracks include the **Bright Angel Fault**, which made possible the corridor hiking trails between the South and North rims, and the **Toroweap Fault** downstream. The side canyons tend to be so barren and dry that visitors are inclined to think of them as somehow peripheral to the Grand Canyon proper; see them roar into life after a storm, and you'll be in no doubt as to the important part they've played in its creation.

The effects of erosion vary according to the different rock strata. **Cliffs** are usually composed of sandstone or limestone deposited in broad bands, which erode slowly, whereas **slopes** comprise constantly crumbling shales. Assorted combinations of rock, piled up like a layer cake and eroding at differing speeds, have resulted in the bizarre monuments so conspicuous toward the eastern end of the canyon. Broad, flat, hard-capped **mesas** erode to form smaller **buttes**, taller than they are wide, or potentially the pyramids known at the Grand Canyon as **temples**. It was Clarence Dutton, a student of comparative religion who wrote the first Geological Survey report on the canyon in 1881, who started the custom of naming prominent canyon features – **Brahma Temple**, **Shiva Temple**, **Vishnu Temple**, and so on – for religious architecture. Honoring his tradition were later cartographers such as François Matthes, who named **Krishna Shrine** and **Walhalla Plateau**.

To return finally to the Colorado River, even if it hasn't been as instrumental an erosive force, the crucial role it *has* played is to carry all the debris away. It would take around a thousand cubic miles of rock to fill in the Grand Canyon as we see it today, and that's how much the Colorado has removed. Originally the debris was deposited toward the river mouth in the Gulf of California, thus renewing the sedimentation cycle. After 1935, the Colorado set about filling in **Lake Mead**, behind the Hoover Dam. What now worries scientists is that the Colorado simply isn't itself anymore. Flash floods still sweep the side canyons and hurl debris into the river, but the cold steady stream that's allowed through the Glen Canyon Dam no longer experiences surges of its own, and it no longer has the brute strength necessary to clear away obstacles thrown into its path. Any year now, some new debris flow may create a monster rapid the Colorado can't remove.

The creation of the canyon

Despite their success in explaining how the canyon's building blocks were put in place, and even how they subsequently eroded away again, geologists have yet to agree how the canyon itself came into being. At least they know what set the ball rolling: the **Laramide Orogeny**, which began at the end of the Mesozoic Era, 65 million years ago. An orogeny is an ongoing period of upheaval and mountain-building; this one, sparked when the Pacific plate collided with and slipped beneath the North American plate, was primarily responsible for creating the Rocky Mountains, but also delineated the **Colorado Plateau**. Within the past five or six million years, the plateau has rapidly risen several thousand feet, while its rivers, the Colorado among them, have carved ever deeper into the earth.

The crucial mystery, however, is that the Colorado Plateau in the Grand Canyon region is not flat. It's an enormous hill, known as the **Kaibab Plateau** (from a Paiute word meaning "mountain with no peak"), which slopes southward from a ridge that runs roughly a dozen miles north of the North Rim, more or less along the national park boundary. The Colorado has eaten away a chunk of the hillside, about a third of the way up the southern slope – which explains why the North Rim is a thousand feet higher than the South. The pivotal point in the course of the modern Colorado comes when it hits the Kaibab Plateau, close to Desert View, where rather than veering away, perhaps to the southeast, it turns west and cuts directly into the plateau.

Why, or how, the Colorado River slices straight through that hill has long taxed the scientific imagination. The oldest serious theory proposed that the Colorado was what's called an "antecedent" river, which has always followed its modern course and simply remained in place as the plateau rose around it. A more subtle refinement describes a process of "superposition," suggesting that the river previously ran atop new, even layers of sediment that had smothered the hills and uplifts we see today, and that when the plateau rose, it wore away those upper layers to reveal the hills, including the Kaibab Plateau, that we find so puzzling today. The trouble with both theories is that the Colorado predates neither the recent uplift nor the canyon; they have all grown up together.

All hypotheses currently in favor argue for some form of "**stream piracy**," in which the Colorado originally followed some other course, but was later "captured" by another river and began to flow in that direction instead. Such a capture might have occurred when a powerful stream, at the head of its own canyon, eventually cut so far back that it breached the stone barrier that separated it from the Colorado. The Colorado would then rush through, abandoning its own course and usurping this alternative channel.

While it has been shown that until five million years ago, the ancestral Colorado River did indeed skirt the Kaibab Plateau, it's not known quite where it went. Suggestions that it used to flow down the gorge of the Little Colorado to meet the Rio Grande have largely been abandoned due to lack of evidence, as has the idea that all of northern Arizona's rivers may once have flowed in the opposite direction. It's now thought most likely that the Colorado circled the southern edge of the Kaibab and then continued northwest. As ground levels to the southwest subsided, in tandem with the uplift of the Colorado Plateau, new rivers began to flow down to the Gulf of California. In some long-disappeared spot, one such river eventually captured, and thus became, the Colorado. The Grand Canyon was born.

Flora and fauna

Considering that the Grand Canyon measures almost three hundred miles in length and ranges eight thousand feet in depth from the highest point on the North Rim to the lowest elevation at Lake Mead, it's hardly surprising that it shelters a tremendous assortment of plant and animal life. Naturally, all share one basic trait: They've adapted to survive in a **desert**, where the low rainfall – around fifteen inches per year on the South Rim and twice that on the North – ensures that the soil cover is poor where it exists at all. Within those parameters, however, the range of life forms and environments is breathtaking, with such treats in store for visitors as the spectacle of an amazing **California condor** soaring above the rim or the lush hidden oases that punctuate the cactus-studded plateaus of the inner canyon.

It was at the Grand Canyon, with its clearly stratified layers, that scientists first realized that just as different groups of plants and animals inhabit different latitudes between the equator and the poles, so too are different collections of species found at the various levels of a mountainside or canyon. The crucial factor is, of course, **temperature**. In the canyon, altitude substitutes for latitude; the higher the elevation, the cooler the temperature.

The first scientist to describe and name the distinct **life zones** was Clinton Merriam of the US Biological Survey. After visiting the Grand Canyon in 1889, he announced that its range of habitats corresponded to those encountered in a trip from the deserts of Mexico to the forests of the Canadian mountains. His work remains the basis for accounts of canyon wildlife to this day, though, as he pointed out, much more than just elevation determines what will survive where. The temperature at any one spot also varies according to how much direct **sunlight** it receives, which itself depends on the angle of the slope and the direction in which it faces; localized **moisture**, from springs or streams; and how exposed it is to the hot and cold air currents that rise and fall within the canyon.

Early explorers imagined that miraculous creatures might lurk in the canyon's recesses. Sadly, twentieth-century expeditions disproved tales of tiny horses, finding only some rather stunted and very thirsty ones, and of "lost worlds" atop such lone, isolated summits as Shiva Temple. The canyon does, however, offer some fascinating cases of **divergent evolution**, such as the distinct species of squirrel that inhabits the North and South rims.

North Rim

At between 8000 and 9000ft above sea level, the highest portions of Grand Canyon National Park, along and just back from the **North Rim**, belong to the **boreal zone**. As in the forests of Canada, the tree population here consists largely of **aspen**, **spruce**, and **fir**, though higher elevations also hold **Douglas fir** – which is not a true fir but is capable of growing 130ft tall – while **ponderosa pines** appear closer to the rim. Relatively high precipitation has resulted in richer soil, and the dense woodlands of the plateau are interspersed with alpine **meadows**. These support wildflowers such as asters and sunflowers and also hold burrowing creatures like weasels and voles, which in turn attract their own predators.

In the hundred years since Theodore Roosevelt first protected it within a national monument, the ecology of the North Rim has been particularly affected by Park Service attempts at management. The longstanding policy of suppressing **wildfires** has had an adverse effect on the ponderosas. Without the natural fires that should sweep through regularly to eliminate needles and brush from the forest floor, debris accumulates to levels where it can fuel a major conflagration that burns long enough to kill the pines. In recent years, the park has moved toward setting its own "controlled burns" and allowing natural fires to blaze away – even though the charred landscape spoils the look of the place for visitors.

A notorious example of early **wildlife management** techniques centers on the **mule deer** of the North Rim. Roosevelt's priority in "protecting" the deer was to preserve them for sport hunters such as himself. Natural predators like mountain lions, wolves, and coyotes were therefore to be eliminated; a single warden, James Owens, shot 532 lions over twelve years. History records that the deer population then mushroomed from four thousand to a hundred thousand and stripped the Kaibab Plateau bare before starving to death en masse during the winter of 1924–25. Although those figures are now being questioned, with scientists suggesting that such boom-and-bust cycles may be a normal feature of wild deer herds, the Park Service has abandoned the idea of culling predators, and hunting is no longer permitted. The wolves never returned – and as yet, there's been no move to reintroduce them, as at Yellowstone – but there are now thought to be around a hundred lions on the North Rim, as well as plentiful coyote.

South Rim

A thousand feet lower than the North Rim, the **South Rim** occupies what's called the **transitional zone**. Here spruce and fir give way to **ponderosa pines**, interspersed with such species as **Gambel oak**, the only tree to lose its leaves in winter amid all the canyon's evergreens.

The largest inhabitants of the ponderosa forest are **elk**, for which the only pure ponderosa stand on the South Rim itself, near Grandview Point, is a favored haunt. Among smaller species, which include skunks, chipmunks, rabbits, and porcupines, perhaps the most ubiquitous is the **Abert's squirrel**, which exists in mutual dependence with the ponderosa, eating its bark, pollen, and seeds; by failing to find all the seeds it buries, the squirrel unwittingly plants new generations of trees. In the best-known instance of how distinct species have evolved on opposite sides of the canyon, the corresponding **Kaibab squirrel** is only found on the North Rim. Once the river separated these two populations, no further interbreeding could take place. Both species have tasseled ears, but the Abert's squirrel has a reddish back and a dark tail with a white underbelly, while the Kaibab squirrel is dark gray with a white bushy tail.

Below the ponderosas comes the stunted **pygmy forest** of **piñon** (also spelled pinyon) pine and Utah **juniper** that's characteristic of the **Upper Sonoran zone**, which starts above the South Rim but beneath the North Rim. Each of these gnarled, desiccated trees, which grow to between twenty and thirty feet and live for hundreds of years, depends for survival on its own attendant **bird** species. The piñon jay harvests and buries nuts from the piñon, while the Townsend's solitaire eats juniper berries and then excretes the seeds they contain.

Just to illustrate that the demarcation lines between these various zones seldom strictly follow map contours, small groups of Douglas firs, normally found at much higher elevations, occupy north-facing alcoves below the South Rim, while if you hike down from the North Rim, you'll find that ponderosa reappear at cooler spots below the piñon-juniper level.

Inner canyon

The piñon-juniper forest thrives at elevations between approximately 7500ft and 4000ft, which means it extends far below the rim on both sides of the canyon. While the plant and animal life of the inner canyon remain within the broad category of the Upper Sonoran zone as far down as the Tonto Platform, as conditions become hotter, drier species progressively replace the piñon and juniper.

First come the **prickly pear** cacti so noticeable on the Bright Angel Trail and flowering shrubs such as cliff rose and Apache plume. Soon the landscape is dominated by desert scrub, particularly **blackbrush**, so named because its stems turn a deep black when wet. The Tonto Platform is also scattered with agave, yucca, and mesquite. Small **mammals** like mice and shrews are abundant, though as most are nocturnal, visitors rarely spot them. Snakes, too, come out at night, most notably the pink-hued and poisonous **Grand Canyon rattlesnake**, which is endemic to the inner canyon. (Two distinct but related species occupy opposite rims: the Hopi rattlesnake atop the South Rim and the Great Basin rattlesnake on the north side.)

Around five hundred **desert bighorn** sheep, which grow up to six feet in length, inhabit remote side canyons. Because no domestic sheep have ever been introduced into the region, this remains a remarkably pristine population, free from the imported diseases that have decimated bighorn numbers elsewhere in the West. For many years, they shared their range with wild descendants of **donkeys** released by prospectors around 1900, but few donkeys remain. To protect grazing for the bighorn, the Park Service killed thousands of burros and eventually, after protests from wildlife campaigners, airlifted the rest out by helicopter in 1980.

Wherever **water** is present in the inner canyon, the picture becomes very different. Majestic **willows** and **cottonwoods** line natural springs and tributary streams such as Bright Angel Creek; **hummingbirds** and **canyon wrens** dart through the air; mosses and maidenhair ferns cling to damp crevices; and there are even **tree frogs**, preyed upon by skunks and raccoons.

The **Lower Sonoran zone**, which starts below the Tonto Platform, is home to the hardiest of desert survivors. Hikers along the corridor trails experience little of this world, as where the sheer inner gorge walls are breached at all, it's usually by watercourses that have their own microenvironments. Toward the western end of the canyon, however, where elevations are lower and broad, dry side canyons reach right to the river, the flora and fauna are significantly different. Sadly, you won't encounter anything as distinctive as the multiarmed saguaro cacti found in the Sonoran Desert of southern Arizona, but many characteristic species are present, including **scorpions**, **king snakes**, large brown lizards known as **chuckwallas**, and **kangaroo rats**, which are so finely adapted to the desert that they need never drink.

Colorado River

The banks of the Colorado form a **riparian** environment of the kind described above, lined with rich vegetation, alive with insects and amphibians, and a magnet for whole echelons of predators. However, the river now represents the least natural part of the canyon; nowhere in the Grand Canyon has human impact had a more dramatic effect.

The Colorado today is a very different creature to the river that flowed through the canyon before completion of the **Glen Canyon Dam** in 1963. It

△ Glen Canyon Dam

used to range in temperature from close to freezing in winter up to as much as 80°F (27°C) in summer. Now it remains a chilly 48°F (9°C) year-round. What's more, where formerly the river was charged with colossal quantities of silt and subject to massive floods, it now runs almost crystal-clear at flow rates that fluctuate within a much more limited spectrum, according to the demand for electricity from the dam.

The effect of those changes has been to eliminate four of the canyon's eight native **fish** species, including the six-foot **squawfish**, and leave the remainder barely clinging to life. The once ubiquitous **humpback chub** can now only find the murky waters it requires for spawning by swimming up the Little Colorado River. It has been supplanted, and often literally eaten, by species introduced for sport, such as **rainbow trout**, **carp**, and **striped bass**. **Crayfish** too, introduced as food for the trout, are now thriving, while **bald eagles** have turned up to prey on the trout in turn.

Before the dam went up, regular flooding ensured that the banks of the Colorado were unable to sustain growth below the high-water mark. Now they've become lined by coyote willow trees and almost taken over by alien **tamarisk**. Many riverside beaches have disappeared altogether, as sand swept away by the river can't be replaced by the silt that now settles instead to the bottom of Lake Powell. A much-publicized **artificial flood** in 1996, engineered by simply turning up the valves at the dam for a few days, briefly regenerated several beaches, but they were soon washed away again. The Park Service constantly proposes more such floods, more carefully designed to produce positive results within the canyon, while vigorous political campaigns aim at tearing down the dam altogether (see p.214).

Books

F ollowing is a selection of books that proved useful, interesting, or entertaining during the writing of this guide. Many of those listed are only available in the US, and most you'd be lucky to find in bookstores anywhere outside the immediate vicinity of the Grand Canyon.

Bruce Babbitt (ed) *Grand Canyon: An Anthology* (Northland Press, o/p). A collection of classic canyon writing, put together in 1978, that includes firsthand exploration accounts from centuries past, as well as entertaining, seldom-seen pieces by the likes of Theodore Roosevelt and JB Priestley. Well worth seeking out.

Pedro de Castañeda *The Journey of Coronado* (Dover). An invaluable historic document; the journals of a Spaniard who accompanied Coronado to the Southwest in 1540, including the first written report of the Grand Canyon.

Christopher M. Coder *An Introduction to Grand Canyon Prehistory*; **Rose Houk** *An Introduction to Grand Canyon Ecology*; **L. Greer Price** *An Introduction to Grand Canyon Geology* (all Grand Canyon Association). These three slim, very readable, and beautifully illustrated volumes, sold individually or as a discounted set in the national park bookstores, jointly form an ideal introduction to the canyon.

Edward Dolnick *Down the Great Unknown* (HarperCollins). Deft retelling of the saga of John Wesley Powell's first canyon voyage that takes great pains to make it all intelligible to modern readers, with a thick and fast flow of analogies.

Colin Fletcher *The Man Who Walked Through Time* (Vintage Books). Enjoyable account by the first man to hike the full length of the Grand Canyon.

Philip L. Fradkin *A River No More* (University of California Press). The definitive account of the intricate and shadowy political maneuverings that went into the ultimate taming of the Colorado River, from John Wesley Powell to modern-day water management issues.

Michael P. Ghiglieri *Canyon* (University of Arizona Press). A highly experienced river guide reveals the lore of the Colorado River, mile by mile; an enjoyable read, even if he tells a bit more about his personal life than many might prefer.

Michael P. Ghiglieri and Thomas M. Myers *Over the Edge: Death in Grand Canyon* (Puma Press). In their bid to account for the demise of every single person known to have died within the Grand Canyon, the authors transcend the merely morbid to throw fascinating light on every aspect of canyon history and provide masses of useful advice on how to avoid becoming another fatality. The morbid stuff's good too.

J. Donald Hughes *In the House of Stone and Light* (Grand Canyon Natural History Association). A comprehensive human history of the Grand Canyon in words and pictures, filled with fascinating yarns about the early days of tourism.

Robert H. Keller and Michael F. Turek *American Indians and National Parks* (University of Arizona Press). What happens when the federal park system appropriates land from its former indigenous inhabitants; the Grand Canyon and Pipe Spring

National Monument are among examples considered in great detail.

John D. Lee *Mormonism Unveiled* (Fierra Blanca Publications). In his "Life and Confession," John Lee, of Lees Ferry fame, doesn't quite tell all he knows – like where he buried the gold – but there's a lot of eye-opening material in here.

Russell Martin *A Story That Stands Like a Dam* (Henry Holt). Meticulously chronicled indictment of the West's last great dam, which inundated Glen Canyon in the 1960s.

Lisa Michaels *Grand Ambition* (WW Norton, US; Hodder and Stoughton, UK). Gripping novelistic reconstruction of a true-life romantic mystery: Just what did happen to honeymooners Glen and Bessie Hyde in the winter of 1928, when they tried to become the first couple to row down the Grand Canyon?

Barbara J. Morehouse *A Place Called Grand Canyon* (University of Arizona Press). Fascinating academic analysis of how the canyon has been defined and exploited.

Stephen Plog *Ancient Peoples of the Southwest* (Thames and Hudson). Probably the best single-volume history of the pre-Hispanic Southwest, packed with diagrams and color photographs.

John Wesley Powell *The Exploration of the Colorado River and Its Canyons* (Dover). Powell certainly embellished his original journals in adapting the details of his first epic journey down the Colorado for public consumption, but they still make exhilarating reading.

Stephen J. Pyne *How the Canyon Became Grand* (Penguin). Historical analysis of how the canyon has been perceived over the centuries, with particular reference to the artists of the late Victorian era. Some of the ideas are intriguing, even if the prose style isn't.

Wayne Ranney *Carving Grand Canyon* (Grand Canyon Association). An up-to-the-minute, well-illustrated overview of how geologists have attempted to explain the formation of the canyon.

Marc Reisner *Cadillac Desert* (Penguin). The damning saga of the twentieth-century damming of the West.

Jeremy Schmidt *Grand Canyon National Park: A Natural History Guide* (Houghton Mifflin). A superb single-volume account of the canyon's environment, ecology, and geologic origins.

Stephen Trimble *The People* (SAR Press). Excellent introduction to all the Native American groups of the Southwest, bringing the history up to date with contemporary interviews.

Stewart L. Udall *Majestic Journey* (Museum of New Mexico Press). Lively, well-illustrated chronicle of Francisco Coronado's 1540–42 *entrada* into the Southwest, written by a former US Secretary of the Interior.

John C. Van Dyke *The Grand Canyon of the Colorado* (University of Utah Press). First published in 1920, Van Dyke's work represents a determined attempt to apply academic rigor to developing a new aesthetic for appreciating the canyon; it's more interesting than it sounds.

Ted J. Warner (ed) *The Domínguez-Escalante Journal* (University of Utah Press). The extraordinary diary of the two Franciscan friars who crossed Utah in 1776 in search of a new route to California and came back via the Grand Canyon (see p.135).

Richard White *It's Your Misfortune and None of My Own* (University of Oklahoma Press). Dense, authoritative, and all-embracing history of the American West that debunks the notion of the rugged pioneer by stressing the role of the federal government.

★ **waterproof**

★ **rip-proof**

★ **amazing value**

CITY MAPS

Amsterdam · Athens · Barcelona · Berlin · Boston · Brussels · Chicago · Dublin
Florence & Siena · Frankfurt · Hong Kong · Lisbon · London · Los Angeles
Madrid · Marrakesh · Miami · New York · Paris · Prague · Rome · San Francisco
Toronto · Venice · Washington DC and more...
US$8.99   Can$13.99   £4.99

COUNTRY & REGIONAL MAPS

Algarve · Andalucía · Argentina · Australia · Baja California · Brittany · Crete
Croatia · Cuba · Cyprus · Czech Republic · Dominican Republic · Dubai · Egypt
Greece · Guatemala & Belize · Iceland · Ireland · Kenya · Mexico · Morocco
New Zealand · Northern Spain · Peru · Portugal · Sicily · South Africa · South
India · Sri Lanka · Tenerife · Thailand · Trinidad & Tobago · Tuscany · Yucatán
Peninsula · and more...
US$9.99   Can$13.99   £5.99

MAPS

Visit us online

www.roughguides.com

Information on over 25,000 destinations around the world

- **Read** Rough Guides' trusted travel info
- **Share** journals, photos and travel advice with other readers
- Get exclusive Rough Guide **discounts** and travel deals
- Earn membership points every time you contribute to the
  Rough Guide community and get free books, flights and trips
- Browse thousands of **CD reviews** and artists in our music area

ONLINE

Small print and

Index

A Rough Guide to Rough Guides

Published in 1982, the first Rough Guide – to Greece – was a student scheme that became a publishing phenomenon. Mark Ellingham, a recent graduate of English from Bristol University, had been traveling in Greece the previous summer and couldn't find the right guidebook. With a small group of friends he wrote his own guide, combining a highly contemporary, journalistic style with a thoroughly practical approach to travelers' needs.

The immediate success of the book spawned a series that rapidly covered dozens of destinations. And, in addition to impecunious backpackers, Rough Guides soon acquired a much broader and older readership that relished the guides' wit and inquisitiveness as much as their enthusiastic, critical approach and value-for-money ethos.

These days, Rough Guides include recommendations from shoestring to luxury and cover more than 200 destinations around the globe, including almost every country in the Americas and Europe, more than half of Africa and most of Asia and Australasia. Our ever-growing team of authors and photographers is spread all over the world, particularly in Europe, the USA, and Australia.

In the early 1990s, Rough Guides branched out of travel, with the publication of Rough Guides to World Music, Classical Music, and the Internet. All three have become benchmark titles in their fields, spearheading the publication of a wide range of books under the Rough Guide name.

Including the travel series, Rough Guides now number more than 350 titles, covering: phrasebooks, waterproof maps, music guides from Opera to Heavy Metal, reference works as diverse as Conspiracy Theories and Shakespeare, and popular culture books from iPods to Poker. Rough Guides also produce a series of more than 120 World Music CDs in partnership with World Music Network.

Visit www.roughguides.com to see our latest publications.

Many Rough Guide travel images are available for commercial licensing at www.roughguidespictures.com

Rough Guide credits

Text editor: David Lauterborn
Layout: Ajay Verma
Cartography: Katie Lloyd-Jones
Picture editor: Harriet Mills
Production: Aimee Hampson
Proofreader: Margaret Doyle
Photographer: Greg Ward
Cover design: Chloë Roberts
Editorial: London Kate Berens, Claire Saunders, Geoff Howard, Ruth Blackmore, Polly Thomas, Richard Lim, Clifton Wilkinson, Alison Murchie, Karoline Densley, Andy Turner, Keith Drew, Edward Aves, Nikki Birrell, Helen Marsden, Alice Park, Sarah Eno, David Paul, Lucy White, Joe Staines, Duncan Clark, Peter Buckley, Matthew Milton, Tracy Hopkins, Ruth Tidball; **New York** Andrew Rosenberg, Richard Koss, Steven Horak, AnneLise Sorensen, Amy Hegarty, Hunter Slaton, April Isaacs, Sean Mahoney
Design & Pictures: London Simon Bracken, Dan May, Diana Jarvis, Mark Thomas, Jj Luck; **Delhi** Madhulita Mohapatra, Umesh Aggarwal, Jessica Subramanian, Amit Verma, Ankur Guha, Pradeep Thapliyal

Production: Katherine Owers, Sophie Hewat
Cartography: London Maxine Repath, Ed Wright; **Delhi** Manish Chandra, Jai Prakash Mishra, Ashutosh Bharti, Rajesh Mishra, Animesh Pathak, Jasbir Sandhu, Rajesh Chhibber, Karobi Gogoi, Amod Singh
Online: New York Jennifer Gold, Kristin Mingrone; **Delhi** Manik Chauhan, Narender Kumar, Manish Shekhar Jha, Lalit K. Sharma, Rakesh Kumar, Chhandita Chakravarty
Marketing & Publicity: London Richard Trillo, Niki Hanmer, David Wearn, Demelza Dallow, Louise Maher, Jess Carter; **New York** Geoff Colquitt, Megan Kennedy, Katy Ball; **Delhi** Reem Khokhar
Custom publishing and foreign rights: Philippa Hopkins
Manager India: Punita Singh
Series editor: Mark Ellingham
Reference Director: Andrew Lockett
PA to Managing and Publishing Directors: Megan McIntyre
Publishing Director: Martin Dunford
Managing Director: Kevin Fitzgerald

Publishing information

This second edition published May 2006 by
Rough Guides Ltd,
80 Strand, London WC2R 0RL, UK
345 Hudson St, 4th Floor,
New York, NY 10014, USA
14 Local Shopping Centre, Panchsheel Park,
New Delhi 110017, India
Distributed by the Penguin Group
Penguin Books Ltd,
80 Strand, London WC2R 0RL, UK
Penguin Putnam, Inc.
375 Hudson Street, NY 10014, USA
Penguin Group (Australia)
250 Camberwell Road, Camberwell,
Victoria 3124, Australia
Penguin Books Canada Ltd,
10 Alcorn Avenue, Toronto, Ontario,
M4V 1E4, Canada
Penguin Group (New Zealand)
Cnr Rosedale and Airborne Roads
Albany, Auckland, New Zealand
Cover concept by Peter Dyer.

Typeset in Bembo and Helvetica to an original design by Henry Iles.
Printed and bound in Italy by LegoPrint S.p.A
© Greg Ward 2006

240pp includes index
A catalogue record for this book is available from the British Library
ISBN 13: 978-1-84353-667-3
ISBN 10: 1-84353-667-6

1   3   5   7   9   8   6   4   2

Help us update

We've gone to a lot of effort to ensure that the second edition of **The Rough Guide to the Grand Canyon** is accurate and up to date. However, things change – places get "discovered," opening hours are notoriously fickle, restaurants and rooms raise prices or lower standards. If you feel we've got it wrong or left something out, we'd like to know, and if you can remember the address, the price, the time, the phone number, so much the better.

We'll credit all contributions, and send a copy of the next edition (or any other Rough Guide if you prefer) for the best letters. Everyone who writes to us and isn't already a subscriber will receive a copy of our full-color thrice-yearly newsletter. Please mark letters: **"Rough Guide to the Grand Canyon Update"** and send to: Rough Guides, 80 Strand, London WC2R 0RL, or Rough Guides, 4th Floor, 345 Hudson St, New York, NY 10014. Or send an email to **mail@roughguides.com**

Have your questions answered and tell others about your trip at
www.roughguides.atinfopop.com

Acknowledgments

Thanks as ever to my wife Sam Cook, for a fabulous year, and to everyone at Rough Guides, especially Chris Barsanti for his tenacious editing on the first edition, and Dave Lauterborn this time around; Harriet Mills for her work on the pictures; Steven Horak and Andrew Rosenberg for overseeing the whole thing; Katie Lloyd-Jones for the maps, Ajay Verma for typesetting; and Margaret Doyle and David Paul for proofreading. I also owe a great deal of thanks to all those who helped with my research at the canyon, especially Bruce Brossman and Mona Mesereau at Xanterra; Gina Yager at Grand Canyon West; Hylton and Robert at Papillon; Donald Goodson of Scenic Airlines; and the many fellow hikers I met out on the trails.

SMALL PRINT

Photo credits

All photos copyright Rough Guides except the following:

Introduction
p.8 Tranquil stretch of the Colorado © National
   Park Service

Color insert: Grand Canyon Trails
Grand Canyon hikers © Michael Clark/Getty
   Images

Things not to miss
03 Toroweap Point © National Park Service
12 Rafting the Colorado © National Park Service
19 Lobby of the El Tovar hotel © National Park
   Service

Black and white photos
p.56 Mary Colter showing a blueprint c.1935
   © Alvina Zimmerman Collection/Grand Canyon
   N. P. Museum Collection/National Park Service

SMALL PRINT

Index

Map entries are in color.

E

F

G

H

Map symbols

maps are listed in the full index using colored text

State boundary		⊞	Hospital
Interstate		▣	Parking
US highway		▣	Toilets
State highway		⊠	Gate
Unpaved/dirt road		⧫	Point of interest
Minor road		✗	Domestic airport
4WD road		✈	International airport
Trail		⬕	Lodge
Railway		⬆	Ranger station
▲ Peak		⬆	Entrance station
Mountain range		⛷	Ski area
Overlook		∴	Ruins
Waterfall		▨	Building
Spring		▨	Forest
Rapids		▨	Beach
Campground		▨	Indian reservation
ⓘ Information office		▨	National monument/park
⊠ Post office